THE VAT IN DEVELOPING AND TRANSITIONAL COUNTRIES

Value-added tax (VAT) now dominates tax systems around the world. But should every country have a VAT? Is the current VAT always as good as it could be in economic, equity, and administrative terms? In developing and transitional countries the answers to such questions are critical to stability, growth, and development. VAT is a critical fiscal tool in most countries. But VAT can sometimes be better designed and almost always better administered. The key questions that must be answered in designing and implementing VAT are essentially the same in all countries. But different tax designs may best suit different countries facing different circumstances. This book reviews experiences with VATs around the world and assesses how the choice of particular design features may affect outcomes in particular contexts.

Richard M. Bird is Professor Emeritus, Department of Economics, and Adjunct Professor and Co-Director of the International Tax Program at the Joseph L. Rotman School of Management, University of Toronto. He is a Fellow of the Royal Society of Canada and currently holds appointments as a Fellow at the C. D. Howe Institute and Distinguished Visiting Professor at the Andrew Young School of Public Policy, Georgia State University. He has served in the Fiscal Affairs Department of the International Monetary Fund; been a visiting professor in the United States, the Netherlands, Australia, and elsewhere; and been a frequent consultant to the World Bank and other national and international organizations, working in more than 50 countries around the world. He has written and edited dozens of books and hundreds of articles, especially on public finance in developing countries. He was awarded the Daniel M. Holland Medal of the National Tax Association in 2006 for outstanding contributions to the study and practice of public finance.

Pierre-Pascal Gendron is Professor of Economics, The Business School, Humber College Institute of Technology & Advanced Learning, Toronto, and Research Associate, International Tax Program, Joseph L. Rotman School of Management, University of Toronto. He has served in the federal government of Canada; been a consultant in progressive positions with tax practices of professional services firms in Canada and the Netherlands; and served as consultant on fiscal matters for international, governmental, and nongovernmental organizations. He has written extensively on public economics, especially in the area of taxation. He regularly speaks on the subject at conferences and seminars.

The VAT in Developing and Transitional Countries

RICHARD M. BIRD
University of Toronto

PIERRE-PASCAL GENDRON
Humber College Institute of Technology &
Advanced Learning, Toronto

CAMBRIDGE
UNIVERSITY PRESS

CAMBRIDGE
UNIVERSITY PRESS

32 Avenue of the Americas, New York NY 10013-2473, USA

Cambridge University Press is part of the University of Cambridge.

It furthers the University's mission by disseminating knowledge in the pursuit of
education, learning and research at the highest international levels of excellence.

www.cambridge.org
Information on this title: www.cambridge.org/9780521877657

First published 2007

A catalogue record for this publication is available from the British Library

Library of Congress Cataloguing in Publication data
Bird, Richard Miller, 1938–
The VAT in developing and transitional countries / Richard M. Bird, Pierre-Pascal Gendron.
p.   cm.
Includes bibliographical references and index.
ISBN 978-0-521-87765-7 (hardback)
1. Value-added tax – Developing countries.   I. Gendron, Pierre-Pascal.   II. Title.
HJ5715.D44B57   2007
336.2′714091724 – dc22   2006101757

ISBN 978-0-521-87765-7 Hardback
ISBN 978-1-107-40144-0 Paperback

Contents

Tables

Preface

The value-added tax (VAT) has been around for more than 50 years. A large literature dealing with various aspects of this most important fiscal innovation of the last half-century exists. One aim of this book is to review this literature and suggest some avenues for further research that should prove rewarding and yet more questions that need further examination. A more important aim is to review the extensive practical experience with VAT around the world in recent decades and suggest some ways to improve its design and implementation in developing and transitional countries.

A first version of some of this material was prepared for a project on Fiscal Reform in Support of Trade Liberalization supported by USAID. We are grateful for numerous comments received from participants in several workshops held at USAID and the World Bank during the course of this project. In addition, we are grateful to the many colleagues in governments around the world and in the International Monetary Fund, the World Bank, and the Inter-American Development Bank who have, over the years, contributed so much to our knowledge of VAT both in theory and especially in practice. Duanjie Chen, Sijbren Cnossen, Glenn Jenkins, Michael Keen, David Sewell, Carlos Silvani, Emil Sunley, and several anonymous reviewers were also most helpful in providing comments and materials that have helped us in writing this book. We are especially grateful for a very close reading of an earlier draft by Michael Keen that has, we hope, saved us from some pitfalls as well as for the helpful editorial efforts of Scott Parris, Janis Bolster, and Susan Thornton. Most of all, we are grateful for the forbearance and patience of our families in putting up with us, not just during the writing of this book but in general.

ONE

Why This Book?

Few fiscal topics are more important than the value-added tax (VAT).[1] Over the last few decades, VAT has swept the world. With the notable exception of the United States most countries around the world now have a VAT. In many developing and transitional countries VAT is the most important single tax. But should every country have a VAT? Is the VAT in place in most countries as good as it should be in economic, equity, and administrative terms? Can it handle the fiscal tasks imposed by trade liberalization and other factors in recent years? Can it deal adequately with the novel issues arising from digital commerce and decentralization? Can it be administered sufficiently effectively by the already hard-pressed revenue administrations of developing and transitional countries?[2]

The answers to such questions are critical not only to fiscal stability in developing and transitional countries but also to their growth and development. Are the VATs now in place in most of these countries the efficient, simple revenue-raisers they are often purported to be? Or are they so inequitable that they may exacerbate social tensions and hence undermine

---

[1] We use *VAT* throughout as an abbreviation for both *value-added tax* and *value-added taxation*. The precise meaning should generally be clear from the context.

[2] As Keen and Lockwood (2006) note, the experience with VAT in most of the countries emerging from the former Soviet Union, and indeed to some extent in all the formerly centrally planned 'transitional' countries, differs in some important respects from that in developing countries more generally, essentially because of the very different starting point in transitional countries. We discuss some of these factors briefly with respect to, for example, Ukraine and China later in this book; for a more general overview of the peculiar fiscal starting point for centrally planned economies, see Wanless (1985), and for discussion of some of the fiscal issues more specific to countries in the process of transition from centrally planned to more market-driven economies, see Tanzi (1992, 1993), Bird (1999), Martinez-Vazquez and McNab (2000), Mitra and Stern (2003), and Wong and Bird (2005).

the political equilibrium reflected in a country's fiscal structure? Does VAT provide a feasible way to tap the informal sector? Or may it end up expanding the range of such activities? In this book we consider these and other critical questions about the design and performance of a tax that in recent years has become the mainstay of the revenue system in most developing and transitional countries around the world.

THE KEY QUESTIONS

We consider three key questions in this book. The first is whether developing and transitional countries should have a VAT at all. On the whole, we think that they should. The second question is, What kind of VAT should they have? The answer to this question is by no means as clear. Different forms of VAT may be best for different purposes in different countries, so we consider a variety of possible designs with respect to various issues. Nonetheless, on the whole we conclude that much of the conventional wisdom about VAT design is sound, although we raise a few questions about how some of that wisdom has been applied in practice.[3] Further, we suggest that most developing and transitional countries should not worry unduly about such 'frontier' VAT issues as the treatment of the financial and public sectors or how to cope with electronic commerce. Such issues are at the forefront of VAT discussions in the developed world. They also matter in many developing and transitional economies to varying degrees. As a rule, however, what is much more important for most emerging economies is to concentrate on the difficult task of first getting an appropriate VAT into place and then running it effectively.

Indeed, the final and most important question for the many developing and transitional countries around that world that already have a VAT in place is how to make a tax like VAT – which to work properly relies essentially on self-assessment (as we discuss further in later chapters) – function adequately in environments that often fail to meet most necessary preconditions for a self-assessment system. Our answer involves two stages. In the first place, fiscal experts need to spend even more time and effort than they already do in determining precisely what kind of less-than-perfect VAT may function best in the particular circumstances of each particular country. There is no

---

[3] The best source of the conventional wisdom on VAT is a series of IMF publications: Tait (1988, 1991), Ebrill et al. (2001), and (jointly with the OECD and the World Bank) International Tax Dialogue (ITD) (2005). The most comprehensive of these studies remains Ebrill et al. (2001), which is more subtle and restrained in its analysis than the practical application of the advice contained therein seems to have been in some instances.

'one-size-fits-all' (NOSFA) solution. Secondly, much more attention needs to be paid to working out in detail exactly how countries can move over time from their initial VAT – which is almost certain for political and practical reasons to be unsatisfactory in some respects – to a good (or at least better) VAT.

It is not simple to determine how best to succeed at either of these tasks in the context of any particular country. In 1991, for example, after a careful examination of Egypt's fiscal position, its existing tax structure and its administrative capacity, as well as close consideration of then-recent experience with adopting VAT in other North African countries (Morocco, Algeria, Tunisia), Egypt introduced its first general sales tax.[4] Essentially, this tax was a VAT limited to importers and manufacturers, although the law explicitly provided for the tax base to be expanded to encompass the distribution sector at a later date. It all seemed quite reasonable at the time. Looking back, however, it is now clear that this approach was wrong.

The critical issue in VAT design relates not to the *stage* at which the tax is imposed but to the *size* of the registered firms. In 2001, when Egypt finally did extend its VAT to include wholesale and retail trade, the immediate result was to triple the number of registrants (firms registered as VAT taxpayers) with no concomitant gain in revenue. The need to deal with so many new, and mostly very small, taxpayers inevitably resulted in some loss in administrative efficiency. What had seemed a decade earlier to be a good design decision based on experience elsewhere as well as Egypt's own prior experience with manufacturers' level consumption taxes (and its limited administrative capacity) turned out to have been mistaken for at least two reasons.

First, further experience has made it much clearer than it was 15 years ago that one of the most critical VAT design decisions is the level of the threshold above which firms must register. For most developing and transitional countries we now know that it is likely wiser to set that threshold too high than too low. We discuss this issue further in Chapter 7. Secondly, experience in many countries has also shown that tempting and apparently logical as it may often be to build upon what exists – as was done in Egypt by choosing to start VAT at the manufacturers' level – countries are more likely to end up with good VAT administration if they start fresh with a VAT. One key reason is precisely that doing so reduces the likelihood that the 'stage' of the production-distribution chain is thought of as a critical element in tax

---

[4] While many other countries could be used to make the same point, the Egyptian example is used here largely because one of the authors was partly responsible for the initial 'mistake' discussed.

determination. Current 'best practice' advice is thus to make a clean break with old taxes and to include all firms above a (fairly high) threshold in the tax base. As the Egyptian case suggests, this advice seems generally sound. Nonetheless, it may not always be feasible to follow this advice at those rare moments in any country in which such a major tax reform as the adoption (or major reform) of a VAT becomes feasible. What should one do then? We consider this question in some detail in this book.

The key questions that must be answered in designing and implementing VAT are essentially the same in all countries. But the context within which these questions must be answered may differ significantly from country to country and may also vary over time within any one country. Different tax designs may be best for different countries or for the same country at different times. Some features of VAT design sometimes considered to be inherently desirable – such as a single rate, zero-rating instead of exemptions, or full and immediate refund of input tax credits that cannot be offset against taxes due on outputs – may not be attainable or even desirable in the context of a particular country at a particular time. Similarly, some 'bad' features – such as too high or too low thresholds, overly extensive exemptions, or multiple rates – may be essential to successful adoption in the first place. Later on, however, such features may prove to be extremely difficult to remove. Difficult choices need to be made.

In the case of Jamaica, for example, a country that introduced VAT in 1991 as did Egypt, a clear 'exemption cycle' is evident with the initial exemptions (and domestic zero-rating) being gradually expanded over time until a major reform in 2003 eliminated many of these concessions. Within a year, however, pressure to reestablish much of the relief just removed was already beginning to build up (Edmiston and Bird 2004). Similar cycles are not unknown in other countries. Nonetheless, though one may regret it later, some 'bad' initial VAT features may be an essential element in getting the tax accepted in the first place. Whether the price is worth paying is a question that countries need to consider carefully.

Anyone who has been involved in attempting to design and implement VAT in any country is well aware of such realities. Nonetheless, surprisingly little effort appears to have been made so far to help those engaged in such tasks in dealing with some vital questions. For example, precisely which factors are critical in defining the VAT design that makes most sense for a particular country at a particular time? Over the years, numerous studies have cited many factors that may affect tax level and tax structure such as industrial concentration, literacy, openness, 'tax morale,' the size of the public sector, the existence of certain political institutions, and administrative capacity.[5] Many of these same factors have a role to play in determining how a VAT should be designed. Nowhere, however, can one find either a clear picture of the relationship between such features and VAT design or any solid basis for assessing the extent to which the choice of particular design features may affect outcomes in particular contexts. This book begins the task of providing such a basis.

WHAT LIES AHEAD

We begin in Chapter 2 with a brief review of how and why VAT has come to cover the world in recent decades. In Chapter 3 we step back a bit and consider whether the (relatively few) developing countries – mainly small islands and countries in the Middle East – that do not as yet have a VAT (as well as, perhaps, regional governments in large federal states [see Chapter 8]) should adopt one. How does a jurisdiction, national or subnational, decide when it should adopt a VAT? In Chapter 3 we discuss this question first by considering briefly the pros and cons of consumption and income taxes for developing and transitional countries and then, in more detail, comparing VAT to other forms of general sales tax, such as a turnover tax and a retail sales tax.

In Chapters 4 and 5 we turn to several critical questions about the desirability of the move to VAT and the role and effects of VAT in developing and transitional countries that have been raised in recent literature, illustrating portions of the argument with recent experiences in such countries as Ukraine and Jamaica. As mainstream economists have begun – at last – to turn their attention to VAT some recent analysis has raised questions about the trade and revenue effects of VAT, as we discuss in Chapter 4, as well as the critical distributional and developmental effects we discuss in Chapter 5.[6] We do not have clear answers yet to all these questions. Nonetheless, on the whole the best path for most developing and transitional countries is not to reject VAT but rather to attempt to understand it better and to improve its design and implementation to fit their particular circumstances.

---

[5] Of course, many of the items listed are themselves conceptually imprecise and difficult to measure. Still, many attempts have been made to do so: for a recent summary of such studies 'explaining' tax ratios, and a recent example, see Bird, Martinez-Vazquez, and Torgler (2006). We return to some of these issues in later chapters.

[6] As Keen (2006) notes, two important reasons why so little serious analytical and empirical work has been done with respect to VAT are (1) that the United States, still the main source of economic research, does not have a VAT and (2) that so few analysts actually understand how VAT works. Our aim in this book is in part to rectify the second of these problems.

Almost without exception, developing and transitional countries need both more revenue and better revenue systems.[7] A good general consumption tax is almost always a critical element in such systems, and a VAT is the best form of general consumption tax available. In the immortal words a World War I cartoonist (Bruce Bairnsfather) once put into the mouth of a soldier responding to another who is complaining about the inadequacy of the foxhole to which he has been assigned: "Well, if you knows a better 'ole, go to it." We are as enthusiastic as the next expert about well-designed selective consumption taxes (excises), moderate income and payroll taxes, sensible property taxes, and good user charges.[8] But we do not think there is a better fiscal 'hole' than VAT for most emerging countries.

The equity and distributional effects of VAT and its potentially distorting economic effects are always matters of concern. But the simple reality is that most developing and transitional countries cannot finance the education, health, and infrastructure development they need to sustain growth in the world in which we live without recourse to some form of general consumption tax. The revenue possibilities of both personal income taxes and corporate income taxes are so limited in most developing and transitional countries that the key revenue choice is generally between payroll taxes and VAT.[9] Given the critical role of the so-called informal sector in most developing and transitional countries and the extensive use in some developing countries (e.g., in Latin America) and most transitional countries of the payroll base to finance social security, VAT – despite its limitations – still seems the best road for most such countries to follow.[10] Most experienced analysts of development taxation – regardless of their political persuasion – have reached similar conclusions.[11]

Better theory should provide better guidelines for much-needed empirical analyses. To date, however, the relatively few such analyses made of VAT are based on inevitably questionable cross section or (limited) panel data

---

[7] Of course, they also generally need to spend the revenues that they have in better ways, but we cannot pursue this critical question further here.

[8] For earlier discussions of these and many other issues related to development taxation, see, for example, Bird and Oldman (1990) and Bird (1992).

[9] See, for example, the detailed discussion of the limited potential of personal income taxes in developing countries in Bird and Zolt (2005). Although Bird (2002) argues that the corporate income tax constitutes an essential ingredient of the revenue system, this does not imply that much revenue can or should be expected from this source in most developing countries, particularly in light of increased international competition for capital.

[10] For an interesting recent analysis of (high) taxes on payrolls in a developing country, see Alm and López-Castaño (2005).

[11] See, for recent examples, Toye (2000), Moore (2004), and Heady (2004).

and are difficult to relate in policy practice to relevant country settings. Empirical work is hampered by the fact that good data are often unavailable. Continued development of both theoretical and empirical analysis of VAT will presumably provide better 'optimal' policy designs in the future. Still, the optimal tax approach (Newbery and Stern 1987), though sometimes suggestive, has not as yet proved to be of much practical help in tax policy design in the real-world setting of any developing or transitional country. One reason is that this approach has not as yet managed adequately to include the administrative considerations that are often dominant in such countries (Slemrod 1990). Moreover, the approach does not encompass adequately the even more important political economy dimension (Moore 2004).[12] We do not attempt here to fill these important analytical gaps. Instead, one of our aims is to set out in some detail a few of the many tasks that remain to be tackled as VAT becomes, as we think it should, as important a focus for future academic and policy research as the income tax has long been.

In Chapter 6 we turn to several important issues in choosing the base of a VAT that have proved troublesome not only in developing countries but more generally – the treatment of real property; the treatment of public sector, nonprofit, and charitable activities (the PNC sector); and the treatment of financial services. We consider a number of alternative designs in each of these areas. In principle, as always when considering any real-world fiscal institution, it is obvious that more could generally be done with respect to each of these topics in even the poorest and least developed countries. Nonetheless, we conclude that even the most advanced emerging economies should not try to pioneer in such matters. One reason we do so is that we think that the distortions arising from the present admittedly imperfect bases of most VATs are unlikely to be very important quantitatively in most developing and transitional countries. However, this statement like so much else we (or others) say about VAT is at this stage necessarily a belief based more on our own (inevitably limited) experience than on solid empirical evidence.

In Chapter 7 we consider some key elements of VAT structure such as rates, thresholds, exemptions, and zero-rating, again illustrating some points with reference to experience in several countries. We conclude that in most cases

---

[12] See, however, Munk (2006) for a recent contribution. Even this interesting paper, however, does not take adequate account of the real world of VAT administration, in which what is done is often very different from what reading the law suggests should be done, as Keen (2006) notes in a useful argument on the need for more systematic 'second-best' analysis of VAT. For an interesting example of the uses and limitations of another analytical approach – CGE modelling – in this context, see Rutherford, Light, and Barrera (2005).

there are excellent reasons for the prevailing conventional wisdom of one rate, a fairly high threshold, and as little use of exemptions and (nonexport) zero-rating as one can get away with (ITD 2005). Again, however, we note that there is surprisingly little evidence supporting much of that wisdom and that there are plausible reasons for diverging from its prescriptions in at least some instances.

Much recent discussion of VAT in the developed world has related to two relatively new phenomena. The first is the rise of digital (electronic) commerce. The second is the apparently increasing interest in a number of countries in subnational VATs. We discuss each of these questions briefly in Chapter 8. As with the frontier tax base issues of the PNC sector and financial services discussed in Chapter 6, we conclude that 'e-commerce' is not at present a matter of great concern for most developing and transitional countries and is unlikely to become a significant factor in shaping their VATs for years to come. On the other hand, we suggest that there may indeed be a limited role for some forms of subnational VAT at the regional level in at least a few such countries, especially larger federal states such as India.[13]

We conclude our review of how VAT really works in Chapters 9 and 10 by discussing a few critical administrative issues.[14] In most developing countries, as Milka Casanegra once put it, "tax administration *is* tax policy" (Casanegra de Jantscher 1990, 179). The real tax system is that which is administered, not that which appears in the formal law. It is thus critical that VAT design take into account real administrative limitations. It is equally critical that constant attention be paid not only to the many administrative design and implementation issues needed to make VAT work but also to maintaining and adapting VAT administration as necessary to confront the realities of changing countries and a changing environment. No developing or transitional country starts with a good VAT administration; all have to 'grow' one (Bird 2005). We set out some ideas on how this may best be done, again illustrating with examples from a variety of jurisdictions. In Chapter 10 we go on to consider briefly such current 'hot' topics as VAT refunds, VAT fraud, and VAT withholding systems as well as the pervasive problem of how to deal with 'semivisible' enterprises – those hidden in the 'small'

---

[13] As Bird (2003) argues, a different form of VAT may have a role to play as a useful addition to local taxation at least in larger metropolitan areas (as it does in Japan and Italy and as is currently being considered for implementation in Colombia and South Africa), but we do not discuss this possibility further here.

[14] For a good general discussion of VAT administration that covers aspects (such as organization) not covered in this book, see Ebrill et al. (2001).

and (more critically) 'shadowy' sectors that loom large in most developing and transitional countries.

Political considerations rule most tax policy decisions in every country. We turn in Chapter 11 to some aspects of the role that VAT and VAT design may play in sustaining 'political equilibrium' in the sense of balancing equity, efficiency, and sustainability in the fiscal sphere. We focus especially on evidence from Latin America, the region of the developing world with by far the longest experience with VAT. Finally, in Chapter 12 we consider briefly the variety of VATs found in some Asian countries and offer a few suggestions on how best to approach VAT issues in developing and transitional countries.

Even the best VAT cannot be the answer to all the fiscal problems facing the many and varied developing and transitional economies around the world. Like most human institutions, VAT is neither perfect nor perfectible. Nonetheless, some form of VAT almost certainly constitutes a critical ingredient in the fiscal answer for most countries. VAT may not always work well. In some cases, VAT can certainly be designed better to fit the context of the country. In many instances, VAT can definitely be better administered even in the face of adverse political and capacity factors. But as long as a general consumption tax makes sense as a key part of a country's fiscal system, as is surely true in most developing and transitional countries, VAT remains the best way to do the job. Our aim in this book is thus neither to praise nor to bury VAT but to pull together much of what we now know about this important tax, which has become the mainstay of revenue systems around the world, and to suggest some further lines of inquiry that seem likely to reward more detailed and deeper investigation in the future.

TWO

The Rise of VAT

In this chapter, we consider four simple questions. First, what exactly is a VAT? Second, which countries have VATs, and how important is VAT in these countries? Third, why has VAT spread around the world so quickly and so broadly? Fourth, is there one 'VAT world' or two?

WHAT IS A VAT?

What exactly is a VAT? A recent definitive statement defines a *value-added tax* as "a broad-based tax levied at multiple stages of production [and distribution] with – crucially – taxes on inputs credited against taxes on output. That is, while sellers are required to charge the tax on all their sales, they can also claim a credit for taxes that they have been charged on their inputs. The advantage is that revenue is secured by being collected throughout the process of production (unlike a retail sales tax) but without distorting production decisions (as a turnover tax does)" (International Tax Dialogue 2005, 8; emphasis omitted). The same name, however – whether *value-added tax* (VAT) or the more recently favored *goods and services tax* (GST) – may cover a variety of taxes in different countries. Like the personal income tax, a VAT is not so much a single tax as a set of taxes that share certain characteristics. To put the point in zoological terms, VAT is neither a gorilla nor a chimpanzee but rather a genus like 'primates.' The Annex to this book contains a country-by-country summary of some characteristics of the VATs found around the world as of about mid-2006.[1] Here we discuss

---

[1] It should be noted that the list of 'VAT countries' found in Annex Table A.1 differs in some respects from the similar information contained in other recent sources such as ITD (2005) and Annacondia and van der Corput (2005) – which also differ from one another. Such differences are inevitable, given the fast-changing nature of the VAT universe and some fuzziness around its definitional edges. For instance, one can differ as to what should be

the question in general terms, leaving a more comprehensive treatment of the similarities and differences between VAT and other sales taxes to the next chapter.

VAT in the European Union

Some seem to think that the only 'real' VATs are those that resemble the VATs found in the European Union (EU).[2] The member states of the EU have all necessarily adopted essentially the same model of VAT as set out in the Sixth VAT Directive of 1977. While Cnossen (2003) argues persuasively that this directive needs major revision to cope with the realities of the expanded, more integrated, and more developed EU of today, it remains the basic EU VAT framework. The 10 new member states that joined the EU in 2004 thus had to adapt their VATs to fit the Sixth Directive as an important condition of membership.[3] All countries in the EU thus in a sense have the 'same' VAT. Nonetheless, even within the 'old' 15 member states of the EU, important differences exist from country to country in both the structure and the operation of VAT.

For example, Table 2.1 illustrates the range and variety of VAT rates applying in the 'old' EU countries. Two points are immediately obvious from this table. Firstly, the unitary (single) rate structure usually recommended to developing and transitional countries is found only in one country, Denmark.[4] Most countries have two reduced rates. Secondly, even leaving aside such vestiges of the colonial era as Spain's two small African territories, the range of rates found in the EU is astounding – from a low of 0.9% in Corsica to a high of 25% in Denmark and Sweden. Indeed, the differences

---

considered a separate taxing jurisdiction worthy of inclusion in such a table: Is French Polynesia to be considered separately from France? What about Madeira and Portugal? Should Indian states or Canadian provinces be listed separately? It is also not always clear exactly what is considered a 'VAT': Does India have a central VAT? Does Brazil? Does Myanmar? Did Colombia adopt a VAT in 1966 (as Bird [1970] suggests) or in 1975 [as shown in Annex Table A.1). This difference arises because Bird (1970) considered a tax that used the invoice-credit method as a VAT even when it was applied only at one stage of production, whereas according to ITD (2005) the tax must be applied at multiple stages to be a VAT. Since to some extent the answers to such questions lie in the eyes (and purpose) of the beholder, lists may differ.

[2] See, e.g., the emphasis on 'crediting' as an essential element of VAT in the definition quoted from ITD (2005), which would seem to rule out 'subtraction' VATs such as that in Japan and perhaps even VATs like that in China with very limited input crediting.

[3] Cnossen (1998) provides an excellent discussion of the 'pre-EU' state of VAT in most of the accession countries.

[4] Even in Denmark, as noted in Table 2.1, there is an exception.

Table 2.1. *VAT in the 'Old' Member States of the European Union*

Country	Standard Rate	Additional Rates	Regional Rates	Domestic Zero-Rating
Austria	20.0	10.0, 12.0	16.0[a]	No
Belgium	21.0	6.0, 12.0	—	Yes
Denmark	25.0	—[b]	—	Yes
Finland	22.0	8.0, 17.0	—	Yes
France	19.6	2.1, 5.5	0.9 to 19.6[c]	No
Germany	16.0	7.0	—[d]	No
Greece	19.0	4.5, 9.0	3.0, 6.0, 13.0[e]	No
Ireland	21.0	4.4, 13.5	—	Yes
Italy	20.0	4.0, 10.0	—[f]	Yes
Luxembourg	15.0	3.0, 6.0, 12.0	—	No
Netherlands	19.0	6.0	—	No
Portugal	21.0	5.0, 12.0	4.0, 8.0, 15.[g]	No
Spain	16.0	4.0, 7.0	0.5 to 13.0[h]	No
Sweden	25.0	6.0, 12.0	—	Yes
United Kingdom	17.5	5.0	—[i]	Yes

[a] This rate applies in two border regions (Jungholz and Mittelberg).

[b] Although the first sales of artists' products is subject to the standard rate in Denmark, only 20% of the taxable base is taken into account so that the result is a special reduced rate of only 5%.

[c] Rates of 0.9%, 2.1%, 8.0%, 13.0%, and 19.6% apply in Corsica, and a standard rate of 8.5% and a reduced rate of 2.1% apply in France's 'overseas departments' (DOM) with the exception of French Guyana.

[d] For VAT purposes, Germany does not include the island of Heligoland or the territory of Büsingen.

[e] These rates apply in the following regions – Lesbos, Chios, Samos, Dodecanese, Cycladen, Thassos, Northern Sporades, Samothrace, and Skiros. Mount Athos is excluded from the scope of the VAT.

[f] Italy excludes from scope of the VAT Livigno, Campione d'Italia, and the territorial waters of Lake Lugano.

[g] Rates apply in Azores and Madeira.

[h] Rates apply in Ceuta and Melilla. The standard rate in the Canary Islands is 8%, with additional rates of 2% and 12%.

[i] A reduced rate of 5% is applied to renovation and repair of immovable property only in the Isle of Man.

Source: OECD (2004), updated by European Commission (2006).

are even greater than shown in Table 2.1 as a result of the wide variation in the extent to which domestic goods and services are zero-rated in different countries.[5]

When differences in the scope of zero-rating – a practice that is much more extensive in the United Kingdom (UK) than in France, for example – are first combined with the differences in rate structure shown in Table 2.1 and

---

[5] 'Zero-rating' under a VAT is exemption under other taxes, while 'exemption' from a VAT is really 'input taxation,' as we discuss in Chapter 7.

Table 2.2. *Deviations between Standard and Weighted Average VAT Rates in the European Union*

	Standard Rate (%)	Weighted Average Rate (%)	Gap as % of Standard Rate
Belgium	21	16.9	19
Denmark	25	25	0
Germany	16	14.7	8
Greece	18	14.2	21
Spain	16	10.9	32
France	19.9	15.5	22
Italy	20	15	25
Luxembourg	15	11.1	26
Netherlands	17.5	14.6	17
Austria	20	17.3	14
Portugal	17	13.2	22
Finland	22	19.9	10
Sweden	25	21.4	14
United Kingdom	17.5	13.7	22
Mean	*19.4*	*15.9*	*19*
Coefficient of Variation	*16*	*24*	*45*
Minimum/Maximum	*15/25*	*10.9/25*	*0/32*

Source: Mathis (2004).

then weighted by the differing shares of the tax base to which these different rates apply in different countries, the result is that the average 'effective' VAT rate varies greatly among EU member states. This rate is often significantly different from the standard rate, as shown in Table 2.2.[6] With the notable exception of Denmark, where 25% means 25%, the gap between this implicit weighted rate and the standard rate varies from a low of 8% in Germany to a high of 32% in Spain. The so-called nonstandard rates (including domestic zero rates) apply, on average, to less than one-third of the VAT tax base in the EU. Most (but not all) of the favoured transactions consist of final household consumption (Mathis 2004). For example, in Ireland, a country that makes extensive use of zero-rating, 12% of the total VAT base is zero-rated, and 93% of the items thus freed of tax are final consumer goods and services. The UK makes even more use of such zero-rating, with as many as one-fifth of all transactions being zero-rated. Some other EU countries such as Spain,

---

[6] OECD (2004) provides a detailed look at the many special rates and treatments to be found in almost every VAT system in the developed world. France, for example, actually applies 10 VAT rates (many in specific territories) and, as do many OECD countries, also applies special methods of base determination ('margin schemes') to a number of activities. Even in the EU the VAT is neither simple nor uniform.

Portugal, and Greece make little use of zero-rating but subject a significant fraction of the VAT base to low rates.

Of course, differential rates are by no means the end of the tale. Without exception – even in Denmark (see note to Table 2.1) – every country in the EU has a range of different treatments and special features in its VAT that further affect the impact of the tax (OECD 2004). For example, as we discuss in Chapter 7, registration thresholds vary from being nonexistent in some countries (Spain, Italy, Netherlands, and Sweden) to about U.S.$108,000 in the UK.[7] Moreover, thresholds differ across sectors in some countries (France, Greece, and Ireland) and differ with respect to registration and collection in others (Belgium, Netherlands, and Portugal). Exemptions vary even more widely from country to country. Strict Denmark, for example, exempts passenger transport, burials, and travel agents, while generous Ireland goes further and also exempts public water supply, broadcasting, child care, and admissions to sporting events. Portugal exempts all agriculture. Similarly, some countries apply special administrative systems to certain types of transactions or activities: for example, while it is common to tax travel agencies on a 'margin' basis, in France the same treatment is also extended to real estate agents.

Finally, VAT administration in different EU countries obviously works with varying degrees of efficiency. Gebauer, Nam, and Parsche (2003) estimate from national accounts data that the average 1994–96 ratio of tax evasion (as a share of VAT revenues) for 10 EU countries ranged from a low of 4.2% in (no surprise) Denmark to a high of 34.5% in Italy.[8] While – as the Danish case illustrates – these authors found no clear correlation between the height of the standard VAT rate and the extent to which the tax was evaded, evasion was nonetheless found to be fairly closely related to the size of the 'underground economy.' We return to this issue in Chapter 5 and again in Chapter 10.

A VAT Is a VAT Is a VAT?

Even though the 'old' EU countries have had essentially similar VATs in place for up to 40 years, VATs in the EU differ in many important respects from

---

[7] Currency conversions throughout are made at exchange rates prevailing at the end of October 2006.

[8] These calculations are of course only estimates and are obviously open to some question. For example, how accurate is the assumption that the national accounts of each country include the same extent of 'underground' activity? But they are very carefully done with adjustments for differential coverage of different VAT rates and other factors and are probably fairly reliable.

country to country. Such differences are even more marked in the world as a whole – not least among the developing and transitional countries with which we are principally concerned. Nonetheless, in an important sense a VAT is indeed a VAT no matter where it is found or exactly what form it may take. In principle, many types of VAT may exist with variations in the breadth of the tax base (gross product, net income, consumption); the treatment of foreign trade – origin, destination; and the method of collection – addition, subtraction, invoice-credit (Shoup 1990). In practice, however, almost every VAT in the world today follows the EU model in several important respects: it is in principle intended to tax consumption on a destination basis (imports taxed, exports zero-rated), and it is applied on a transaction basis using the invoice-credit (output tax less input tax) method.[9] Not only the recent 'accession' countries but all countries aspiring to EU membership or influenced predominantly by EU experience – for example, those in francophone Africa – have followed the EU VAT model to a significant extent.

Elsewhere in the world, however, while the influence of the EU model is still clear – for instance, in most of the early VAT adopters in Latin America – other models have been developed and adopted, notably in New Zealand and Japan. The principal distinguishing feature of the New Zealand (and to a lesser extent Australian) model is the breadth of the base (e.g., with respect to the public sector, as we discuss in Chapter 6), while the Japanese VAT uniquely takes the 'subtraction' form for most VAT taxpayers (Schenk 1995).[10]

One factor that seems to have shaped the type of VAT found in many developing and transitional countries has been the nature of the expert advice they have received from abroad. In many former French colonies, for example, some key features of their VATs to this day reflect the structure of the French VAT at the time the country in question first adopted a VAT (Hill 1977). The role of the Fiscal Affairs Department (FAD) of the International Monetary Fund (IMF) has been even more important, during both the early

---

[9] A major exception not discussed in this book is the origin-based income-type VAT that exists in various forms in Italy, Japan, and several American states and that has been suggested as a local business tax more generally (Bird 2003). In addition to the Japanese tax discussed subsequently, two other significant deviations from this rule are the common application of the 'margin' approach in some industries (mentioned earlier) and, more importantly, the prevalence of 'special' regimes for 'small' taxpayers (see Chapter 10).

[10] For further discussion of the Japanese tax, see Tamaoka (1994), Ishi (2001), and Beyer (2001). Initially, the VATs adopted in the countries emerging from the former Soviet Union also were imposed to some extent on a subtraction basis: see, for example, the discussion of Belarus in Bird (1995). During the 1990s, however, almost all these VATs moved to the invoice-credit approach (see Baer, Summers, and Sunley 1996).

phase of VAT adoption in Latin America and the later spread of VAT around the world. Indeed, FAD has clearly been the leading 'change agent' in tax policy in many developing and transitional countries. Although FAD has never formally set out its own 'model' of an appropriate VAT for a developing country, its preferences have, over the years, been set out in some detail in a series of important publications.[11]

Regardless of the initial basic model adopted, however, as time passed and circumstances changed many countries have introduced home-grown variations in their VATs.[12] No one VAT is identical to any other VAT: each has its special features. Nonetheless, compared to the income tax, most VATs found around the world are essentially cut from the same mould, reflecting their relatively recent, and related, origins. As Thuronyi (2003, 312) noted, "while there are differences in VAT from one country to another, compared with the income tax VAT laws are remarkably similar."

HOW VAT HAS SPREAD

Two detailed tables summarizing the status of VAT around the world are presented in the Annex to this book. The first, Table A.1, is a summary table on the present status of VAT – essentially a revised version of a similar table in International Tax Dialogue (2005). The second, Table A.2, shows the importance of VAT in the revenue systems of those countries that have it and provides some VAT indicators that we discuss further in Chapter 4.[13]

As of early 2006, there were around 140 countries with a VAT of some sort.[14] According to Annacondia and van der Corput (2005), 26 additional

---

[11] See Tait (1988, 1991), Ebrill et al. (2001), and ITD (2005). See also the three model VAT statutes in IMF (2003) as well as the model VAT law set out in Schenk (1989). The Basic World Tax Code developed at Harvard under USAID auspices also set out a 'model' VAT law for developing countries (Hussey and Lubick 1992), although it does not appear to have had much direct influence on any country.

[12] An interesting example, though one that should not be emulated, was Canada's initial adoption of many 'income tax' concepts (e.g., with respect to the valuation of automobiles provided by businesses) in its Goods and Services Tax (GST) (Bird 1994). Given this starting point, it is not surprising that over the years the legislative and regulatory apparatus of the GST in Canada has come to resemble in complexity and size that of its income tax.

[13] We are grateful to Bayar Tummenasan at Georgia State University for his kind assistance in assembling these data.

[14] VAT may well lurk in the future even of many of those few countries that are now VAT-free. Bahrain and the United Arab Emirates, for example, have recently considered adopting a VAT; Swaziland has announced it will do so in the next few years; Hong Kong has issued a consultation paper proposing a 5% VAT; and VAT is now reportedly under consideration in a number of Pacific islands (Grandcolas 2005). No doubt still more jurisdictions have leaped, or soon will leap, onto the VAT bandwagon.

Table 2.3. *The Spread of VAT*

	Sub-Saharan Africa	Asia and Pacific	EU15 plus Norway and Switzerland	Central Europe and FSU	North Africa and Middle East	Americas	Small Islands[a]
Total	33 (43)[b]	18 (24)	17 (17)	27 (28)	9 (21)	23 (26)	9 (27)
1996–Present	18	7	0	6	2	1	3
1986–1995	13	9	5	21	5	6	6
1976–1985	1	2	0	0	2	6	0
1966–1975	0	0	11	0	0	10	0
Before 1965	1	0	1	0	0	0	0

Note: Regions defined as in Ebrill et al. (2001), except Serbia and Montenegro, included in Central Europe.
[a] Island economies with populations under 1 million, plus San Marino.
[b] Figure in parentheses is number of countries in the region.
Source: International Tax Dialogue (2005).

countries still have some other form of general consumption tax, and about the same number have no such tax. In general, however, the normal thing these days is to have a VAT. The few countries that do not have one constitute a heterogeneous grouping that includes the United States; a few odd cases like Iraq, Iran, and Cuba; some oil-rich countries; and a fairly large number of small island countries in the Caribbean and the Pacific. Although most countries have already made the leap to VAT, we nonetheless discuss in Chapter 3 the conditions under which it makes sense for a jurisdiction to adopt a VAT. We do so in part to emphasize that VAT is simply a way of collecting a sales tax – a fact that sometimes seems to be lost in translation when it comes to the political arena in which tax policies are ultimately decided. In the same chapter we also introduce some of the considerations that come into play when a subnational jurisdiction considers levying a VAT, an issue to which we return in Chapter 8.

Table 2.3 provides a summary picture of the spread of VAT, while Table 2.4 shows the rapid expansion of domestic consumption taxes as a share of total tax revenue in developing and transitional countries in recent decades.[15]

VAT is now the single most important source of tax revenue in some countries, and one of the most important sources in many more. For

[15] For a sample of country experiences, see Gillis, Shoup, and Sicat (1990); OEA (1993); Yoingco and Guevara (1988); Gonzalez (1998); and OECD (1988). A particularly topical and important case is that of India, on which see, for example, Shome (1997), Chelliah et al. (2001), Empowered Committee (2005), Bagchi (2005), Sthanumoorthy (2005), and Purohit (2006).

Table 2.4. *Tax Structure by Region (as percentage of total tax revenue), 1975–2002*

	Income Tax			Social Security	Domestic Goods and Services			International Trade
	Total	Individual	Corporate		Total	General Consumption	Excises	
North America								
1975–1980	61.0	44.3	15.9	21.4	11.7	6.0	5.1	5.2
1986–1992	57.3	46.2	10.5	26.8	12.4	7.1	4.6	3.1
1996–2002	82.4	65.6	15.7	41.2	14.7	8.7	5.1	1.8
Latin America								
1975–1980	25.9	8.8	13.9	21.3	32.0	13.6	15.3	21.2
1986–1992	25.3	7.0	14.4	18.6	38.5	17.0	17.1	17.5
1996–2002	29.2	5.9	17.8	24.9	54.0	32.6	15.5	12.8
Western Europe								
1975–1980	27.5	21.4	5.5	30.8	32.6	18.4	10.6	4.3
1986–1992	28.0	21.3	6.0	31.2	34.4	21.6	9.6	2.1
1996–2002	44.4	30.8	12.2	50.1	49.3	29.8	14.1	0.3
Asia								
1975–1980	37.2	22.0	19.7	0.1	35.7	13.7	17.6	23.1
1986–1992	37.2	19.7	18.20	0.4	37.4	16.4	15.8	20.1
1996–2002	44.6	23.0	20.3	3.7	38.2	18.6	14.5	12.3
Africa								
1975–1980	28.9	13.4	14.5	6.5	26.7	16.6	12.1	34.4
1986–1992	24.7	13.2	10.3	5.9	28.8	16.5	10.7	36.7
1996–2002	29.6	17.1	11.2	6.2	35.0	21.1	10.9	32.0
CEEME								
1975–1980	—	—	—	—	—	—	—	—
1986–1992	34.9	10.1	23.1	20.9	30.6	23.3	11.3	11.3
1996–2002	29.0	130.9	14.8	40.2	52.1	31.8	14.2	14.2

Note: 'CEEME' (Central and Eastern Europe and the Middle East), although it includes a number of countries in North Africa and the Middle East, essentially reflects changes in the transitional countries of Central and Eastern Europe and the countries emerging from the former Soviet Union. To maintain consistency of measurement and to allow cross-country comparisons of tax structures, the table reflects consolidated central government revenue for most countries. However, if these data were unavailable, national budget data, or some combination of national, state, and local revenues, were used. To even out annual fluctuations, the figures are averaged over 1975–1980, 1986–1992, and 1996–2002.

Source: Calculated (mainly from GFS data) by Bird and Zolt (2005a).

example, in Latin America general consumption taxes (mainly VAT) rose from only 14% of tax revenues in the 1970s to close to one-third by the end of the century (Table 2.4). While less marked, similar increases may be seen in Africa and Asia. In no region does the rise of VAT appear to have been at the expense of income taxes: VAT and income tax have in general proved to be more complements than substitutes. The relative expansion of VAT has been accommodated in most countries to a considerable extent by the decreasing relative importance of other consumption taxes such as excises and especially taxes on foreign trade. We discuss the revenue aspects of VAT further in Chapter 4.

VAT growth has thus been both extensive across countries and intensive within countries. Once in place, VAT in many countries has grown in revenue importance for several reasons. Firstly, as countries develop, a larger proportion of transactions would generally be expected to fall within the scope of the tax.[16] Secondly, VAT rates have tended to creep up over time. For example, even in the well-established EU system, the standard VAT rate increased in 6 of the 15 'old' countries during the decade 1994–2003 (OECD 2004). Thirdly, as already mentioned with respect to Egypt and Jamaica in Chapter 1, reforms – or at least changes – in the base of VAT and other features (e.g., registration, simplified systems) that may affect revenues are not uncommon. For example, to take only the period between June and August 2005, in June Romania was reported to be increasing its VAT rate while oil-wealthy Venezuela said it was going to lower its VAT rate, in July Portugal increased its standard rate from 19% to 21% (and from 13% to 15% in Madeira and the Azores), and in August Greece announced its intention to introduce a 19% VAT on new home sales.[17]

WHY VAT HAS SPREAD

The principal reasons for the rapid spread and success of VAT are twofold. The first reason is undoubtedly the early adoption of VAT in the EU and the perceived success of both the EU and its VAT. The second is the key role played by the IMF in spreading the word to developing countries. The demonstrated success of VAT in the EU showed that VAT worked. The consistent support

---

[16] For an early analysis of the changing composition of consumption tax bases in Colombia, see Levin (1968). Unfortunately, no similar analysis has apparently decomposed the subsequent growth of VAT revenues in Colombia (or any other country) into, for example, automatic base growth, discretionary base growth, rate changes, and administrative improvement. One reason is probably the unavailability of needed data, as we discuss further in Chapter 9.

[17] Information from Tax Analysts Web services, August 8 and July 11, 2005 (<www.taxanalysts.com>).

and advocacy of this form of taxation by the IMF in emerging countries, first in Latin America and then around the world, introduced the idea of VAT and facilitated its adoption even by countries with much less developed economic and administrative structures.[18] At the same time, for reasons of their own, all the non-EU countries of the Organisation for Economic Co-Operation and Development (OECD) – other than the United States – have also, one by one, introduced VATs of their own in recent years – New Zealand in 1986, Japan in 1989, Canada in 1991, and Australia in 2000.[19]

VAT has been an enormous success. It has swept away other contending general sales taxes in most of the world. Only five countries have ever repealed a VAT, and all either have since reintroduced one or reportedly plan to do so soon.[20] In many countries VAT has come to rival and even dominate the income tax as the mainstay of national finances. No fiscal innovation has ever spread so widely so rapidly or been so successfully adopted in such a wide variety of countries. Not all is sunshine in 'VATland,' however. Increasingly, clouds of varying sizes and shapes seem to be looming on the horizon – some in all VAT countries, but some more particularly in the developing and transitional economies that have become particularly dependent on VAT and are hence most vulnerable to looming or emerging problems with VAT.

Some problems such as the relatively high compliance cost for small firms and the vulnerability of the refund system to fraud have always been inherent in the structure and operation of VAT.[21] These problems have been exacerbated in recent years by the increased fiscal weight being placed on this tax in many countries, particularly in emerging economies seeking fiscal revenues to respond to new pressures arising from the need to reduce tariffs to accord with the requirements of the WTO and regional trade arrangements.[22] Apart from the structural and administrative difficulty of

---

[18] As Keen and Lockwood (2006) show, countries are more likely to have adopted a VAT if they have an IMF program, are relatively open to international trade, and have neighbours that have already done so.

[19] The other non-EU members of the OECD – Turkey, Korea, and Mexico – all had VATs in place before they joined the OECD. Norway and Iceland, though not members of the EU, were early adopters of VATs on the EU model. On Norway, see Bryne (2002).

[20] The five are Belize, Ghana, Grenada, Malta, and Vietnam (Keen 2006).

[21] We discuss these problems at more length in later chapters.

[22] For an early discussion, see Greenaway and Milner (1993). The conventional recommendation for consumption taxes – notably VAT – as the main replacement source is nicely developed in Ebrill, Stotsky, and Gropp (1999); see also Keen and Ligthart (2001). As Baunsgaard and Keen (2005) show, however, in practice this formula appears to work much better in developed than in less-developed countries.

dealing with 'the small and the shadowy' (see Chapters 5 and 9), even the economic merits of VAT relative to alternative forms of taxation have recently been subjected to serious question, as we discuss further in Chapters 4 and 5. New issues with respect to subnational VATs and the effects of cross-border digital trade have also become important in some countries (see Chapter 8).

Experience in a variety of countries suggests that several conditions are needed for success in such major tax reforms as adopting and implementing VAT.[23] Among the factors commonly mentioned are political commitment, thorough advance preparation, adequate investment in tax administration, an extensive public education program, consideration of local conditions – the 'NOSFA principle' we mentioned in Chapter 1 – and the need for visible offsets to perceived distributional downsides, support from the business community, and, by no means least, good timing.[24] In particular, political commitment to reform and the ability to put together sufficient political support are necessary conditions for sustainable success, as we discuss further in Chapter 11. On the technical level, thorough advance preparation, adequate investment in tax administration, and extensive public education have all proved critical to success in some countries.

Unfortunately, few of the developing and transitional countries in which revenue constraints bite hard can fulfill this laundry list of requirements. Few countries have managed to do it all. One result is that most countries have encountered many problems in implementing VAT. Problems range from such flaws in tax design as inappropriate thresholds (Chapter 7) to failures in implementation such as weak registration procedures, poorly functioning refund systems, and insufficient audit (Chapters 9 and 10). Nonetheless, VAT is definitely here to stay.

---

[23] For examples, see Terkper (1996, 2000) and Chapman (2001) on Ghana; Schatan (2003) on Mexico; Jenkins and Kuo (2000) on Nepal; Jenkins and Khadka (1998) on Singapore; Jenkins, Kuo, and Sun (2003) on Taiwan; and Waidyasekera (1998) on Sri Lanka. For a more systematic analysis of VAT adoption, see Keen and Lockwood (2006), and for a brief general discussion of tax reform, see Bird (2004).

[24] The case of Canada is interesting in this respect. It introduced its VAT – the Goods and Services Tax (GST) – in 1991 right in the midst of a tough recession. The result was a political disaster for the party in power, which was obliterated in the subsequent 1993 election. On the other hand, as Dungan and Wilson (1993) note, one result of this timing was that the much-discussed 'inflationary' impact of GST (e.g., Whalley and Fretz 1990) was imperceptible. The limited effect of VAT on price levels has also been noted for other countries (Tait 1988; Pagan, Soydemir, and Tijerina-Guajardo 2001; Valadkhani and Layton 2004). We do not discuss the 'price level' effect of VAT further in this study, except briefly in the context of foreign trade in Chapter 4.

TWO WORLDS OR ONE?

Indeed, as we mentioned earlier (and discuss further in Chapter 3), VAT is almost certain to spread even further in the future. But what kind of VAT? We turn to this question in some detail in Chapters 6 through 10, but to put it most starkly, are there two VAT worlds or one? Is VAT in developed countries such as the EU really the same animal as VAT found in most developing countries? What lessons might the extensive experience of EU countries and other developed countries (e.g., New Zealand, Canada) have to offer for VAT design, reform, and implementation in developing and transitional countries?

The First Global Conference on VAT held in Rome in March 2005 was illuminating in this respect.[25] This initial attempt to establish an 'international tax dialogue' in the sense of creating a community that shares knowledge about mutual problems with respect to VAT was not completely successful. One reason was precisely that in some respects developed and developing countries are in such different worlds that it was not always easy to communicate with each other. Those concerned with improving how financial sector activities are taxed in a complex developed economy (e.g., Pallot 2005; Pallot and White 2002) or with extending the scope and reach of electronic invoicing (see Chapter 8) are not operating in the same reality as those coping with the initial task of introducing a VAT in an environment in which tax payments are still generally made in person at tax offices and the idea that tax administrations should first collect a tax and then pay (much of) it back is completely novel.

Nonetheless, this conference also demonstrated that in many ways all countries do face many of the same problems with respect to VAT – though the mix and weight of problems may be quite different. This point was nicely brought out, for example, in a session during which a British official made an interesting presentation of VAT fraud strategy in that country (Leggett 2005).[26] During the discussion following this presentation, an official from an African country asked how the United Kingdom dealt with the major problem his own country faced, namely, the undervaluation of imports. The answer was that the UK had not yet dealt adequately with this problem – but it was next on their agenda. Circumstances differ and so do priorities.

Another example of mutual incomprehension occurred when a presenter from Barbados noted in passing that her country was concentrating on

---

[25] See the conference Web site at <http://www.itdweb.org/vatconference>
[26] See also National Audit Office (2004).

reducing arrears rather than on applying fines for various infractions in accordance with the law (Weekes 2005). Some discussants from developed countries seemed to have considerable difficulty in understanding why such a choice had to be made – that is, why Barbados did not simply apply the law in all cases. They did not appear to understand the reality of scarce resources (and often equally scarce political support) within which tax administrators in many developing countries must often operate on a daily basis. Officials in Barbados may be making a perfectly rational decision in choosing to chase those already in the system rather than tackling the much more difficult task of seeking those who are in hiding.

The point of both these stories is simply that the relative importance of different problems, the priorities attached to resolving them, and the resources available to deal with them differ so widely from country to country that communication across borders may sometimes be difficult. Still, while those concerned with VAT in different countries may sometimes feel that they are speaking to people from another world – and in some respects, they are – there is much that developing and transitional countries can and should learn from the considerable experience that has now been accrued around the world with respect to VAT design and implementation.

For example, we all now know that good VAT design makes good VAT administration easier and that bad design may make good administration almost impossible (International Tax Dialogue 2005). Similarly, it is now well understood that VAT as do all modern taxes, requires both taxpayers and tax officials to behave properly if it is to work correctly – that is, it must be 'self-assessed' (Ebrill et al. 2001). In the new language that those concerned with taxation are learning all over the world, to apply a tax effectively, one must know one's 'clients' (taxpayers) in depth – their strengths, their weaknesses, and their needs. In principle, how to proceed is simple. First, one must understand the problem, and doing so requires measurement and analysis. Next, one must develop an appropriate strategy and policies to deal with the problem and then implement those policies effectively. Finally, one must evaluate and appraise outcomes and adapt as necessary to changing realities.

All this is easy to say. But it is of course much easier to do all these good things in developed countries that have highly developed formal sectors and good data, where the political legitimacy of the government is generally accepted and where the tax administration is experienced and capable, than it is to do them in developing and transitional countries that too often lack all these critical ingredients. Moreover, the problems at the forefront of the VAT list are unlikely to be the same in all countries. In the EU, for example, the current 'hot' problems with VAT include such matters as coping with relatively sophisticated fraud schemes, dealing with the complexities generated by cross-border trade in digital services, coping with the nuances of financial and nonprofit activities, and developing modalities within which to facilitate the apparently increasing need for international cooperation to resolve many of these issues. On the other hand, in countries such as those in sub-Saharan Africa with huge informal sectors, very limited administrative resources and, in many cases, little apparent political will to support effective tax administration, the problems with VAT are often both more fundamental in nature and more difficult to resolve in practice.

Nonetheless, despite these differences, there is much that countries can learn from each other. Almost all countries, for example, continue to worry about the equity aspects of VAT. Although developed countries are unlikely to face political unrest on this issue at the levels seen in recent years in countries such as Mexico, Colombia, and the Philippines, it is clear that VAT in all countries has in many ways been shaped by concern about distributional issues.[27] Indeed, it is striking that the conventional 'expert' opinion that the fewer VAT rates and exemptions the better seems to have had less influence in some EU countries than in some of the recent VAT adopters in the developing world who are more susceptible to expert (usually FAD) guidance. Recently, for example, Sweden's minister of finance explicitly rejected a well-argued analytical report that suggested replacing the country's present multiple rate VAT system (rates of 6%, 12%, and 25%) by a single flat VAT rate of 21.7%.[28]

In practice, the balance between equity and administration in any particular country at any specific time, like that between efficiency and political reality, is almost always struck more by luck than by science. For a country to

---

[27] This protest took quite different forms in the three countries mentioned. In Mexico, there were massive street protests against a proposed VAT reform, and it did not proceed. In Colombia, a similar reform resulted in such prolonged congressional debate and opposition that the reform law was withdrawn. In the Philippines, the Supreme Court issued a restraining order halting implementation of a VAT reform that had actually been passed by the legislature. But the result in all cases was the same: VAT reform was blocked. Interestingly, although the Philippine law was finally passed at the end of 2005, it was done in such a manner that the legislature was able to pass the 'blame' for increasing the VAT rate to the president by stipulating that the executive had to implement the increase if and only if certain fiscal conditions existed – knowing full well that the stipulated conditions did exist.

[28] As reported on June 29, 2005, at <www.taxanalysts.com> Note that the recommended flat rate is very close to the 'effective' rate for Sweden shown in Table 2.2 and, incidentally, to the EU average rate.

be able to introduce VAT, it may be politically necessary to introduce some degree of explicit progressivity within the VAT itself. If so, how should this best be done: through zero-rating, exemption, or reduced rates? Although there is no conclusive evidence on this critical issue, we suggest in Chapter 7 that perhaps the last of these options (reduced rates) may sometimes be the least of these three 'evils' (as they all are, viewed from an administrative perspective). The best (the ideal model – uniform rate, minimal exemption, no domestic zero-rating) may be the enemy of the 'good' (what is politically and administratively feasible).[29] It is unfortunate that so few attempts have been made to measure the real trade-offs in such design decisions.

Much the same can be said about VAT compliance costs. While many studies have attempted to measure these costs in a few (mainly developed) countries (Hasseldine 2005), it is by no means obvious what, if anything, one can or should learn from such studies with respect to VAT design and administration in developing and transitional countries. Why, for instance, is the now standard advice for high thresholds in such countries (Keen and Mintz 2004) – advice that is based at least in part on the common finding of compliance cost studies with respect to the relatively much higher costs imposed on smaller firms – so generally ignored? A related issue about which much has been written but little is known is the implication of the important 'shadow economy' found in most developing and transitional countries for the design and operation of VAT. Both VAT thresholds (Chapter 7) and the more general question of special VAT rules for small businesses (Chapter 10) are closely related to this issue. As yet, however, little thought has been devoted either to the implications and modalities of running parallel 'special' and 'general' regimes or indeed to the more basic question of the extent to which the size and nature of the informal economy are themselves functions of the interaction between the tax system and prevailing norms and customs.[30]

VAT fraud has come to be the focus of much discussion in developed and developing countries alike. All seem to agree that a better policy framework, better risk management and audit, and more and better international cooperation are key ingredients in the solution to this problem in developed

---

[29] As we discuss further in Chapters 5 and 7, a uniform VAT rate is unlikely to be economically optimal (Newbery and Stern 1987), but it is nonetheless often argued to be the 'best' choice, for example, for the reasons set out persuasively by Cnossen (1999, 2004).

[30] As we discuss later, the literature on both these subjects provides little useful guidance to tax policy. See Keen (2006) for ideas on how to introduce both rigor and common sense into this discussion.

countries. Presumably the same is true, if less attainable, in less developed countries as well.[31] Some countries have reportedly had success with such devices as recourse to the cash method, VAT withholding systems, 'tax lotteries,' and temporary closures of premises that do not issue proper VAT receipts. While we discuss some of these issues later (Chapter 10), there has not yet been any systematic assessment of the relative merits of such methods or of their possible transferability to other settings.[32] Similarly, much has been written about the use of new technologies to assist tax administration, but again there is little clear empirically based guidance for developing and transitional countries with respect to what works best where or why.

In short, while much has been learned from decades of experience with VAT in a variety of countries around the world, there is also much that we do not yet know as well as many areas in which the guidance that can be provided to emerging economies leaves much to be desired. Even in the EU, VAT is now showing signs of age and may need rejuvenation if it is to continue to serve as well as it has in the past (Cnossen 2003). Indeed, some have argued that VAT administration in EU countries needs fundamental reconsideration if the revenue base is to be protected from increasing fraud (Sinn, Gebauer, and Parsche 2004).

Paradoxically, the fraud problem may in at least some ways be a bit simpler to tackle in less developed economies. In many such countries VAT evasion is a much more serious problem than in the EU. But most of this evasion is considerably less sophisticated and could be resolved simply by devoting more resources to enforcement and using them better (Engel, Galetovic, and Raddatz 2001). What should be done is not difficult to determine. The problem is that it is usually politically very difficult to do it. Most developing and transitional countries can, for example, gain a great deal by 'benchmarking' on good developed-country administrations (Vázquez-Caro 2005) and by applying (simpler) versions of risk management strategies such as those set out in Leggett (2005). Indeed, most such countries have so many obvious things to do along these lines that they probably should not worry much about some of the issues now plaguing VAT in the EU. First, they have to overcome the critical initial hurdles of implementing VAT effectively – a task in which the political dimension usually swamps the technical one. By the time sophisticated fraud moves to the top of their VAT

---

[31] As Toro (2005) shows in his discussion of Chile, one does not have to be rich to have a good tax administration. But it helps – a lot.

[32] For a rare exception, see the critical analysis of two such special approaches to checking VAT evasion (in Bolivia and North Cyprus) in Berhan and Jenkins (2005).

agendas, no doubt there will be much they can learn from whatever turns out to work best in developed countries in dealing with such problems. 'Second movers' have an advantage in the world of policy and administrative reform. Not everyone may be on the same page at the same time, but all are reading the same book.

THREE

Is VAT Always the Answer?

Will VAT continue to spread? We think so. One reason we say this is that we think that income taxation offers an increasingly shaky fiscal foundation for many developing and transitional countries. Income taxes are usually more technically complex, more administratively demanding, more vulnerable to erosion and competition, and even less politically popular than consumption taxes (Bird and Zolt 2005). While there is much that can be said in support of income taxes and we think that such taxes continue to have a potentially important role to play in emerging countries, that role is unlikely to be as the mainstay of the fiscal system.[1] General consumption taxes are increasingly likely to rule the fiscal roost, and in most circumstances a VAT is the most sensible form of general consumption tax – both in efficiency terms and, with some qualification, as we discuss later, also in equity, administrative, and revenue terms.

But is VAT always the right answer? Here, we are less certain. For some large subnational jurisdictions (Chapter 8) and some countries, introducing VAT may both make sense and be administratively feasible. However, for some relatively small jurisdictions in which the combination of the 'border problems' discussed later and the relatively high cost of administering a consumption VAT may outweigh the economic or revenue gain from doing so, it may not.[2] For example, in small islands in which the entire tax base is effectively imported, introducing a VAT to do what a simple uniform import tax would do as well serves no purpose.[3] When much of the potential

---

[1] As Bird (1992) discusses in detail, other revenue sources such as user charges, excises, property taxes, and payroll taxes are also relevant and useful in most circumstances.

[2] As mentioned in passing earlier, a quite different kind of VAT may make sense as a low-rate local business tax even in these cases (Bird 2003).

[3] An important issue in some such cases relates to the appropriate method and level of tourist taxation. This issue is mentioned briefly in Chapter 7 but we do not discuss it in detail. For an earlier treatment, see Bird (1992a).

domestic consumption base is subsidized, as in some of the oil-rich Gulf States, imposing a VAT may also make little sense unless such subsidies are simultaneously removed.[4]

Still, the fact is that most sales taxes today take the form of VAT. Is VAT likely to spread even further? Up to now very few jurisdictions that have imposed VAT have reversed their decision, and most that did so have subsequently jumped back on the VAT train. Recently, however, a few transitional countries such as Ukraine have been discussing the possibility of turning away from VAT to some other form of general consumption tax (Lanovy 2005). Is anyone likely to do this? We think not. No jurisdiction with a VAT is likely to find it sensible to replace the VAT, as we discuss in the next section.[5] We then turn to the question of the pros and cons of VAT for a country (or region) still without one.[6]

IF YOU HAVE A VAT, KEEP IT

There are essentially only three types of general sales taxes: turnover tax, single-stage sales tax, and VAT. A turnover tax is in some ways the easiest to administer. Tell me your turnover, and I'll tax you on it. Alternatively, a tax can be levied on 'turnover' (gross sales receipts) as estimated by tax officials or even as self-reported by taxpayers, as is often done with respect to local business taxes, for example (Bird 2003). In either case, the basic

---

[4] If services such as electricity and housing that are largely financed from the budget are taxed, presumably there would be pressure to increase the subsidy rate to offset the tax. As we note in Chapter 6 with respect to the issue of imposing VAT in the public sector, imposing VAT in order to make the real budgetary cost of such subsidies transparent is logical but governments are seldom keen to be this logical. A less obvious problem is that if a subsidized output (e.g., electricity) is taxed, the inputs acquired by the electricity supplier become creditable and the result may be a net revenue loss to government. We owe this point to David Sewell.

[5] One never knows which way the political winds will blow. Some countries have recently reduced VAT rates. In Canada, for example, the Conservative (minority) government elected in January 2006 decreased the GST rate from 7% to 6% (effective July 1, 2006) and intends to reduce it further to 5% in the future. Given the popularity of these cuts, no opposition party has dared to oppose them in public.

[6] We do not discuss here whether U.S. states (or some Canadian provinces) should consider changing their retail sales taxes to VATs. Bird and Wilson (2004) argue that such a change for the province of Ontario would definitely make sense on competitive grounds. Dahlby (2005) goes further and suggests that all Canadian provinces with retail sales taxes should move to VAT, following the model set out in Bird and Gendron (1998, 2001). Bird (2005b) suggests that even if the United States does not have a national VAT, it would nonetheless be smart for many states to consider introducing 'VAT-like' elements into their retail sales taxes, essentially for the reasons set out in the present chapter.

administrative problem is to determine and verify the turnover (sales) of a taxpayer and to collect the tax. The idea is simple. Its execution can be difficult. The basic way to evade such a tax is also simple: hide (underreport) sales. The easiest way legally to avoid a turnover tax is by integrating vertically with one's suppliers, since 'within-firm' sales are not taxed. The other side of this coin, however, is that a turnover tax is by far the economically most distorting form of sales tax. For example, sales of investment as well as consumption goods are taxed. Indeed, often (as in the former Soviet Union) even export sales are taxed. If one wishes to discourage exports and investment and to induce firms to integrate up and down the supply chain, one may perhaps welcome the effects of such a tax. Even so, since the final tax burden borne by any particular transaction depends essentially on how many prior taxed transactions are embodied in its sales price, few are likely to understand either its final effects on prices or its distributional impact. Governments that impose turnover taxes have little idea of the effects of such taxes on either allocation or distribution.

To avoid all these problems, one obvious solution is to impose a single-stage sales tax – commonly called a retail sales tax (RST) – on the final sale to consumers (households or nonregistered firms).[7] Investment goods purchased by registered firms, like other inputs purchased for business purposes, would then in principle be freed from tax, as would exports. The allocative and distributional effects of such a tax are much clearer than those of a turnover tax. The government can figure out what it is doing.

Unfortunately, experience with RSTs even in countries with good tax administrations demonstrates that this promising approach has two fatal flaws. First, it is extremely difficult to ensure that interfirm purchases used to produce taxable goods and services – and only those purchases – are exempt from tax. The 'ring' (or suspension) system used to achieve this result – under which tax is 'suspended' on sales by one registered firm to another, and so on and on, until there is a sale to someone outside the ring of registrants – is both cumbersome to police and easy to abuse. Second, the entire tax collection process rests on the least dependable link in the chain – the final sale to a consumer (that is, someone outside the ring of licensed firms). The fragmented and usually small-business–dominated retail trade sector is notoriously difficult to police in any country.

---

[7] We do not discuss other forms of single-stage sales taxes (those imposed prior to the retail level) here. Few such taxes now exist, and all suffer from the problems long ago analyzed by Due (1957).

Hence the dilemma: turnover taxes are easy to administer but have bad economic effects; single-stage retail sales taxes in theory may avoid these bad effects (though in practice they are unlikely to do so very cleanly) but they are difficult to administer well. Enter the VAT. In principle – and, when properly set up and run, in practice – VAT combines the good features of both its competitors while avoiding most of the bad features. How does it do this? Essentially, through two features: Firstly, VAT imposes what is economically equivalent to a single-stage retail sales tax through a multistage process that in effect 'withholds' tax at each stage of the chain of production and distribution preceding the final sale to households. By doing so, it ultimately achieves the (presumed) goal of taxing only consumption. Moreover, even if evasion occurs at the final retail stage, only that part of the potential tax base consisting of the retail margin escapes tax. Secondly, by crediting taxes on inputs including capital goods, VAT avoids distorting economic choices with respect to production technology. It also eliminates taxes on exports by crediting taxes paid on inputs at prior stages.

With an RST, as with a turnover tax, the basic way to evade is simply to avoid reporting sales. This can be done by remaining in the shadow economy, by not keeping proper books, or by not reporting correctly to the tax authority. It takes only one to evade. With VAT, however, there are two ways to evade: by underreporting sales or by overreporting taxable purchases (thus claiming excess input tax credits and, in some cases, even refunds). On the other hand, with VAT it also takes two to evade – a seller and a buyer. Moreover, since the two sides of the transaction are (for interbusiness trade) in principle recorded in two sets of books, the task of the administration in detecting evasion should be easier with VAT.

Indeed, the task of the tax collector is made even simpler in principle when it comes to sales between businesses because the two parties involved in any potentially taxable transaction (buyer and seller) have conflicting incentives. Buyers want to overstate purchase prices to inflate credits, while sellers want to understate sales to reduce output taxes. For this reason, some early writers even claimed that VAT was at least to some extent 'self-enforcing' (National Economic Development Office 1969). In reality, however, this apparent strength of VAT has in some instances proved to be a weakness since it perhaps induced some countries to rely too heavily on tax design (the VAT approach to sales taxation) to do the work that only good tax administration can really do. A major form of VAT evasion plays on this feature of VAT: a firm creates a 'shell' company and then 'sells' inputs to itself at a false price that then serves as the basis for an input tax credit or refund claim.[8]

It is easier to get away with this dodge when the alleged supplier is in another country, as in the case of the so-called carousel frauds in the EU (Sinn, Gebauer, and Parsche 2004). But when the tax administration is as weak as it is in many developing and transitional countries, it is not hard to create and register fictitious firms domestically in order to operate such frauds. As we discuss further with respect to refunds in Chapter 10, one reaction to such practices has been to disallow refunds with respect to capital purchases by new firms until a reasonable pattern of economic activity has been established (e.g., for a year).[9] Despite such problems, however, and regardless of the competence of the administration and the honesty of both officials and taxpayers, both in principle and in practice it remains simpler to enforce a sales tax applied in an incremental 'value-added' form to a chain of transactions than to have a system in which all stands or falls on honest reporting of a single transaction (the final sale). The lesson is this: if you have a VAT, keep it.[10]

THE ECONOMICS OF TAX CHOICE

But what if you do not have a VAT? Should you adopt one? Why not go for the apparently simpler economic equivalent of a retail sales tax (RST)? The conceptual equivalence of VAT and RST has frequently been noted. Provided that the tax base is identical and that each is equally well administered, the two are essentially alternative ways of imposing the same tax.[11] The choice between the two is thus often said to turn essentially on which can be better administered in the particular setting in question (which in

---

[8] The procedure just described can also be used to manipulate intercompany transfer prices. Tax authorities sometimes use indirect tax audits to uncover evidence of non–arm's length transfer prices between members of the same corporate group.

[9] The denial or delay of export refunds is, as we discuss later, another and even less attractive response.

[10] Since (as we discuss later) VAT is a relatively complex and costly tax from both administrative and compliance perspectives, this advice of course presumes that the initial VAT adoption paid for itself in revenue and efficiency terms, as discussed next.

[11] For a rigorous comparison of a VAT and a retail sales tax (RST), as well as with two possible alteratives, a manufacturers' level tax and a turnover tax in a simplified setting, see Das-Gupta and Gang (1996). This article shows that such comparisons are sensitive to conditions in both intermediate and final goods markets. Nonetheless, the consensus of professional opinion ignores such subtleties and concludes that VAT is unquestionably a better way to tax consumption than an RST.

turn may be related to the amount of revenue expected from the tax). This argument is obviously technically correct. If two taxes tax the same base equally effectively, they are indeed equivalent in an economically relevant sense. However, the argument is incomplete since in reality the bases of a VAT and an RST are most unlikely to be equivalent. This point is critical because the economic effects of a tax depend primarily on the size and nature of its base. The size of the tax base determines the rate needed to generate any given revenue, and the precise nature of the base determines both the precise nature of the way in which the tax affects economic efficiency and the potential effectiveness of the tax's administration in any given setting. The two most important and critical differences between VAT and RST are the extent to which business inputs are 'untaxed' and the extent to which services are taxed. In principle, such differences need not exist. However, in practice they almost invariably do, and for good reason.

Business Inputs

There are a number of reasons, persuasive at least to economists, for *not* taxing business inputs under a consumption tax. The first and in many ways the critical argument from an economic perspective is simply that since, by definition, only consumers consume, then only consumers should be subject to a consumption tax. To the extent that some 'consumption' tax in fact falls on intermediate production inputs, the actual burden imposed on final consumption will vary in proportion to the extent to which such inputs are used in producing final consumption goods. The resulting uneven pattern of tax incidence is unlikely to accord with any policy intent. It will affect consumption choices and hence reduce market efficiency. A second argument is that input taxes also affect production efficiency by altering the choice of inputs and perhaps even the choice of production techniques – for example, by delaying new investment because of the higher cost of capital equipment.[12] The result is to reduce not only economic efficiency but also investment and growth.[13]

Further reasons for untaxing business inputs are not hard to find. For instance, since most firms are too small to influence prices of goods sold to other jurisdictions, to the extent that taxes on production inputs are

---

[12] The classical argument on the importance of not distorting input prices and hence creating production inefficiencies is Diamond and Mirrlees (1971). While there are 'second-best' exceptions to this rule, they do not seem very persuasive in practice (Keen 2006).

[13] Initially, China's VAT did not allow input credits for capital goods precisely in order to *discourage* investment!

not rebated on exports the relative profitability of exporting is reduced. Consequently, the export sector is smaller than it would otherwise be.[14] Moreover, because firms can generally avoid such 'cascading' taxes if they produce inputs themselves, an undesirable incentive to vertical integration is created. Even the size and structure of productive organizations may thus be affected by consumption taxes that are not confined to taxing consumption. Finally, firms in jurisdictions that impose relatively heavier taxes on business inputs are clearly penalized relative to firms in areas that tax such inputs less heavily. A recent study in Ontario (Canada), for example, found that removing the 'cascading' effect of the provincial (retail) sales tax on business would have a larger marginal incentive effect on new investment than would lowering the provincial corporate income tax from 12.5% to 8% (Chen and Mintz 2003).

On the other hand, there are also some reasons that appear often to be persuasive in the political arena as to why inputs *should* be taxed. The major reason is simply that there is a lot of potential revenue in taxing business inputs. Many U.S. states and Canadian provinces collect between a third and half of RST revenues from such inputs (Ring 1999; Kuo, McGirr, and Poddar 1988). Clearly, if these items are excluded from the tax base (as they are with VAT), then to meet an immediate revenue target either the tax rate has to be higher or the tax base has to be expanded.[15] Related to this argument is the simple fact that it is always politically attractive to tax something vague called 'business' – usually understood to mean 'the rich' or at least 'someone other than me' – rather than final consumption, which all too obviously means 'me' to most voters. Finally, in addition to these political arguments, it may also be argued that it is administratively complex to 'untax' business inputs. Indeed, it is complex to do so with an RST; that is one important reason that so many countries have adopted a VAT in recent decades – precisely because it is hard to relieve business inputs from tax with any other form of sales tax.

---

[14] Even if taxed firms can shift some tax to foreign buyers, the same result would ensue unless demand were completely inelastic. In general equilibrium, of course, exchange rate changes would also have to be taken into account (Chapter 4).

[15] In the long run, if one accepts the Diamond-Mirrlees (1971) approach, presumably taxing business inputs will of course *reduce* potential revenue – but governments seldom look that far ahead. On the other hand, as Technical Committee (1997) argues, we might want to tax some business inputs such as fuel if they are associated with externalities, and, as Bird (2003) argues, to some extent such taxation may even be viewed as a sort of 'generalized user charge.' These and many other subtle points are being left aside here both to keep things simple and to keep the reader's eye on what matters most in VAT practice.

On the whole, viewed from a strictly economic perspective business inputs should be 'untaxed' under any decent consumption tax. To do so with RST, one can proceed in two ways. First, the definition of 'taxable sale' found in most jurisdictions with RSTs – essentially most U.S. states and some Canadian provinces – excludes 'sales for resale.' While it is not always clear exactly what this term means, the usual interpretation excludes from tax those goods that are physically incorporated into other goods, which are then in turn sold for final consumption – for example, wood used to build a desk.[16] There are, however, many borderline cases (consumables and fuel, containers, repairs and maintenance, construction, etc.) and the tax treatment of many of these items varies widely under RSTs in the United States, for example (Due and Mikesell 1994).

Secondly, some products, notably machinery and equipment, may be specifically exempt from tax. For instance, the exemption approach is often applied to major agricultural inputs (feed, seed, fertilizer, agricultural equipment) under the RST. Such exemptions are generally administered by requiring the purchaser to provide to the seller an official certificate of exemption – a document certifying that the buyer is a registered vendor and showing its sales tax registration number. As a rule, the purchaser is held liable for any misuse of this exemption – for example, if the buyer makes a tax-free purchase that is not for resale (or not physically included in a product that is sold). Some U.S. states require similar certificates for purchases of industrial equipment and even in a few cases for tax-free purchases of agricultural inputs, although farmers are seldom if ever registered for sales tax purposes. The purpose of such certificates is to facilitate control by providing a more complete 'paper trail' for sales tax auditors. The efficacy of this system depends entirely on the quantity and quality of sales tax audit. The strength of this pillar of the RST generally leaves much to be desired.[17]

A further problem with the RST approach arises from the existence of a considerable group of 'exempt purchasers' in the form of a wide variety of both public sector and nonprofit organizations. The tax status of nonprofit entities is a complex and difficult issue under the VAT (Chapter 6). It is arguably more so under an RST – or it would be if such taxes were ever enforced to VAT standards. Ideally, for full audit control, exempt purchasers

[16] Similar rules are found in some VATs in developing countries and give rise to the same problems.
[17] One thorough review in the United States concluded that "most states need to at least double their audit staffs, increasing their audit coverage threefold to maximize revenue" (Due and Mikesell 1994, 244).

should be registered as such and their registration numbers quoted on the relevant invoices. No U.S. state appears to do this.[18] Indeed, some states do not even register nonretail enterprises (manufacturers and wholesalers) that make occasional taxable sales, although again such registration is necessary for control over purchases for resale. The theoretically correct solution, although not necessarily the most cost-efficient, would be to register more, not fewer, entities under either RST or VAT. However, most U.S. states seem more concerned to reduce 'overregistration' than 'underregistration' because of the ability of registered firms to purchase many items tax free (Due and Mikesell 1994).[19]

Sales of taxable goods and services that take place within the 'ring' of those holding registration (or exemption) certificates escape RST. RST applies only when sales are made to those outside this magic circle – that is, to final consumers or, perhaps (and by no means unimportantly) to unregistered or 'informal' producers. This approach is obviously potentially subject to abuse – for example, by using equipment such as vehicles or computers purchased for businesses for personal purposes. A so-called use tax exists to capture such personal use but is not very effective.[20] In part because of the considerable potential for abuse, in practice most RSTs restrict the operation of the suspension system in a number of ways – for example, excluding certain products (such as vehicles or personal computers).[21]

No tax is perfect. Certainly no existing RST is perfect in excluding all tax elements from the price of business inputs (Ring 1999). It cannot be done. Most RSTs further exclude most important services and also permit a wide variety of other exemptions and exclusions, with the result that many business purchases are not subject to tax in the first place. However, to the extent that such exempt and excluded activities incorporate taxed elements – even accountants and consultants use computers, desks, and pencils that are taxed, for instance – nominally untaxed business inputs generally incorporate some tax element. The fees a firm pays for accounting services may thus be $100 higher because the accountant is passing on the

---

[18] Nor do those Canadian provinces with RSTs. Since many nonprofit activities are registered under the federal GST in principle, such provinces could use the GST number for control purposes, but we are not aware that any does so.

[19] The same concern arises under VAT because a registered firm can make a false claim for input tax credits.

[20] Due and Mikesell (1994, chap. 10) discuss the use tax in some detail, setting out the different ways in which it operates in different U.S. states and its widely varying importance in revenue terms.

[21] Due and Mikesell (1994, chap. 3) discuss state treatment of production inputs in detail.

RST he or she has paid on various inputs. The firm in turn incorporates this additional $100 in its cost base in determining the price it charges for its own product, assuming it can pass the tax on fully.

The tax that is paid by the final consumer on any product thus depends not simply on the RST explicitly levied on the final price but also on the extent to which that price incorporates earlier taxes levied in the production process. Depending on market conditions, in some instances the producer may have absorbed some tax costs, thus reducing profitability and making investment less attractive. If such costs impinge on the acquisition of new capital, businesses may be at a competitive disadvantage with respect to competitors located in other countries and regions.[22] If such costs reduce the profitability of exporting, the export sector will be disadvantaged. The extent to which and the manner in which the hidden taxes imposed by the RST echo down the supply chain distort both consumption and production decisions, alter the distributive impact of the tax in a complex way, and reduce economic efficiency, investment, and growth in the economy as a whole.

From the perspective of tax design, a principal reason for adopting a VAT is precisely that it reduces many of these unintended consequences. The extent of the multifaceted distortions resulting from the RST approach to sales taxation is difficult to assess, but the VAT approach should be less distorting simply because it substantially reduces the taxation of business inputs. Paradoxically, precisely because most inputs pay VAT, no additional tax element is included in the VAT levied on the sale to the final consumer. Sellers deduct VAT previously paid on inputs (including purchases of capital goods) before remitting VAT due on sales (assuming VAT takes the conventional income-credit form). From an economic perspective, this ability of VAT to 'untax' business is one of its most attractive features: VAT is the form of consumption tax that approaches most closely taxing consumption at the explicit tax rate stated in the law.

Taxing Services

Untaxing business inputs reduces the tax base, however. Even if more growth ensues over time, the immediate result is that the tax rate has to be increased

---

[22] Over time, as resources shift in response to demand shifts reflecting price differentials, such disadvantages may be reduced, but (as we argue in Chapter 4), even when taxing jurisdictions have separate currencies and there can also be exchange rate adjustments, such effects are unlikely to be offset fully.

to raise a given amount of revenue, and higher tax rates create distortion. Fortunately, a VAT usually expands the tax base from the usual goods-oriented RST base to encompass a much wider range of services. 'Services' may take many forms. Some services are ancillary or incidental to the production or supply of goods, while others stand alone. In many cases the line between goods and services is thin, and taxes that fall only on 'goods' are open to abuse and can be administratively intractable.[23] The recent growth of digital technology has blurred this line even more (Chapter 8). VAT does not resolve these problems, but it does make them more manageable.

VAT usually encompasses a much wider range of services than most RSTs, ranging from services associated with the purchase and use of goods (repairs, transportation, insurance, consulting) to a wide spectrum of other services. Some services – such as accounting, legal, and other professional services – are consumed largely by firms and are creditable against output tax, thus reducing cascading and distortions. The VAT approach to service taxation – taxing all services and allowing credits to legitimate business users (registered VAT payers) – is, experience suggests, more effective, equitable, and efficient than the RST approach of taxing only certain specific services (dry cleaning, barbers, preparation of personal income tax returns) that are assumed to be provided mainly to consumers.

A survey a few years ago found that 164 different named services were subject to RST in different U.S. states, ranging from only one in Alaska, which has only a local sales tax, to 157 in Hawaii, where the so-called general excise tax is actually imposed on 'turnover' or gross receipts rather than just on 'retail sales'and hence has a much broader base (as well as even more cascading) than the usual RST.[24] Unfortunately, since many of the services taxed are those frequently used by businesses – credit reporting, advertising, printing, computer and data processing, maintenance and janitorial services, and so on – the impact of including more services in the RST tax base has

---

[23] Automobile and other repairs, for example, usually require both parts (goods) and labour (services). The potential for rearranging the bill to minimize tax is obviously great when only 'goods' are taxed.

[24] Although State of Hawaii (2002) makes much of the difference between what Hawaii calls its 'excise tax,' which it alleges is imposed on business, and a sales tax that would be, it assumes, imposed on consumers, the Hawaiian excise is of course only another variety of sales tax. Unlike most RSTs, however, it is imposed at three rates: 0.15% on insurance commissions, 0.5% on wholesale sales, and 4% on retail sales. The low rate on wholesale sales is presumably intended to reduce cascading. In 2000, 'wholesale sales' were defined a bit more broadly to include, for example, certain telecommunications and transportation services in a further attempt to reduce cascading.

probably been to increase the extent to which the tax falls on business inputs rather than final consumption.[25]

In contrast, VAT both taxes a considerably wider range of services and clearly 'untaxes' services to the extent they are used by registered taxpayers for business purposes. Of course, as we discuss in later chapters, many problems remain in taxing services under a VAT, for instance, with respect to financial services and cross-border services.[26] Moreover, it remains true in principle that exactly the same base could be reached equally well with a properly designed and administered RST. That most RSTs are defective does not mean that any consumption tax taking this form must inherently be similarly imperfect. In practice, however, most RSTs do appear to be much more economically distorting than most VATs.[27] The relatively lower rates of RSTs (and the considerably greater availability of administrative and fiscal resources) may make the resulting problems tolerable and affordable in U.S. states and Canadian provinces. Developing and transitional countries do not have the luxury of making similar bad choices.

Other Economic Aspects

VAT thus wins on economic grounds. Or does it? When it comes to other factors sometimes mentioned in this connection, the case for VAT seems less strong. For example, while on balance the evidence is that VATs may have increased revenues to some extent in developed countries, it is not all that clear, and the proposition seems especially weak in the least developed countries (Keen and Lockwood 2006). Certainly, VAT is not always a sure way to increase the total tax take (Chapter 4). The revenue yielded by any sales tax is the product of its base and rate. Abstracting from administrative

---

[25] Federation of Tax Administrators (1997) discusses the situation in the U.S. states. There have been few changes in the situation in the last few years. For an interesting exploration of the extent to which RSTs might be extended to encompass services more successfully, see Hendrix and Zodrow (2003). As these authors note, there is a strong economic case for taxing more consumer services but none for taxing business services. They do not, perhaps, emphasize strongly enough the considerable administrative difficulties that arise under the RST approach in distinguishing between the two. The 'dual use' system they suggest as a possible replacement appears to combine the problems of the VAT approach – the need for refunds, etc. – with those of the RST – the need to distinguish 'dual use' inputs.

[26] For a good general discussion of VAT on services, see Kay and Davis (1990).

[27] While as is so often the case when it comes to sales taxes there is surprisingly little empirical evidence to support such statements, Kuo, McGirr, and Poddar (1988) estimated (some aspects of) the distortion costs of RSTs in Canada in the 1980s.

issues (and any long-term effects on growth), the size of the respective bases depends upon (1) the extent to which business inputs are taxed under the RST and 'untaxed' under the VAT, (2) the extent to which final (consumer) services are taxed under the two forms of tax, and (3) the relationship between these two magnitudes for each tax. If, as suggested earlier, more services are taxed under the VAT approach than under the usual RST, then arguably the elasticity of a VAT (with respect to GDP) should be higher since the share of services in consumption usually rises more quickly as income rises than does the share of goods. Still, as already mentioned, the evidence is that VAT is a 'money machine' remains cloudy (Chapter 4).[28]

Similarly, it is occasionally asserted that an RST is more prone to 'erosion' by exemptions than a VAT. There is no obvious reason this should be correct unless one believes that the administrative cost of particular exemptions is relatively higher with an RST than that of similar exemptions under a VAT. This issue has not been systematically examined by anyone. Of course, as we argue in Chapter 7, governments introducing any form of sales tax are well advised to establish as few exemptions and exceptions as possible because, once granted, such concessions invariably prove hard to reverse and invite demands for more concessions. Since an RST is (often, although not necessarily) more visible than a VAT, perhaps one might argue that concessions are more likely in the case of the former. Again, however, there is no evidence to support this argument.

Much the same is true of the common argument, mentioned earlier, that VAT is easier to administer because it is 'self-enforcing.' No tax is self-enforcing.[29] The argument to the contrary sometimes made with respect to VAT rests on the fact that the output tax payable by one firm is to some extent another's creditable input tax. Firms may thus have conflicting interests – one to underreport (output tax) and the other to overreport (input tax) – and

---

[28] It is sometimes asserted that VAT confers a short-term revenue advantage to government because it 'gets the money earlier' (that is, in stages during the production process rather than only at the end when a good is finally sold to consumers). But this argument is clearly wrong. At the end of each tax period the government must (so to speak) pay back input tax credits so the net flow of revenue to government depends entirely on the amount that is collected on the final sales – that is, 'sales to others than VAT registrants' – taking place in the economy in that period (OECD 1988). If the VAT payment period is identical to the normal commercial payment period, as is often the case, and the level of activity of VAT taxpayers is constant over time, the same arithmetic applies even in the case of a single VAT taxpayer: neither the taxpayer nor the government gains or loses in revenue terms by moving to a VAT.

[29] Earlier 'self-enforcing' tax ideas may be found in, for example, Kaldor (1956), Higgins (1959), and Strasma (1965). For an evaluation of these ideas, see Shoup (1969).

the result may be, on balance, more accurate reporting. If sellers and purchasers were (1) equally liable for each other's accurate tax reporting and hence concerned to police each other's honesty and (2) subjected to a credible threat of monitoring by the tax authorities, this argument might perhaps carry some weight. As a rule, however, neither party is liable for errors of either commission or omission by the other party in the transaction, and tax auditing in most developing and transitional countries is as sporadic as it is ineffective.[30] VAT does have some administrative advantages over an RST, as we discuss later, but these advantages are not necessarily decisive.

Finally, while it has often been suggested that VAT is a more effective way to reach the so-called informal sector, this too is unclear as we discuss later in this book. The extent to which any form of consumption tax reaches the elusive denizens of this hidden sector is a function of both design and – especially – administration. In practice, however, even if one could conceive of an equally well-administered RST on the same base, the VAT approach is likely more effective in this respect essentially because it taxes imports of the informal sector as we note in Chapter 10.

ADMINISTRATIVE ASPECTS OF TAX CHOICE

On balance, we think the economic advantages seem clearly on the side of VAT. As just discussed, however, the issue is less clear with respect to the administrative dimension of tax choice. Some think, for example, that a major difference between a VAT and an RST is that the former requires dealing with a much larger number of taxpayers. Any form of general tax on final consumption does require dealing with considerably more taxpayers than does, say, a manufacturer's sales tax, but VAT does not require dealing with many more registered entities than a similar tightly controlled RST. The issue cannot be settled by comparisons between the number of 'retailers' and the total number of firms. The former number is by definition smaller, but this does not mean VAT is more administratively demanding than a retail sales tax. Not only 'retailers' make 'retail sales.' Since manufacturers (e.g., Dell) and importers and other distributors to business (e.g., big 'box' outlets such as Home Depot or Costco in North America) also sell directly to

---

[30] As we discuss later in Chapter 8, the question of who is liable is particularly important with respect to cross-border digital commerce. If the liability is to be placed on the party within the taxing jurisdiction, whether the buyer (who can credit only taxed purchases) or the seller (with respect to sales to exempt entities), each party to the transaction requires accurate information about the status of the other party. The EU (like Singapore, Canada, and others) aims to provide such access through computerized registration systems.

consumers, they too should be registered for RST purposes. In addition, as we mentioned earlier, if an RST is administered as tightly as VAT, a substantial number of 'nontaxpayers' should be registered to ensure adequate audit control of 'tax-free' sales.[31]

Both forms of consumption tax are identical in one important respect. Both operate by distinguishing between those who are 'inside' the system and those 'outside' the system. An RST 'suspends' tax on sales between those inside the system and taxes sales to those outside. A VAT taxes all sales but then credits taxes levied on sales made 'inside' the system (input tax credits) against taxes levied on those made outside (output taxes). If the tax base is the same – same items taxed, same exemptions, and so forth – and the two taxes are administered equally effectively, then exactly the same entities (including those 'exempt' under an RST) should be 'inside,' that is, registered (or otherwise recognized) for sales tax purposes. It is true that in practice most RST jurisdictions do not follow this path. Instead, they download the task of dealing with exempt purchasers (other than 'tax-free' sales to other registered firms) to sellers. However, since sellers seldom bear any liability for mistakes, the efficacy of this way of operating a sales tax is doubtful.

In principle there should thus be little difference in the number of firms to be dealt with under either the VAT or RST form of consumption tax, *provided* the same level of administrative control is achieved under both systems. In practice, however, there are often important differences in the nature and scope of the tasks facing the tax administration. One reason is that the VAT approach downloads much of the burden of administration to the private sector. For example, under an RST if a registered entity purchases a product, no tax is collected. For the tax administration to determine whether tax should have been collected, it must determine the facts of the case: was the purchaser a legitimate (licensed) activity and did it put the product purchased to a legitimate use? If some impropriety is uncovered, it is up to the authorities to chase down the guilty and attempt to collect any tax due. This is not easy, and it is not surprising that most RST administrations seem to do little along these lines. All the cost is borne by them and successful outcomes are elusive.

With a VAT, tax is collected on many more transactions, and the government keeps the revenue unless taxpayers demonstrate both that they are legitimate taxpayers and that they have a legitimate claim to credit against tax due on their sales. The onus is on the taxpayer, not the government, to act. If the government doubts the legitimacy of a claim for credit, it can

---

[31] We return to some of these issues when we discuss VAT thresholds in Chapter 7.

demand documentation (invoices) that by law must be maintained by the taxpayer. Further, it may also follow the chain of invoices as necessary by using documentation that should be readily available – and if it is not available, the game is over for the taxpayer. Life for tax administrators may thus in some respects be somewhat easier under a VAT than an RST. The obverse, however, is that VAT is correspondingly more onerous for taxpayers, who must maintain more records to aid the hand that smites them.

Sandford et al. (1981) argued that anyone who runs a sound business needs to maintain 'VAT-like' records in any case, so that imposing a VAT may even yield so-called management benefits by encouraging businesses to do their job better. Such minor consolations are unlikely to cut much ice with taxpayers faced with what undoubtedly is perceived by them to be a new and onerous fiscal obligation. Complaints are likely to be particularly great from smaller firms, for which the fixed costs of establishing required new accounting or reporting systems constitute a proportionately greater burden (Cnossen 1994). However, since if anyone ever actually tried to administer an RST at the standards of the average VAT, taxpayers would presumably be required to maintain exactly the same records, this particular 'anti-VAT' argument should be regarded with some skepticism.

BORDER ISSUES

A final set of policy-cum-administrative issues that arise in choosing which form of general sales tax makes most sense in any particular context may be (loosely) labeled 'border issues.' 'Borders' may arise not just between taxing jurisdictions but between classes of taxpayers and types of transactions. As we note in Chapter 8, for example, VAT is clearly better than RST when it comes to 'e-commerce' not because it can tax direct sales to consumers effectively – it cannot – but because it is more effective in relieving business inputs from tax and thus reducing the economic distortions created by so-called consumption taxes that in practice actually tax much production (as do most RSTs). We shall concentrate here, however, on geographical borders. Such borders are particularly important in subnational jurisdictions that by definition do not control their frontiers.

Even in the United States, where many seem to think that states have no alternative to the RST, two states (Michigan and New Hampshire) do in fact have a variety of VAT, although neither calls it a VAT nor seems very keen about it (Bird 2003). Two other U.S. states (Louisiana and Mississippi) also have an important 'VAT-like' element in their RSTs. In the case of Louisiana, for example, 'wholesalers' – a term that includes manufacturers, jobbers, and suppliers selling to anyone for sale at retail – are required to collect advance sales taxes from such purchasers. Retailers who have made such advance payments can then deduct such payments from the tax they collect on their own sales, provided that the deductions are supported by invoices from wholesalers showing the advance payment.[32] This is of course exactly the way a VAT works.

As Canadian experience demonstrates, even a full-fledged invoice-credit VAT can work well at the subnational level in the right conditions (Bird and Gendron 1998). For domestic sales provincial VATs in Canada work exactly as the Louisiana tax does. For cross-border (out-of-province) sales, taxes are not collected on import except with respect to international imports. The same is true, however, even with respect to those provinces that have RSTs since the Canada Border Services Agency (CBSA) has made arrangements with most provinces to collect provincial sales taxes (regardless whether they are imposed in VAT or RST form) on imports for final consumption.[33] For imports by final consumers (or nonregistrants) from other provinces, provincial sales taxes rely on provisions similar to, and probably no more effective than, the so-called use tax common in the United States.[34] However, 'commercial' imports made by registered importers are not subject to any provincial tax on import from other provinces or from abroad. Tax on such imports is in effect 'deferred' until resale. In this case even if a province has a VAT, its tax acts as a 'suspended' RST in the sense that tax is deferred at import and collected on the first subsequent taxable transaction. This 'deferred VAT' procedure is exactly the way VAT has long worked in some European countries with respect to cross-border transactions (Cnossen and Shoup 1987).

One argument sometimes made in favor of VAT in developing countries is that this approach offers a more effective way to collect consumption taxes both because the first 'chunk' of the tax is collected at the border when goods are imported and because a relatively higher proportion of taxable consumption is likely to be imported than in more developed countries. If a country has no effective tax collection system other than at its borders,

---

[32] For a description of the Louisiana tax, see U.S. Chamber of Commerce (2004).

[33] Provincial taxes are also applied by CBSA to goods delivered by courier or post, subject to a *de minimis* rule.

[34] Bird and Gendron (1998) argue that this process may be somewhat more effective in provinces with VATs because the overarching national VAT (the GST) and agreements between the federal and provincial authorities permit information exchange and therefore more effective audits.

such arguments are attractive. Indeed, they seem so attractive that a recent study actually went so far as to say that "so central is the role of customs in relation to the VAT that Hong Kong, so committed to free trade that it currently has no customs administration, has been advised to consider creating one if it decides to adopt a VAT" (Keen 2003, 8). Such arguments can be overdone.[35] As noted earlier, subnational jurisdictions can get around having border controls simply by not attempting to collect the tax at the border (since they cannot do so) but instead trying to collect it on the first taxable transaction that occurs after the border. This is the way an RST works and is also common practice with VAT. Of course, at the limit a 'deferred VAT' is conceptually identical to a 'suspended RST' and raises similar problems.[36] In the conditions of most developing and transitional countries, as we note later, it is generally advisable from both revenue and development perspectives to impose VAT at the border instead of hoping (as with an RST) to be able to collect it later in the distribution process.

In a jurisdiction that does not control its borders, an invoice-credit VAT works with respect to cross-border transactions in much the same way as an RST in the same jurisdiction would work with respect to similar transactions. In both instances no tax is imposed at the border. Hence no tax is collected until (and unless) a subsequent 'in-jurisdiction' transaction attracts the attention of the authorities. The 'deferred VAT' approach is also sometimes used with respect to imports that are subsequently reexported. While such treatment is most common with respect to export processing zones and similar 'enclaves,' it is occasionally applied more widely to well-established exporters.

In Singapore, for example, under what is called the "major exporter scheme" (MES), approved VAT registrants can import without paying tax at the time of import (Inland Revenue Authority of Singapore 2003). The basic requirements to qualify are that over half of total sales are for export and the firm is in good compliance with all tax requirements. In some instances, the tax authorities may also require a letter of guarantee. MES status, once

---

[35] The recent consultative paper on a VAT for Hong Kong makes no mention of them (Hong Kong 2006).

[36] To illustrate, a difficult (though seldom discussed) 'border problem' arises under any sales tax with respect to verifying exports. Whether input taxes are refunded on export or deferred, as is sometimes done for major exporters under both RST and VAT (see later discussion), the problem of adequately documenting and verifying exports remains.

granted, is good for three years. The rationale for this approach is that since exports are zero-rated, any VAT collected on imports would in any case have to be refunded. It is less costly to all concerned simply not to collect tax in the first place. In addition, it is sometimes argued that deferral alleviates the disadvantage that would otherwise be faced by exporters who had to pay VAT on imports and then wait – sometimes for a very long time – for the tax to be refunded after export. Such schemes are simply a variant of the usual 'duty-free' ('bonded') treatment common in many customs systems. They are hence subject to all the problems commonly associated with controlling abuse, fraud, and leakage in such systems (Goorman 2005). The Achilles' heel of this approach in most developing and transitional countries is the lack of any creditable system of 'post-import audit' (e.g., of duty-free stores).

Another 'border' issue related to exports concerns 'pre-export' taxation. Under an RST, goods exported from the jurisdiction are not taxed but tax elements may be included as a result of prior taxes on inputs. Under a VAT, taxes previously paid on inputs would be credited and in many cases refunded. Since an input tax credit is conceptually equivalent to a check drawn on the Treasury but issued by the private sector, potentially serious frauds may arise from fraudulent (or overvalued) exports (Chapter 10). In such cases VAT may create a better 'audit trail' than would an RST. Regardless of the form of a sales tax, however, it is always difficult to verify the reality and value of exports reported by taxpayers, especially when (as with most subnational jurisdictions) there are no physical border controls or (as with digital commerce) there is no physical transaction (Chapter 8).

Finally, developing and transitional countries seldom want to create barriers to new capital investment. They are also likely to want to reduce troublesome refund claims. One way to achieve both goals may be to defer VAT on imported capital goods (Chapter 10). Any such system should presumably apply only to low-risk VAT registrants who import large capital goods. Such imports (like domestic capital goods) would continue to be subject to standard VAT, and imports by non-VAT registrants (or by high-risk registrants) would still have to pay VAT before clearance of goods. 'Qualified' VAT registrants – those with good compliance records and, perhaps, financial bonds – would, however, be permitted to defer payment until the next VAT return filed after import clearance. In that return they would have to report VAT liable on imported purchases as a liability. At the same time, however, they can claim an input tax credit for this amount (for 100% of VAT if equipment used exclusively for taxable activities). As with a deferral scheme for major exporters, the major practical problem with this approach is that it requires a level of administrative efficiency and competence that seldom exists in developing and transitional countries.[37] As we discuss in more detail in Chapters 9 and 10, even the cleverest VAT design cannot make up for deficient VAT administration.

---

[37] With respect to large projects, it might be easier (and no more risky) just to exempt capital goods imports. Of course, as with all deferral schemes, ideally interest should be paid on deferred taxes at some appropriate rate although it appears that no one actually does this.

FOUR

Trade and Revenue

Almost every country now has a VAT. But is the VAT now in place in most developing and transitional countries as good as it could be? Must 'good' VATs always follow the same pattern? Can every country administer VAT sufficiently well to make the introduction of the tax worthwhile? Is VAT always the best way to respond to the revenue problems arising from trade liberalization? Can VAT be adapted to cope with the rising demands in some countries, especially federal countries, for more access to revenues by local and regional governments? Can VAT deal with such new problems as those arising from changes in business practices with financial innovations and digital commerce? The answers to such questions are critical in many emerging economies. VAT is too important for them not to get the answers right – or at least as right as possible.

VAT remains the best form of general consumption tax available. If a developing or transitional country needs such a tax, as most of them do, then, as we suggested in Chapter 3, VAT is the one to have in almost all cases. Of course, this does not mean that the VAT most such countries already have has been either designed or implemented in the best possible way, as we discuss in Chapters 6 through 10. In addition, some serious criticisms have recently been leveled against VAT as a source of revenue for emerging economies. We consider many of these criticisms in this and the next chapter. We conclude that although there is much we still do not know about VAT, some authors (e.g., Riswold 2004) have given far more weight to these criticisms than the evidence suggests is warranted.

VAT AND TRADE

The most important rationale for the original adoption of VAT in Europe was to facilitate trade within the then-new European Community by turning the sales taxes that had long existed in all member states into true destination-based consumption taxes by both 'untaxing' exports (and removing hidden subsidies) and placing the taxation of imports and domestic production on the famous level playing field.[1] However, some recent empirical work suggests that VAT may deter rather than facilitate trade (Desai and Hines 2002). Others have uncovered disquieting results as they have explored more carefully the theoretical framework linking VAT, tariff reform, trade, trade costs, and welfare (Keen and Ligthart 2001, 2005). Countries with VATs are unlikely to shed them regardless of what theorists may argue, but much room remains for further work in this area.

VAT as Competitive Advantage

A view that surfaced recently in the United States is that a destination-based VAT provides a competitive advantage to the country that implements it.[2] It seems obvious to many that VAT must favor exports since it does not tax them while subjecting imports to tax at the border. Indeed, not only are domestic exporters not required to charge VAT on their foreign sales, but because they are 'zero-rated' (subject to tax at a rate of zero), they are able to obtain full credit for VAT they pay on business inputs. Some international economics textbooks even classify VAT as a nontariff barrier from the standpoint of U.S. firms doing business with EU countries (Appleyard, Field, and Cobb 2006). To a U.S. firm trying to sell in the EU, VAT looks like a tariff and the refund paid to EU exporters looks like an unfair export subsidy. The result seems clear: the United States ends up being penalized for its supposed relatively greater reliance on direct taxation than EU countries essentially because refunds of indirect taxes (but not direct taxes) are allowed by the WTO.[3]

Both VAT and tariffs do tax imports. However, VAT taxes all domestic consumption including imports, while tariffs tax only the latter component of

---

[1] For detailed discussion of the various ways in which fiscal issues came into play in the early days of what later became the EU, see Shoup (1967).

[2] See, e.g., Westin (2004) and Hartman (2004, 2004a). Similar views received considerable attention, again largely in the United States, in the 1970s; for a particularly detailed empirical exploration, see Dresch, Lin, and Stout (1977).

[3] Actually direct taxes (as a share of GDP) are often higher in many EU countries than in the United States (although they may be lower as a share of total taxes): see Messere, de Kam, and Heady (2003). Much of this discussion also arguably distorts the history and rationale of the GATT rules on indirect taxes as carried forward under the WTO: see, for example, the interesting arguments of Floyd (1973) and the more recent discussion in Daly (2006). However, such side issues – like the prolonged controversy about the U.S. use of direct taxes to foster exports (Daly 2006) – cannot be discussed further here.

consumption. Unlike a tariff, VAT has no protective effect and hence does not distort domestic production for such small economies as most developing and transitional countries.[4] Indeed, setting aside the issue of relative collection costs, a VAT is clearly superior to a positive tariff for a small economy not only because it reduces economic distortions but because consumption provides a wider tax base than imports so that a tax on consumption has a smaller deadweight loss per dollar of revenue collected (Desai and Hines 2002).

A quite different way in which VAT may perhaps be seen as conferring a competitive advantage is from the perspective of a country contemplating replacing some other form of sales tax by VAT. For example, one important reason Canada preferred VAT to the country's then existing manufacturers' sales tax (MST) was not only that it would remove a hidden tax on Canadian exports (the 'cascaded' – and unrefunded – MST imposed on transactions prior to final sale) but also, more subtly, that it would remove a bias favouring imports. VAT, unlike MST, would extend to the retail level. Thus, it was argued VAT "would ensure a uniform tax on both imports and domestic goods and services, regardless of when costs (e.g. marketing costs) are added to imports" (Canada 1987, 35).[5] The argument here is not so much that VAT promotes competitiveness on the export side but rather that replacing an economically flawed tax with a VAT removes some distortions from the system and levels the playing field between imports and domestic production.

In an article published in the late 1980s, three authors then with Canada's Department of Finance estimated the effective federal and provincial tax rates for final demand commodities, taking into account taxes on both intermediate inputs and capital goods (Kuo, McGirr, and Poddar 1988). Using this framework and data from 1980 the authors demonstrated that there were indeed quantitatively significant nonneutralities not only in the (then) MST but also in other commodity taxes such as the provincial retail sales taxes. Many goods and services that bore no direct taxes were, in effect, being taxed through hidden taxes imposed on their inputs. The resulting pattern of effective rates by product and industry was unsystematic and bore little relation to any legislative intent.[6] For example, the indirect tax content of exports was estimated to be 1.3% of export revenues. Subsequent analysts correctly pointed out that to some extent the 'cascading' demonstrated by

---

[4] A 'small' economy is one unable to influence the world prices at which it trades.

[5] Under the MST, since importers as such did not generally bear local marketing costs, while manufacturers often did (so that these costs were included in their sales tax base), the MST was not in practice imposed equally on importers and competing manufacturers.

[6] Essentially the same results hold for U.S. state sales taxes (Ring 1999). The importance of this point with respect to subnational VATs was discussed in Chapter 3.

this analysis may have served to correct the narrowness of the sales tax base and that there was no clear evidence of the social costs of the measured difference in effective rates (Whalley and Fretz 1990, 44).[7] Nonetheless, there appears to have been general acceptance of these results.[8]

Did the adoption of VAT actually remove the 'antiexport bias' attributed to Canada's MST? From 1980 (the year of the estimate cited) to 1996 (five years after the introduction of the GST), federal sales tax as percentage of GDP rose from 2.1% to 3.5%. In 1980, about one-third of the price impact of the MST was estimated to be passed through to exports. However, the equivalent figure for 1996 was estimated to be only 2%.[9] Federal sales taxes increased by 65% as a share of GDP over this period, but the impact on exports had been essentially eliminated. At least in the case of Canada, it appears that a move to VAT may indeed have encouraged trade – at least if one accepts the rather strong assumptions on tax incidence underlying the studies just cited.

Feldstein and Krugman (1990) examine the trade effects of VAT using a theoretical trade model. An 'idealized' VAT in the form of a tax applied at a uniform rate on all production for consumption, with border adjustments (imports subject to VAT and VAT on exports fully rebated), would have no allocative effects and be neither pro- nor anticompetitive, essentially because all prices rise so as to offset the VAT. For the same reasons, a VAT without border adjustments (an origin-based tax) would also be neutral with respect to trade. However, in the case in which an idealized VAT replaces an income tax, a temporary expansion in trade might result because of the reduction in the taxation of savings. The relevance of such arguments is limited, however, in a world in which VAT generally complements reliance on income taxes in developed countries (Messere, de Kam, and Heady 2003) and is perhaps more likely to precede such reliance in developing and transitional countries (Bird and Zolt 2005)

VAT as Neutral or Even Trade Reducing

The view that VAT may confer some competitive advantage has been challenged for several reasons. As just noted, the common argument in the

---

[7] This is much the same analytical point recently emphasized, in a somewhat different context, by Emran and Stiglitz (2005), as we discuss later.

[8] For example, a general-equilibrium analysis of the tax substitution (Hamilton and Whalley 1989), although carried out by one of the authors of the critical analysis just mentioned, used the effective tax rates calculated by Kuo, McGirr, and Poddar (1988).

[9] The estimate is from an unpublished study by Hasheem Nouroz (personal communication) using an analytical framework similar to that employed by Kuo, McGirr, and Poddar (1988).

theoretical literature is that VAT is neutral, that is, has no real effects on trade. For example, Frenkel, Razin, and Sadka (1991) show that free trade in both goods and services will equalize the after-tax price of tradable goods and services *if* both countries not only use the destination principle but also apply identical taxes – as is of course not the case. More generally, with balanced trade, provided tax rates do not vary over time, taxes on either exports or imports are equivalent and either form of trade tax will discourage trade by driving a wedge between producer and consumer prices (the Lerner symmetry theorem). As Van den Berg (2004, 194), puts the point: "an import tariff, by raising opportunity costs to exporters, is a tax on exports as well as imports."

Two mechanisms bring about this result. First, in a general equilibrium setting a tariff on imports in any domestic sector X will reduce imports and allow the sector to expand. Assuming that costs increase in X as its output expands, this expansion will drive up the demand (and price) of resources for that sector. But input prices will also increase for other sectors, reducing their ability to produce and export. Second, a tariff that increases the price of imports and induces domestic consumers to buy fewer imports will reduce the demand for foreign exchange. The result will be an appreciation of the domestic currency, thereby making the country's exports more costly in foreign countries. As Feldstein and Krugman (1990) show, this equivalence holds even with a (highly unusual) VAT that taxes imports and does not feature an export rebate. In this case, however, if there is either price flexibility or an appropriate exchange rate adjustment, VAT becomes a protectionist measure and would likely reduce the size of the traded goods sector.

This so-called equivalence result has played a large role in the literature on VAT and trade, but it is based on strong assumptions that are invariably violated in practice, as Ebrill et al. (2001) correctly emphasize.[10] These assumptions include not only uniform taxation but also the absence of both revenue and intergenerational wealth effects as a result of a switch from the origin to the destination principle. Moreover, in the real world, outcomes depend heavily upon the relative size of various elasticities and marginal reactions. Feldstein and Krugman (1990) examine a somewhat more realistic case in which VAT is applied more selectively, for example, with some exemptions and exclusions, especially for nontraded rather than traded goods and services. Unsurprisingly, since such a VAT increases the production and consumption of nontradeable goods and services at the

---

[10] For a sample of the ongoing theoretical discussions of this point, see, for example, Lockwood (1993); Lockwood, de Meza, and Myles (1994, 1994a, 1995); and López-Garcia (1996).

expense of tradeables, they conclude that a typical (selective) VAT reduces both imports and exports. Border adjustments or no border adjustments, VAT is unlikely to be a source of competitive advantage.

Empirical Studies and Considerations

In what may perhaps be seen as a loose test of the argument just stated, Desai and Hines (2002) examine the relationship between the reliance on VAT (VAT revenue as a percentage of total government revenue) and the size of exports and imports. They conclude not only that countries relying on VAT have fewer exports and imports (relative to GDP) than countries that do not, but also that the negative correlation between VAT and trade (the sum of exports and imports) is stronger for low-income countries. They reach this conclusion by regressing measures of trade intensity (openness or export share) on explanatory variables that include indicators of VAT use. Three data sets are used: (1) an aggregate cross section of 136 countries for 2000, (2) an unbalanced panel of 168 countries over 1950–2000, and (3) data on foreign affiliates of large U.S. multinational enterprises (MNEs) in 52 countries in 1999. While the authors employ a variety of specifications, the ordinary least squares results (for the most complete specifications) are that, for the cross-section data, VAT has a negative and statistically significant impact on either openness or trade and that, for the panel data, although VAT continues to be associated with reduced openness and export shares, the size of estimated effects is smaller – for example, openness declines by less than 1% in response to a 10% greater reliance on VAT.

This study is intriguing but hardly decisive. For instance, when openness and export share regressions are run for the 1970–98 period, adding average tariff rates as an explanatory variable, all VAT effects become statistically insignificant (when all fixed effects are incorporated). Tariff rates pick up most of the openness and export restriction effects (i.e., higher tariffs imply higher exports), and that result perhaps suggests that there are model mis-specification problems. Moreover, since over this period VAT has increasingly replaced tariff revenue in many developing and transitional countries (Table 2.4), simultaneity may also be a problem. Other problems concern the extent to which VAT is a substitute for other revenue-raising instruments and such important practical questions as the nonuniform application of VAT (Table 2.2) and the difficulties firms face in some countries in collecting refunds (Chapter 10).

Edmiston and Fox (2006) raise some additional concerns about the way VAT actually operates and the ways in which some of these problems may discourage international trade and exports. Such common problems in many developing and transitional countries as delays in the payment of credits, the opportunity cost of funds that are tied up until rebates are paid, the impossibility of getting refunds in some countries, and the inclusion of VAT paid by nonregistered traders in producer prices may result in some 'taxes' on exports.[11] It is not clear whether such problems are quantitatively more or less significant than the problems associated with the limited range of possible substitute revenue sources available in most countries.

It is easy to dismiss such comments as irrelevant: after all, standard textbook arguments suggest that in theory exchange rate adjustments will offset any effects of VAT on exports or imports.[12] Since reducing the demand for imports through trade restrictions reduces exports by reducing the demand for foreign currencies used to purchase imports, the result will be an appreciation of the domestic currency that makes domestic exports more expensive to foreign customers. After a transitional period, or so the textbooks say, trade will settle down to previous levels.

Actually, real-world exchange rate adjustments (even when domestic price adjustments are also taken into account) are most unlikely to yield such a precisely balanced and clean outcome for the decidedly nonuniform VATs found in the real world. The literature on incomplete pass-through of exchange rates, for example, suggests that exchange rate adjustments will not completely offset price differences associated with tax changes. The extent of pass-through – that is, the extent to which changes in exchange rates are fully reflected in the prices paid by consumers for imported goods – depends on such factors as the responsiveness of markups to competitive conditions and the degree of returns to scale in the production of the imported good (Olivei 2002). Marginal cost and markup effects can interact in different ways to produce various outcomes. In theory, constant returns to scale with constant markups will result in complete pass-through, while constant returns to scale with variable markups will result in a less than complete pass-through. Empirical analysis is the only way to sort these influences, and some recent empirical studies suggest that the prices of imported goods respond less than one-for-one to changes in exchange rates even in the long run.[13]

Purchasing power parity (PPP) theory provides another view on the relationship between nominal exchange rates and relative domestic price levels.

---

[11] Actually, taxes on exports, like taxes on intermediate goods, are not necessarily always a bad idea in the circumstances of some developing countries: for an early argument, not unlike that developed in Emran and Stiglitz (2005), see Sanchez-Ugarte and Modi (1987).

[12] See, for example, Appleyard, Field, and Cobb (2006); Pugel (2004); and Van den Berg (2004).

[13] See Olivei (2002) and Wickremasinghe and Silvapulle (2005).

In a recent survey Taylor and Taylor (2004, 135) refer to PPP as "a disarmingly simple theory that holds that the nominal exchange rate between two currencies should be equal to the ratio of aggregate price levels between the two countries, so that a unit of currency of one country will have the same purchasing power in a foreign country." Of course, transaction costs such as transport costs, taxes, tariffs, and nontariff barriers may cause border effects. Even allowing for such factors, however, absolute PPP – as the version of the theory just stated is called – obviously provides a satisfyingly neat theoretical result.

Unfortunately, absolute PPP is as difficult to test as most nice theories since it is difficult to assess whether the same basket of goods is available in two different countries. What has been examined empirically is 'relative PPP,' a less restrictive version that holds that percentage changes in exchange rates will offset differences in inflation rates between two countries over the same period. Reviewing the evidence, which they emphasize is weak, Taylor and Taylor (2004, 139) conclude that "*relative* PPP seems to hold in a long-run sense." But even relative PPP clearly does not hold in the short run. Other research has attempted to explain the evident slow adjustment of real exchange rates. For example, Kleiman (1997) examined the possible role of taxes in explaining the departure of national price levels from PPP and found that the overall burden of central government taxation, especially indirect taxes, raised the general price level. Although his study did not consider VAT as such, this result can likely be carried over to VAT without stretching matters too far. It thus seems plausible that adjustments in exchange rates (like adjustments in domestic prices) are unlikely to offset differences in relative prices that may arise from the imposition and operation of a VAT quickly and completely. But the only definite conclusion one can reach at present is that the effects of VAT on trade flows are not yet known with any degree of certainty.

VAT AND REVENUE

The effects on revenue of VAT remain as open to interpretation and question as are its effects on trade. Recent empirical studies questioning the capability of VAT to replace revenues from trade liberalization, especially in very poor countries, underscore this conclusion.[14] Some countries may

---

[14] See especially Baunsgaard and Keen (2005). Rajaraman (2004) raises an additional point peculiar to India and a few other countries, namely, that even if revenues increase after trade liberalization, they may accrue to regional governments and not to the central government that has lost tariff revenue.

want to retain taxation on international trade on revenue grounds simply because of the apparent relative inefficiency of VAT administration compared to the administration of taxes (tariffs) at the border.[15] On the other hand, if VAT can be administered adequately, the conventional conclusion that it offers the best way for a country to make up revenue losses from trade liberalization (Ebrill, Stotsky, and Gropp 1999) appears generally to hold – though more convincingly for more developed countries than for less developed countries, in which trade taxes are generally more important and alternative tax bases less accessible.[16]

The critical point is that a country must have the capacity to administer VAT adequately. Whether a country introduces VAT to replace another form of general sales tax or as a new tax, revenues (either from consumption taxes or in general) need not increase, but they are highly unlikely to decrease. Moreover, the economic cost of collecting revenues will decline because the base of VAT is less damaging to production efficiency and is almost always broader than that of the taxes (tariffs or other sales taxes) that it replaces. A country is thus generally better off with a VAT than with most alternative general taxes.[17] Although increasing the effective rate of an existing VAT (either by raising the nominal rate or more usually by reducing exemptions) will neither necessarily increase revenues proportionately nor be costless, it is thus often the economically most sensible way to expand public revenues in developing and transitional countries.[18]

A number of empirical studies have examined the relationship between reliance on VAT and the size of government. In the recent U.S. tax reform discussion, for example, the alleged relationship between VAT and government size was one reason for some opposition to VAT, although a review of the evidence concluded that VAT is not "a money machine that would finance the expansion of government" (Bartlett 2004, 1536). In an earlier

---

[15] For recent detailed treatments of customs administration, see Keen (2003) and De Wulf and Sokol (2005).

[16] On this point, compare the rigorous analysis in Keen and Ligthart (2001) with the equally rigorous analysis of a different theoretical case in Keen and Ligthart (2005) and especially the interesting empirical analyses by Baunsgaard and Keen (2005) and Keen and Lockwood (2006).

[17] We do not discuss here the important actual and potential role of excise taxes in developing and transitional countries: for a recent book-length discussion of this issue, see Cnossen (2006).

[18] Compare, for example, the analysis of the revenue effects of Mexican rate increases in Pagan, Soydemir, and Tijerina-Guajardo (2001) with the considerably less positive results for Jamaica in Edmiston and Bird (2004). Garcia Molina and Gómez (2005) found that the 1974 VAT reform in Colombia increased revenues permanently.

cross-section analysis, Ebrill et al. (2001) noted a number of empirical regularities with respect to trade, country size, and government size:

- Countries without a VAT tend to be small, with the notable exception of the United States and (prior to 2005, when a number of state-level VATs were introduced) India.[19]
- Countries that have implemented a VAT have relatively higher GDP per capita levels and rely less on international trade.
- Both income and openness (defined as the sum of exports and imports divided by GDP) are positively correlated with the ratio of taxes to GDP.
- Government consumption and importance of trade are positively correlated (Rodrik 1998), but government consumption as a share of GDP is smaller in larger countries, and small countries tend to be more open to international trade (Alesina and Wacziarg 1998).
- A relatively high ratio of trade to GDP is conducive to VAT revenue performance, presumably because of the relative ease of collecting VAT at the point of import. However, economies for which international trade is important tend to have higher tax yields whether or not they operate a VAT.

A subsequent update of this analysis cautiously concluded that "there is some evidence that the presence of a VAT has been associated with a higher ratio of general government revenue and grants to GDP" (International Tax Dialogue 2005, 11).[20] This study went on to note that this relationship seems stronger the higher the GDP per capita and the lower the share of agriculture in GDP, though the latter relation may simply reflect the common exclusion of most agricultural activity from VAT. Similarly, although the revenue impact of VAT seems smaller the higher the import ratio, this may simply reflect the fact that tariffs (or other taxes) may be equally effective in such countries. On the other hand, all else equal, the more important is trade, the more revenue can be collected from an existing VAT.[21] International Tax

---

[19] The 2006 budget speech in India announced the intention to introduce a central VAT by 2010. For some interesting thoughts on what needs to be done to achieve this target, see Bagchi and Poddar (2006).

[20] See also the subsequent analysis in Keen and Lockwood (2006), which concludes that, while the impact of VAT on (total) revenue appears generally positive, it is theoretically ambiguous and empirically least clearly positive in sub-Saharan Africa.

[21] Keen (2006a) shows that for 36 developing and transitional countries for which data are available, VAT on imports on average accounts for 43% of gross VAT collections, with the share of import VAT ranging from 33% in Argentina and 36% in Zambia to as high as 83% in Guinea and 81% in Kyrgyz Republic.

Table 4.1. *Ukraine's VAT Is in Trouble: Its Decline as a Revenue Source*

Year	VAT as % GDP	VAT on Imports as % GDP	VAT on Domestic as % GDP	VAT Productivity (VAT as % GDP /20)
1998	7.3	1.6	5.7	.36
1999	6.4	1.0	5.4	.32
2000	5.6	1.8	3.8	.28
2001	5.1	1.8	3.3	.26
2002	6.0	3.0	3.0	.30
2003	4.7	3.5	1.2	.24
2004	4.9	3.5	1.4	.25

Source: Bird (2005c).

Dialogue (2005) properly emphasizes, however, the extreme variation across countries in the revenue performance of VAT, reflecting the different ways in which a wide range of factors – differences in tax design, differences in economic environment, and different characteristics (e.g., literacy) – interact in different economies. Definitive answers with respect to VAT's revenue impact are more difficult to come by than the simple assertions that characterize political debate.[22] We return to this issue later.

A Case Study: Ukraine

As in many developing and transitional countries, VAT has become the workhorse of the revenue system in Ukraine. How well VAT works is a critical determinant of the performance of Ukraine's entire fiscal system. As Table 4.1 shows, however, Ukraine's VAT is in trouble. Revenue has declined relative to GDP. VAT's 'collection efficiency' has also declined. The 'VAT gap' – the gap between potential and actual revenue – remains large (Bird 2007).

The revenue yield of VAT as a share of GDP has declined steadily since the tax took full effect in Ukraine in the late 1990s.[23] Such a prolonged decline in VAT yields is both unusual and disturbing. As a rule VAT yield rises when

---

[22] Of course, definitive answers with respect to, for example, the factors determining tax ratios and tax structure more generally are equally hard to come by (Bird, Martinez-Vazquez, and Torgler 2006).

[23] Although a 'value-added tax' was introduced in Ukraine in 1991, it was only in 1997 that a modern VAT (allowing in principle for freeing both investment and exports from tax) was introduced.

GDP grows (Baunsgaard and Keen 2005). In Ukraine, however, although real GDP rose by 49% from 1998 to 2004, the VAT share (VAT revenue as a share of GDP) actually fell by 33%. Normally a general consumption tax such as VAT should grow at least at the same rate as GDP: its GDP elasticity should be approximately 1.0. In Ukraine, however, the arc GDP elasticity of VAT from 1999 to 2004 was an incredibly low 0.38. The revenue performance of Ukraine's VAT leaves much to be desired.

Another striking fact is that the share of VAT collected at the border in Ukraine rose from less than one-quarter of total VAT revenues in 1998 to almost three-quarters in 2004. The other side of the growing dependence of VAT on imports is that VAT collected on domestic consumption fell sharply from 5.7% of GDP in 1998 to only 1.4% in 2004. Of course, many countries collect much of their VAT revenue at the border, and rapid growth in imports such as Ukraine experienced in this period is likely to be reflected in an increase in the share of VAT collected from imports. However, it is difficult to think of any other instance in which a country has had such a marked and rapid change in the extent to which it depends on imports for VAT revenue. For example, in 2004 two-thirds of the absolute increase in VAT revenues in Ukraine was attributable to increased taxes on imports – even though VAT import revenue actually declined from 6.5% of imports in 2003 to only 3.6% in 2004.

Ukraine's VAT has clearly become less efficient as a revenue producer. As we discuss in more detail in the next section, a crude measure of VAT 'revenue efficiency' is simply to take the VAT share of GDP and divide by the standard rate of VAT (20% in Ukraine throughout this period). The number that results from this calculation depicts the percentage of GDP collected by each percentage point of the standard VAT rate. As Table 4.1 shows, this number has declined sharply in Ukraine since a 'modern' VAT was introduced in 1998, with a particularly marked decline in 2003 and 2004. Although Ukraine's VAT 'productivity' for this period (0.30) is not unusually low (see later discussion), the marked and continuous decline in VAT's revenue productivity that has occurred in Ukraine in recent years is striking.[24] Something is clearly wrong in a country in which both income and trade increase but VAT efficiency declines.

Crude calculations may also be made of the size of the 'VAT gap' – defined as the difference between VAT actually collected and that potentially

[24] The conceptually better measures of VAT 'efficiency' discussed later are highly correlated to VAT productivity in Ukraine.

realizable if all consumption were in fact taxed at the stated rate. To illustrate, if VAT actually taxed all final household consumption in Ukraine at 20%, it would have raised an additional 4.2% of GDP in 2004. The VAT 'gap' (potential less actual revenue as percentage of potential) calculated in this way is thus 46%. This estimate of what has been called the 'gross compliance ratio' (Gallagher 2005) takes into account both evasion and 'base erosion' (in the form of legal reductions of the tax base through exemptions and zero-rating other than for exports).[25] Although even a gap of this size is not out of line with that found (by more refined methods) in countries such as Italy and Uruguay, it is much larger than the gap in countries such as Chile or the United Kingdom that have better VAT administrations.[26]

A more conservative estimate of the VAT gap may get a bit closer to estimating the extent to which the decline in VAT revenues may reflect increasing evasion. If VAT productivity as measured in Table 4.1 had simply remained constant at the 1998 level, VAT in Ukraine would have raised an additional 1.5% of GDP in 2004. The gap measured in this way is about 16%. In other words, if there had been no significant erosion of VAT base in 2004 compared to 1998 – probably not too bad an assumption in Ukraine – VAT evasion must have increased by at least this amount over this period. Of course there was already probably a good deal of evasion in 1998.

Although there are many problems with such crude numbers, the conclusion seems inescapable: something is rotten in Ukraine's VAT. Three broad classes of explanation for such poor performance are possible: changes in economic structure, changes in tax structure, and changes in administrative effectiveness.

VAT does not (in principle) tax either exports or investment.[27] A rise in GDP attributable to either an export-driven expansion or an investment boom may therefore result in an initial decline rather than an increase in VAT revenues because input credits (for exports and investment) may build up more quickly than output taxes. From 1998 to 1999, for example, exports as a share of GDP rose by 29.7% but VAT fell by 11.3%, a result that seems consistent with this story. From 1999 to 2000, however, although exports rose less (14.9%), VAT fell even more (13.9%), and from 2000 to 2001

---

[25] Using somewhat different data, Gallagher (2005) calculates a similar gross compliance ratio (45%) for Ukraine.

[26] Data for the countries mentioned may be found in Gebauer, Nam, and Parsche (2003); Engel, Galetovic, and Raddatz (1998); and Coba, Perelmuter, and Tedesco (n.d.).

[27] Of course, this is precisely why the consumption-based measure of VAT 'efficiency' is conceptually preferable, but as noted earlier, in Ukraine during this period this measure appears to move with the cruder 'productivity' measure (Table 4.1).

both exports and VAT declined. The explanation for VAT's poor revenue performance cannot lie in exports.[28] Similarly, investment has not expanded nearly enough since 1998 to account for the observed decline in net VAT revenues. On the whole, Ukraine's VAT performance cannot be explained by changes in economic structure.

Some of the decline in the VAT-GDP ratio before 2002 may perhaps reflect base 'erosion' in the form of increased exemptions (World Bank 2003). But no base changes occurred to explain the continued marked decline in 2003 and 2004. Some exemptions were eliminated after the change in government in 2005, but it seems unlikely that this policy reversal will be sufficient to reverse the trend of declining VAT yields.[29] Changes in tax structure cannot explain Ukraine's VAT performance.

The conclusion seems inescapable: the major explanation of the decline of the VAT in Ukraine lies in tax administration. There may have been a significant deterioration in the efficiency of VAT administration over this period. But what seems more likely is that VAT administration was never very strong and that, with time, its inherent weaknesses have been increasingly exploited by the growing private sector.

VAT evasion, the size of the underground economy, and corruption are closely linked. A recent study, for example, found a correlation of 0.66 between the estimated level of evasion in different countries and the Transparency International (TI) index of perception of corruption.[30] Of course, nothing is this simple in the policy world. For example, although Ukraine's corruption index is about the same as Chile's, evasion in Ukraine appears to be more than twice as great. Still, when the perceived level of corruption is as high as it is in Ukraine, a high level of tax evasion – about 38%, if one simply extrapolated the regression estimated in the study just mentioned – is only to be expected. As we discuss in Chapters 9 and 10, evasion reflects not just weak administration but more systematic structural problems such as the prevalence of corruption and a large underground economy.

---

[28] As discussed further in Chapter 10, this conclusion is especially strong because Ukraine did not in this period refund most of the input VAT accrued on exports.

[29] World Bank (2003, 53) estimates, for example, that the cost of the regional VAT concessions eliminated in early 2005 was about 3% of VAT revenues in 2001. Although this cost may have expanded a bit in later years, it seems improbable either that these exemptions account for much of the observed decline in VAT revenues or that their elimination will reverse this trend.

[30] The reference is to a study carried out under the auspices of the Administración Federal de Ingresos Públicos (AFIP), the Argentine tax administration; this study was available (in 2004) at <www.afip.gov.ar> but is apparently no longer posted.

VAT Productivity and Efficiency

It is difficult to draw simple conclusions about the comparative revenue performance of VAT in any country from aggregate data such as those discussed with respect to Ukraine, because of such factors as the differing shares of 'informal' activity in different countries and the varying extents to which such activities may be reflected in national GDP statistics. Attempts have therefore been made to develop more comparable measures such as those labelled 'productivity' and 'efficiency' in Table 4.2, which compares VAT performance in the Western Hemisphere.[31]

While it is not easy to interpret the measures in Table 4.2, as we mentioned with respect to Ukraine, 'VAT productivity' is simply the ratio of VAT revenues to GDP divided by the 'standard' rate of the VAT. In other words, this figure shows what percentage of GDP each percentage point of the standard VAT rate collects. On average, for the countries included in Table 4.2, one percentage point of VAT collects 0.36% of GDP, with the range being between a low of 0.10% for Brazil's (very limited) federal VAT and a high of 0.62% in Nicaragua. By this criterion, the VAT in, say, Jamaica looks very good indeed. However, this measure may be misleading since in principle VAT taxes consumption, not production, and GDP measures production, not consumption.

For this reason, the measure shown in Table 4.2 as 'VAT efficiency' – sometimes called 'C-efficiency'(Ebrill et al. 2001) – has come to be used as a more reliable indicator of comparative VAT performance. This figure is calculated as the ratio of VAT revenues as a percentage of (usually private) consumption divided by the standard rate, so it has a unit value for a uniform tax on all consumption. The actual ratios shown in the table, however, range from a low of 0.16 for Brazil's very narrow-based national VAT to a startling high of 0.93 for the VAT (General Consumption Tax, or GCT) in Jamaica. Jamaica's performance as measured by this indicator thus again appears to be well above average.[32]

---

[31] This discussion largely follows Edmiston and Bird (2004). A variant of the 'efficiency' measure, called the "gross compliance ratio" and estimated as the ratio of actual to 'potential' VAT collections (as estimated by applying the standard rate to private consumption), is discussed in Gallagher (2004, 2005).

[32] One study estimated a ratio greater than one for Singapore, attributing this result largely to the considerable volume of taxes imposed on tourists and visitors (who can claim few refunds): see Jenkins, Kuo, and Sun (2003). Our own estimate for Singapore, for a different period (Annex Table A.2), is lower. Such calculations are very sensitive to the period and data used, as we discuss later.

Table 4.2. *VAT Revenue Performance in the Western Hemisphere*

Country	2003 Rate	VAT as % Revenues	VAT as % GDP	VAT Productivity	VAT Efficiency
Argentina	21	30.9	3.9	0.19	0.27
Barbados	15				
Bolivia	14.9	37.1	5.4	0.36	0.47
Brazil[a]	20.5	9.9	2.0	0.10	0.16
Canada[a]	7	13.4	2.7	0.38	0.67
Chile	19	44.4	8.0	0.42	0.64
Colombia	16	42.3	4.5	0.28	0.44
Costa Rica	13	25.2	4.6	0.35	0.53
Dominican Republic	12	—	—	—	0.31
Ecuador	12	—	—	—	0.42
El Salvador	13	52.8	5.6	0.43	0.50
Guatemala	12	45.8	4.5	0.38	0.45
Haiti	10	—	—	—	—
Honduras	12	—	—	—	0.55
Jamaica	15	36.5	9.2	0.61	0.93
Mexico	15	26.5	3.3	0.22	0.33
Nicaragua	15	32.5	9.3	0.62	0.70
Panama	5	—	—	—	0.52
Paraguay	10	43.2	4.4	0.44	0.54
Peru	18	45.9	6.4	0.36	0.50
Suriname	10	—	—	—	—
Trinidad and Tobago	15	—	—	—	—
Uruguay	23	30.2	7.8	0.34	0.46
Venezuela	16	35.3	4.7	0.29	0.43
Average	14.1	34.5	5.4	0.36	0.49

Note: A dash indicates not available.
[a] Central government VAT only.
Source: Edmiston and Bird (2004).

Many questions may be raised about such measures. For example, while differences between countries may be interpreted as reflecting differences in both base erosion (through reduced rates, zero-rating, and exemptions) and tax evasion, the measured differences may be inflated in some countries by such measures as limiting input credits and thus taxing some intermediate as well as final consumption.[33] In Jamaica, as in many countries, input credits for some items (cars, entertainment) are limited and others (capital

---

[33] Note that while this component is in large part what Table 2.2 measures as the gap between implicit and standard rates, it also includes the effect of 'nonstandard' (OECD 2004) exemptions: see also the discussion in Chapter 7.

Table 4.3. *VAT Efficiency at Standard and Weighted Average Rates*

Country	VAT Revenue (% of GDP)	VAT Standard Rate (%)	VAT Efficiency	Adjusted Weighted Rate (%)	Adjusted Efficiency
Argentina	5.6	21	0.27	18.9	0.29
Chile	8.3	19	0.44	18.0	0.46
Kenya	5.5	16	0.35	17.9	0.31
Panama	1.5	5	0.30	5.4	0.22
Turkey	8.2	18	0.45	16.3	0.49

Source: Information for selected countries, for different recent years, was kindly provided by Carlos Silvani.

expenditures) are generally claimable only over a two-year tax period. In countries with differentiated rates, the ratios may also be inflated if some rates – for example, those on vehicles (which are subject to an average GCT rate of over 55% in Jamaica)[34] – are higher than the standard rate, because the revenue produced by such rates is 'scored' as though collected at the standard rate.

Of course, if some rates are below the standard rate, the ratio is biased downwards for the same reason. For example, in Jamaica in 2002, 9.8% of total GCT liabilities were attributable to goods and services taxed at above standard rates – mainly vehicles – and only 2.6% to items taxed at below-standard rates, so the reported ratios are slightly biased upwards for this reason. As we mentioned in Chapter 2, many – indeed most – VAT countries have more than one VAT rate. If the average weighted rate is higher than the standard rate, the resulting calculation may be a bit low, and if it is lower, it will be a bit high.[35] Nonetheless, as Table 4.3 suggests, it is perhaps not unduly misleading to compare countries using standard rates only. Of course, single-year calculations such as those in Table 4.3 may also paint a misleading picture.

In any case, Table 4.2 suggests that both 'VAT productivity' and 'VAT efficiency' in Jamaica are above average for the Americas and indeed for countries at its per capita income level more generally.[36] However, it may

[34] Vehicles account for 5.5% of imports and 21.5% of tariff revenue in Jamaica, considerably higher than the equivalent figures in Barbados, for example, although the latter has a higher average tariff on vehicles than Jamaica (44.5% compared to 34.6%): see IDB (2004).

[35] In addition, if a country (such as New Zealand) subjects a fair amount of public sector consumption to VAT, its 'efficiency' ratio (if measured relative to private consumption, as it often is) may exceed 1.0, i.e., 100%: ideally, of course, public sector consumption should be included in the denominator in such cases.

[36] To illustrate, for the 23 countries with GDP in the range U.S.$1,500–5,000 for which data are shown in Annex Table A.2, the average productivity ratio is 0.36 and the average efficiency ratio 0.55.

Table 4.4. *Jamaica: Productivity and Efficiency of the GCT, 1991–2004*

Fiscal Year	GCT as % Total Taxes	GCT as % GDP	VAT Productivity	VAT Efficiency
1991/1992	11.9	2.7	0.27	0.51
1992/1993	21.4	4.9	0.49	0.80
1993/1994	28.0	7.2	0.57	0.86
1994/1995	28.6	7.2	0.58	0.85
1995/1996	31.4	8.4	0.56	0.80
1996/1997	30.6	7.5	0.50	0.71
1997/1998	30.2	7.3	0.49	0.71
1998/1999	29.2	7.4	0.50	0.74
1999/2000	26.8	7.2	0.48	0.72
2000/2001	25.7	7.1	0.47	0.68
2001/2002	25.7	6.7	0.44	0.64
2002/2003	27.3	7.4	0.49	0.71
2003/2004	27.7	8.3	0.55	0.80

Source: Edmiston and Bird (2004).

be misleading to benchmark performance by averages based on inevitably flawed and somewhat suspect international comparisons.[37] A more useful way to use such 'performance indicators' may be to view a country's performance over time, as we did in Table 4.1 for Ukraine. Table 4.4 shows that the measured performance of the VAT in Jamaica varies considerably from year to year.[38] Until 2003, Jamaica's performance in terms of these measures was gradually deteriorating. The figures shown in the table reflect repeated attempts to increase revenues – notably, rate increases in 1993 and 1995 and a significant reduction in exemptions in 2003. In Jamaica, as in many developing and transitional economies, constant attention and frequent policy changes seem needed simply to prevent VAT revenue from declining.[39] We consider this common phenomenon further in Chapter 11.

Although all measures of VAT 'efficiency' have flaws, such numbers have now begun to be calculated in such abundance that they are beginning to enter into econometric analysis. Examination of raw country data such as that depicted in Annex Table A.2 suggests that there is no obvious relation

[37] For extended discussion of the uses and limitations of 'benchmarking' tax administration, whether quantitatively or qualitatively, see, for example, Gallagher (2005), Vázquez-Caro (2005), and Bird and Banta (2000).

[38] Gallagher (2004) shows that the same is true in other countries such as El Salvador and Guatemala.

[39] Incidentally, Edmiston and Bird (2004) rather daringly extrapolate from Jamaica's revenue experience after two earlier VAT rate increases and estimate that the 'revenue-maximizing tax rate' in Jamaica is only 18%; see also the discussion in Chapter 7. In 2006 the government raised the rate from 15% to 16.5%.

between the level of economic development and the importance of VAT revenues.[40] Similarly, there is no clear relation between the level of economic development and VAT productivity. Although there is also no evident correlation between VAT efficiency and the level of economic development, given the definition of 'productivity,' it is hardly surprising that there does seem to be a definite correlation between VAT productivity and VAT share of GDP.

If income levels alone do not explain variations in VAT efficiency, what does? Work is just beginning on this question. For example, McCarten (2006) estimates that 42% of the variability (adjusted R^2) in the ratio of VAT revenues to consumption is explained when regressed against the standard rate of VAT, a measure of the openness of the economy, the level of illiteracy, and indexes of government capacity to control corruption and the cost of registering a new business. All these variables except the last were statistically significant. Using a smaller sample of transitional countries, McCarten (2006) also finds that an index related to the prevalence of bribery is a significant (negative) explanatory factor. His unsurprising conclusion is that there is substantial room to improve VAT efficiency in many developing and transitional countries by improving governmental institutions and tax administration.

In a more detailed econometric examination focusing specifically on the collection efficiency of VAT, Aizenman and Jinjarak (2005), using an unbalanced panel of 45 countries (including a number of developed countries) for the 1970–99 period, find that VAT collection efficiency increases with urbanization, trade openness, real GDP per capita, and measures of both political stability and the 'fluidity' of political participation but is negatively related to the agricultural share of GDP.[41] For different specifications 55–67% of the variance was explained. The most important explanatory variables were urbanization and real GDP per capita, and all results were

---

[40] As Bird and Gendron (2005) discuss, it seems to make little or no difference whether one uses VAT efficiency based on total or private consumption (correlation coefficient is 0.98) or even which measure of VAT efficiency and VAT productivity (correlation coefficient is 0.91) is used. Using data in the USAID/DAI data base (available at <http://www.fiscalreform.net/index.php?option=com_content&task=view&id=16&Itemid=37>) the correlation coefficient between the 'gross compliance ratio' (Gallagher 2004) and VAT productivity is also high (0.86).

[41] Aizenman and Jinjarak (2005) interpret their measure of 'VAT efficiency' as an indication of the investment by the country concerned in 'tax capacity' and use this measure to test a political model related to this concept that was originally put forward by Cukierman, Edwards, and Tabellini (1992). It is not clear, however, how one can interpret a number that seems to be driven as much or more by economic structure as by political will as constituting 'investment' in this sense.

relatively robust. When high-income countries were excluded from their sample, all coefficients continued to have the same sign and significance. For the high-income countries alone, however, only the level of per capita GDP and the share of agriculture had explanatory power, perhaps in part because the other variables displayed relatively little variability across these countries. Finally, when the relationship between VAT efficiency and income inequality (measured by Gini coefficients) was explored in a simple cross-country ordinary least squares regression, inequality was found to have a significant negative effect.

While interesting, this study is certainly not the last word on the subject. Before it becomes the launching pad for a burgeoning new industry attempting to explain the very considerable variation observable in the measured revenue efficiency of VAT in different countries, considerably more time and effort need to be spent to ensure that the figures used to measure 'efficiency' are more meaningful and comparable than those currently available. For example, some effort should be made to disentangle such factors as those mentioned – multiple rates, statutory exemptions, and evasion.

VAT and Revenue Reconsidered

Potential taxpayers have many ways to escape the fiscal system in most developing and transitional countries. Taxpayers – or their tax base – may flee abroad. Or they may remain but hide in the shadow economy. Or they may secure some form of favorable treatment by exerting influence in various ways (legal or otherwise) to have changes made in tax law or its interpretation. Even if through an oversight they find themselves somehow trapped within the taxation system, they may seek forgiveness through amnesty laws or specific grants of relief. The record over the years in some countries of repeated erosion of the VAT base through concessions at many levels (as well as outright evasion) suggests that many or all of these processes have been at work.

The initial VAT legislation in most developing and transitional countries was usually close to standard international models in part because it was often drafted in whole or part with the participation of international experts. Over time, however, VAT in most countries has tended to become both more complex in structure and often somewhat ad hoc in the way it is actually applied. The structure of VAT becomes littered with concessions of various sorts that reduce revenue and make the tax difficult to manage, requiring frequent 'tune-ups' to keep the revenue flowing. Once concessions enter the system, they are often subsequently enlarged, creating more complexities and costs for both taxpayers and the tax administration. Few developing or transitional countries offer taxpayers much assistance in coping with such complexities or pay much attention to the compliance costs they impose on taxpayers. Nor do most such countries do much to guard against abuse. Most so-called VAT audits in many countries amount to little more than simple numerical checks, for example. Widespread base erosion facilitates evasion and – especially when taxpayers are subject to (bad) 'audit' – corruption.[42] Those with influence often have their tax debts forgiven. VAT reality in many countries clearly fails to live up to VAT's initial promise.

It gets worse. With the tax base being eroded in such ways, governments hard pressed for revenues have sometimes been driven to discretionary and unpredictable enforcement efforts – collecting money where they can and (as the refund problem discussed in Chapter 10 suggests) keeping it when they get it whether they should do so or not. Alternatively, governments sometimes resort to introducing still more legislative changes (such as the 'VAT withholding' also discussed in Chapter 10) to close the very gaps that previous political and administrative decisions have opened. In some countries the results have been an almost continual cycle of changes in the effective tax structure, subsequent erosion of the tax base, and unrelenting pressure on the tax administration to meet revenue targets. The few unfortunate taxpayers who remain subject to the full rigor of the formal tax system in such countries face uncertain tax burdens. No one can say with certainty how any transaction will be taxed today let alone tomorrow. Savings and investment are deterred and misallocated. Trade may be discouraged as VAT refunds to exporters are not paid out but are instead kept in the Treasury and used to meet budgetary needs. Trust vanishes, the shadow economy expands, revenues fall, tax pressure is again increased on those who cannot escape, and the cycle continues.

As we suggested in the case of Ukraine, the underlying problem when VAT performance is this dismal is unlikely to lie solely in poor tax design. Rather, it usually reflects more fundamental problems. One such problem is the existence of a gap between the institutional requirements for good VAT administration and the real fiscal institutions that exist in the country. We discuss this aspect further in Chapter 9. Another problem is the extent to which deviations from 'good' VAT practice are used as rewards for political supporters or – the distinction is often unclear – as instruments of industrial

---

[42] Taxpayers do not need to corrupt tax officials if they never see or hear from them.

or regional policy.[43] As we discuss later, in the economic and political environments of many developing and transitional countries, such policies are perhaps understandable. Unfortunately, the very instability that makes such policies attractive ensures that they are unlikely to yield good results in terms of revenue or anything else – except, perhaps, the desired political goal of garnering support from certain interests.

---

[43] For examples of such policies, see, for example, the references to Kazakhstan and Georgia in IBFD (2004, 54–55) and the cases of Ukraine and China we discuss in Chapter 7. The more general 'political equilibrium' aspect of VAT policy is discussed further in Chapter 11.

FIVE

Equity and the Informal Sector

As anti-VAT protests and demonstrations around the world show, there has always been considerable popular concern about the equity aspects of VATs (Botes 2001).[1] Equity is always and everywhere a central issue in taxation. Indeed, from one perspective the principal rationale for taxes in the first place may be thought of as an attempt to secure equity. Governments do not need taxes to secure money: they print the money. The role of the tax system is to take money away from the private sector in the most efficient, equitable, and administratively least costly fashion possible. One person's conception of what is equitable or fair may differ from those of others. In the end, views of what constitutes an equitable tax system are defined and implemented only through the political institutions within which countries reconcile (if they do) such conflicting views and interests. The result may diverge widely from what an outside analyst may consider to be fair or equitable in terms of some normative standard.

Equity issues may be approached at two different levels. One level focuses on the details of how taxes impose burdens on taxpayers who are in the same or different economic circumstances. At a more fundamental level, what matters are not such details but rather the overall effects of the fiscal system on the income and level of well-being of different people. The policy implications of these two approaches to tax equity may be quite different. Focusing on the implications for equity of details of particular taxes leads,

---

[1] See also the reference in Chapter 2 to protests in Mexico and elsewhere. VAT issues have often played a prominent role in political campaigns, particularly when the tax is introduced. For example, a political slogan heard in Guatemala in the mid-1980s was "el IVA no va" (roughly 'No to VAT'). A key reason for the virtual elimination of the governing political party in Canada in the early 1990s was strong public resentment of Canada's new VAT – the GST (Bird 1994a). Despite its campaign promise to abolish the GST, however, the winning party in the ensuing election soon found the revenue too hard to replace.

for example, to proposals to alter the rates and structures of particular taxes such as VAT. Changes in such details may improve horizontal and vertical equity within the limited group subject to the full legal burden of the tax. At the same time, however, inequity more broadly considered may sometimes be worsened. From the perspective of social and economic inequality it is the overall impact of the budgetary system on the distribution of wealth and income rather than the details of VAT or any other tax that matters. In reality, however, decisions are almost always taken on a tax-by-tax basis with much attention being paid to the alleged distributional effects of this or that particular tax feature considered in isolation.[2]

WHO REALLY PAYS VAT?

Consider a recent analysis of VAT in Jamaica, where the tax is called the General Consumption Tax, or GCT (Edmiston and Bird 2004). Who really pays the GCT in Jamaica? That is, who really bears the burden of this tax in the sense that the real income at his or her disposal is reduced? The person or company legally responsible for paying VAT (the seller) has little to do with who actually pays the tax. Suppose an item sells for $1 before the imposition of VAT. If the seller simply charges the same price as before and adds a 15% VAT, resulting in a final selling price of $1.15, then the buyer pays the tax because it has been shifted completely forward to him or her by the seller. Alternatively, the seller may lower the price to $0.87 after a 15% VAT is imposed, yielding a final selling price of $1.00. In this case the seller would pay the tax. Or the seller may lower the price a bit, thereby shifting part of the tax forward to the consumer and bearing the remainder of the tax.[3] What happens in reality depends on market structure and the relative responsiveness of sellers and buyers to changes in price – the relative price elasticities of supply and demand. We know so little about these magnitudes in most countries, however, that conventional tax incidence analysis generally avoids such complexities and simply assumes the tax is fully shifted forward from the seller to the final consumer.

Even with this simplifying assumption, it is seldom straightforward to determine whether a VAT such as Jamaica's GCT is progressive, proportional, or regressive. To analyze the distributional impact of VAT, one needs

---

[2] See, for example, the detailed account of changes in the British tax system over the last two centuries in Daunton (2001, 2002).

[3] Conceivably under some forms of imperfect competition, sellers may even be able to increase their price by more than the amount of the tax, thus 'overshifting' it forward.

to calculate the average VAT payment as a proportion of an appropriate base for each household group. Often in developing countries the data to estimate tax burdens by income level are simply not available. In the case of Jamaica, for example, only survey data on household consumption are available. Since it can be argued that people derive well-being directly only from consumption, this base of comparison seems reasonable in some ways. Still, since savings provide for future consumption, current income remains the preferred standard against which most people (though probably not many economists) judge tax equity. To approximate more closely this broader (income) base in the Jamaican case, although households were divided into deciles on the basis of average annual per capita consumption, GCT payments were calculated as a proportion of *total expenditure* (a survey item that includes not only consumption but also some nonconsumption items such as contributions to pensions).

Once this and other necessary assumptions are made, it is a straightforward exercise to calculate the estimated impact of Jamaica's GCT for fully taxed and zero-rated items.[4] A recent study found that the indirect tax system in Jamaica was slightly progressive (Edmiston and Bird 2006). Although estimated GCT incidence was roughly proportional in the bottom half of the income distribution, it increased steadily in the upper half. Total spending of the highest consumption group includes 9.0% in indirect taxes or over 40% more than the 6.4% paid in such taxes by those in the lowest consumption group.

If income data had been available for Jamaica, the calculated incidence of consumption taxes would likely have been less progressive and might even have been mildly regressive. However, a recent survey of many similar studies in a variety of developing countries (Chu, Davoodi, and Gupta 2000) found that most recent (post-VAT) studies of the consumption tax incidence found significantly less regressive results than had been reported in earlier surveys (Bird and De Wulf 1973). Indeed, even in instances in which VAT itself appeared regressive, the change from import and excise taxes to general sales taxes such as VAT (Table 2.4) appears to have made tax incidence a little more progressive in most poor countries.[5] Table 5.1 summarizes a number of incidence studies carried out recently in several developing and transitional countries, many of which suggest mildly progressive results. The precise

---

[4] One complication is that it was necessary to estimate the GCT embedded in the price of exempted items (because no credit is allowed for input tax) as the ratio of input tax to total supplies for each industry.

[5] Gemmell and Morrissey (2003) reach a similar conclusion.

Table 5.1. *The Distributive Effects of VAT*

Country	Source	Selective Summary of Findings
Colombia	Steiner and Soto (1999)	VAT found to be slightly regressive
Colombia	Rutherford, Light, and Barrera (2005)	An increase in VAT would be relatively progressive with respect to the lowest-income groups
Colombia	Zapata and Ariza (2005)	VAT appears to be slightly progressive
Dominican Republic	Jenkins, Jenkins, and Kuo (2006)	VAT found to be progressive across all quintiles of household expenditure; includes estimate of different rates of compliance at different income levels
Ethiopia	Muñoz and Cho (2003)	VAT found to be progressive because of exemptions (especially of in-kind consumption)
Mexico	Huesca and Serrano (2005)	A more differentiated rate would both raise revenues and improve equity
Pakistan	Refaqat (2003)	VAT slightly progressive because of exemptions
Peru	Haughton (2005)	VAT found to be somewhat regressive
Russia	Decoster and Verbina (2003)	Indirect taxes were progressive, including VAT rates
South Africa	Botes (2001)	Zero-rating actually made VAT a little more regressive
South Africa	Go et al. (2005)	VAT is mildly regressive

incidence of VAT estimated in such studies depends not only on its design (rates, exemptions) but also on the nature of local consumption patterns (e.g., the distribution of in-kind consumption) and on the effectiveness with which the tax is administered.[6]

BEYOND PARTIAL INCIDENCE STUDIES

Are such attempts to put quantitative flesh on the structure of incidence theory the end of the story? Another common concept of equity in tax

---

[6] Most studies of the effect on incidence of substituting domestic consumption taxes for trade taxes fail to consider that replacing import taxes with domestic consumption taxes also removes an (unbudgeted) 'tax' previously imposed on consumers who paid higher prices to protected domestic producers (Harberger 2006). We know surprisingly little about either the incidence of particular taxes or the overall incidence of government taxing and spending programs anywhere, let alone in developing and transitional countries (Bird and Zolt 2005).

analysis is horizontal equity. A tax system is said to be horizontally equitable if taxpayers with equal capacities to pay taxes pay approximately the same taxes. One way that a tax system may be horizontally inequitable is by excluding a significant portion of taxpayers from the system. In many countries activities taking place in the so-called informal sector of the economy largely escape the direct tax system. Since such activities are less able to escape indirect taxes – even thieves must sometimes buy things – it has often been suggested that one way to impose an appropriate tax burden on those in the informal sector is through indirect taxes.

There are several versions of this story (Bird and Wallace 2004). Some argue that with the exception of services there is a decent tax 'handle' for taxes on retail trade. For instance, most such trade is carried out by large organized firms in Jamaica. An indirect tax such as VAT can tax an important part of the informal sector such as the nonreporting plumbers and other home repair enterprises that buy supplies from a registered taxpayer. Indirect taxes may also reach the informal sector via shifting of the taxes into wages, returns to capital, or consumer prices. Small tax-avoiding manufacturers, for example, may be effectively taxed via indirect taxes if the tax is capitalized in some way that affects the return to capital or labor, which in turn is a function of such factors as capital-to-labor ratios and price elasticities of demand. Even illegal and criminal activities – a not inconsiderable part of the informal sector in some countries – will be subject to at least some taxes. Heavier reliance on indirect taxes, no matter what form such taxes may take, will not move tax-dodging businesses into the formal sector. But it may increase both the equity of the relative tax treatment of the formal and informal sectors and the efficiency of resource allocation in general. In any case, whatever theory may suggest, the reality is that the larger the informal economy, the more countries rely on indirect taxes (Alm, Martinez-Vazquez, and Schneider 2004).

Such issues are important in Jamaica, where the 'shadow economy' has been estimated to be 36.4% of GNP – almost twice the size of the informal sector in Chile and larger than that in neighboring countries such as the Dominican Republic (Schneider and Klinglmair 2004). While such estimates are at best rough approximations, all evidence supports the common idea that there is a relatively large hidden or informal economy in Jamaica. Estimates of the size of this sector commonly range from 30% to 60% of GDP in most developing and transitional countries.[7]

---

[7] These estimates do not mean that the measured GDP is understated by such percentages. GDP is a value-added measure while the usual hidden economy measure is of total activity

The existence of a large sector of the economy effectively not subject to direct taxation is important in assessing the role and effects of consumption taxation. A well-designed VAT might be more progressive than a personal income tax if the latter in practice burdens only a limited group of wage-earners. Increasing the role of indirect taxes in such circumstances may make a tax system more horizontally equitable. It may also make taxation less allocatively distorting by reducing the pressure on market-based activities to move into the less-taxed informal sector. VAT may thus level the competitive playing field to some extent. On one hand, VAT in principle grants relief from taxes on business inputs to those taxpayers who actually pay taxes on their sales. On the other hand, VAT in practice imposes some tax on those businesses that are not VAT registrants. Those who operate entirely in the cash economy may remain largely unknown to the tax authorities, but even they will end up paying some tax when they purchase consumer goods and services (or inputs for their productive activities) from the taxed sector.[8] From this broader perspective, VAT as a component of the tax system may be less regressive than suggested by studies like those discussed in the previous section.[9]

In the real policy world, however, no matter what the calculations of researchers may suggest, people think consumption taxes are regressive.

---

and hence not directly comparable. Double counting must be eliminated to ensure compara-bility to GDP. In addition, some illegal activities (e.g., drug smuggling) usually included in the informal sector estimates are generally not included in GDP. An estimated under-ground economy of, say, 40% may imply an understatement in measured GDP of, say, 20%, depending upon the nature of the informal sector (e.g., the importance of illegal activities), the extent of double counting in the estimate of that sector, and the extent to which the activities measured are included in the measure of GDP. As such factors may vary over time, unquestionably vary over the business cycle and differ from country to country, and may also have very different implications for tax evasion in different circumstances, even good estimates of the size of the informal sector do not provide a useful guide to tax policy. There continues to be considerable controversy over how best to measure the informal economy: for a recent example in a data-rich developed country, see Breusch (2005) and Giles and Tedds (2005).

[8] Fedeli (1998) shows that VAT offers more opportunity for administrative actions to reduce evasion (e.g., penalties are more effective) and is on the whole less conducive to the growth of the informal economy than other forms of general consumption taxation.

[9] As Warlters and Auriol (2005) show in a recent comparative general equilibrium study of 38 African countries, VAT almost invariably scores well in efficiency terms even in the poorest countries. Go et al. (2005), in a more detailed study of VAT in South Africa using a general equilibrium model, also find that VAT is an effective and efficient revenue instrument compared to other taxes, although it is mildly regressive. Somewhat similar results emerge from other recent general equilibrium analyses of Colombia (Rutherford, Light, and Barrera 2005) and Jamaica (Light 2004), although the latter was unable for data reasons to estimate the incidence of the VAT.

Academics may argue that taxes on consumption are less regressive on a lifetime rather than annual perspective (Fullerton and Metcalf 2002). But such refinements carry little weight in the political arena – perhaps rightly so in most developing countries, given the relatively short life expectancies and the subsistence level at which many people live. It is thus not surprising that reduced VAT rates or exemptions for certain 'basic' items such as foods, passenger transport, medical services, and cooking fuel are common, particularly in countries in which substantial differences exist in consumption patterns between income groups. The common expert riposte to such policies is that whatever small degree of progressivity they may achieve could be more effectively attained by making small changes in the income tax or by adjusting transfer payments (International Tax Dialogue 2005). Such principles can and should become practice when countries are sufficiently developed.[10] But in countries in which the poor as a rule neither pay income tax nor benefit from transfer payments (or other properly targeted expenditures) this riposte does not seem very relevant.[11] We discuss VAT exemptions further in Chapter 7.

In that chapter we also discuss further the conventional argument that there is unlikely to be much gain in imposing differential 'luxury' rates under a VAT. In view of the efficiency and administrative costs to which such differentiation gives rise, this argument seems strong even in developing countries. If desired, excise taxes can do more along these lines (Cnossen 1999, 2004). The case for imposing VAT at a uniform standard rate and on as broad a base as possible in such countries is less convincing, however. As has long been known, a uniform VAT is likely to increase the price of many goods essential to the poor (Ahmad and Stern 1987). Because the poor may consume a relatively small amount of such products, it is undoubtedly true that much of the benefit of such exemptions will go to the nonpoor (International Tax Dialogue 2005).[12] Nonetheless, in view of the relatively heavy tax burden of such taxes on the poor and the apparent inability or unwillingness of governments in many countries to provide offsets to such

---

[10] Even then, however, perceptions may rule in the policy arena. Canada is an interesting example. When it introduced its GST, it simultaneously introduced a refundable 'GST credit' under the income tax that offset fully any impact of the new VAT on lower-income groups. Nonetheless, political pressure forced the government of the day to provide a 'double dip' in the form of an extensive zero-rating system for so-called basic foods (Bird 1994a).

[11] It is true that all is required is that some expenditures benefiting those hurt by the tax are *better* targeted than such exemptions, but this test is one that many countries would fail.

[12] For example, Muñoz and Cho (2003) note that most benefits from exemptions (such as utility services) accrue to the rich in Ethiopia and are hence regressive.

tax burdens through other fiscal adjustments, building some relief into VAT design may often be justifiable.[13]

To relieve any good or service completely from VAT, it must be 'zero-rated': that is, not only must the sale of the good itself be free of tax but so must its inputs. As we argue in Chapter 9, domestic zero-rating is a bad idea in countries already facing problems with VAT refunds. On the other hand, exemptions not only increase cascading but by breaking the VAT chain also make effective enforcement more difficult. As we suggest in Chapter 7, a compromise position may sometimes be to impose a reduced rate on some items, although careful analysis is needed to determine what level and form of relief may be best for the particular circumstance of a particular country. There are too many countries in which the items taxed (or not taxed) in different ways seem to have been chosen arbitrarily by fiat rather than in a reasoned fashion to make one comfortable with the state of knowledge on this issue.[14] Even if a country works out sensibly what is best at a point in time, the issue needs to be revisited periodically both because of 'exemption creep' (Chapter 7) and because in the nature of development, circumstances change, and when circumstances change, what is sensible usually changes also.

VAT AND THE FORMAL ECONOMY

Emran and Stiglitz (2005) suggest that in the presence of a substantial informal sector any general tax such as VAT that falls on the formal sector acts to deter the growth and development of the economy as a whole.[15] Hines (2004) concludes that increasing consumption taxes will definitely foster

---

[13] For an earlier detailed analysis of this point in Jamaica see Bird and Miller (1989). A more rigorous analysis for Tunisia along similar lines, although not with special reference to VAT, may be found in Bibi and Duclos (2004). On the other hand, Muñoz and Cho (2003) show that even very poor countries can sometimes deliver the expenditure goods more effectively than poorly targeted exemptions.

[14] Even approaches that may seem sensible and empirically based may prove faulty. Some years ago, for example, the Philippines considered a system that would exempt from its then sales tax items that were most widely consumed by low-income groups, as reported by extensive household surveys. However, when it was found that certain types of cosmetics appeared to be more widely used by even very poor groups than many 'basic' foods, the idea was quickly dropped. Everyone (i.e., those who make policy decisions) 'knows' that cosmetics cannot possibly be 'essential' even if everyone (the populace) persists in buying them.

[15] For an earlier discussion of the issue (though not with special reference to developing countries), see Piggott and Whalley (2001). Munk (2006) extends the argument by explicitly introducing administrative costs.

the expansion of the hidden economy if (as seems plausible in developing countries) the labor intensity of production in that sector is greater than in the formal sector. Nonetheless, another recent study suggests that even governments fully aware of such problems may rationally choose to impose higher taxes (including VAT) on the formal sector of the economy (Auriol and Warlters 2005). The reason is that, given their relatively weak tax administrations, the best way many developing and transitional countries have to raise revenue may sometimes be to increase barriers to entry to the formal sector – for example, by increasing taxes – thus creating 'rents' that may then be taxed. Such arguments about the interaction between VAT and the development of the formal economy are just beginning to be explored empirically.[16] Their significance for those engaged in implementing and improving VATs around the world is as yet far from obvious.

Much recent discussion of taxation in developing and transitional countries has focused on the so-called shadow (underground, informal) economy. Recent studies suggest that the informal sector has been becoming more, not less, important in at least some countries (Chen 2005). In addition, the evidence is that persons and enterprises at all income (and size) levels are engaged to varying extents in the informal sector (de Ferranti et al. 2004). Many businesses appear to operate in both the formal and informal sectors at the same time. As we noted earlier, firms that operate in the shadow economy may escape VAT liability on their sales, but in principle they are also not able to reclaim credit for any VAT paid on inputs. It has therefore been suggested that one way to impose an appropriate tax burden on those in the informal sector is by imposing VAT. On the other hand, as mentioned in the previous paragraph, it can also be argued that thus increasing taxation of the formal sector may expand rather than reduce the amount of hidden economic activity, since some activities now taking place in the market may disappear into the shadow sector.[17]

As is often the case when theoretical arguments are inconclusive, empirical investigations of the relative magnitudes of various elasticities and responses at the margin are needed to assess their relevance in any particular country. A recent study by Warlters and Auriol (2005) of 38 African countries makes a promising start on this task, although, as they properly stress, there remains considerable uncertainty about the key parameter in their analysis – the elasticity of substitution between taxed and untaxed activities. One conclusion of this study is that although the size of a country's informal

---

[16] See also Gordon and Li (2005) and Aizenman and Jinjarak (2006).
[17] We develop a variant of this argument (with respect to 'simplified' taxes) in Chapter 10.

economy is generally more important than its tax structure in determining the marginal cost of public funds, within the formal tax system general taxes on goods (notably VATs) are always more efficient than taxes on factors such as income or payroll taxes. Nonetheless, this study also argues that the most efficient way to increase taxes (ignoring distributional issues) is to increase taxes on untaxed goods. Even when it is costly to impose taxes on firms operating in the informal economy, Warlters and Auriol (2005) therefore suggest that it is more efficient to do so than to increase taxes on the formal sector. If one's goal is a more efficient revenue system in poor countries, the key step is to reduce the size of the informal sector, for instance, by lowering such barriers to 'formality' as high administrative and compliance costs of the tax system. Since such costs are relatively high with VAT, this study lends additional weight to the position we take in Chapter 7 about the undesirability of attempting to dig too deeply into the economy with VAT. On the other hand, it must be remembered that one of the least costly ways of taxing the informal sector is likely through a VAT that taxes at least some of the inputs used by that sector (Keen 2006a).

Under any form of consumption tax, those who operate entirely in the cash economy may remain largely unknown to the tax authorities. Even such 'ghosts,' however, will pay some tax to the extent they purchase either consumer goods and services or inputs for their productive activities from the taxed sector. Both theory and experience suggest on the whole that a VAT is more likely to reduce than increase tax evasion than other forms of general tax, whether on sales or income. To the extent formal-sector entities trade with similar firms, they are of course within the VAT system. If informal-sector enterprises trade only with other nonregistered entities (including final consumers), they are obviously outside the system. To the extent nonregistrants purchase inputs from registered firms, however, they bear some VAT. Both theory and experience suggest that – other factors (such as entry levels to the tax system) being equal – this 'two-way' aspect of VAT implies that it is more likely than other forms of general sales taxes to reduce rather than increase tax evasion. Moreover, if nonregistrants wish to sell to registered firms, their customers may even prefer that they become registered so that the 'tax' part of their price would become 'legal' and hence creditable. Over time, the result may be to induce expansion of the 'VAT sector.'

All this is fine. However, one lesson from recent analysis and experience is that despite such arguments it is likely a mistake to push such expansion too hard in developing countries. As any tax imposed directly on formal sector entities does, VAT may discourage 'formalization' to some extent and thus be 'antidevelopmental' in some sense (Emran and Stiglitz 2005). On the other hand – and economic arguments always have at least two hands – if one accepts, as we do, that every country needs some form of general taxation and that VAT is less likely to have such undesired effects than other forms of general taxation of consumption (let alone income), this argument implies not that VAT as such is a bad idea but rather that care must be taken to ensure that VAT design is appropriate for the country in question. To the extent VAT systems in practice have discouraged 'formalization' – and there is evidence that they have done so in some instances – as a rule the fault lies in specific features of the design and implementation of the tax (such as unwieldy registration and filing requirements) and not in the tax itself.[18] As we discuss in more detail in Chapters 7 and 10, close attention definitely needs to be paid to such devilish details to prevent such undesired outcomes. On the whole, however, while further theoretical and especially empirical research on the effects of VAT in developing and transitional economies is needed, the case for VAT in most such countries remains solid.

---

[18] For example, numerous studies have found that the tax registration process – a purely administrative procedure – is in many countries one of the major barriers to formalization (Djankov et al. 2002).

SIX

What Should Be Taxed?

VAT is often thought of as a relatively simple tax. Admittedly, a VAT is, by definition, simpler than an income tax for reasons of both definition (it is less 'net' so its base is easy to determine) and timing (there are almost no intertemporal issues in applying VAT).[1] Nonetheless, designing and implementing a VAT are far from simple tasks. In this and the next two chapters we consider a number of design issues, leaving some important administrative questions for Chapter 9 and 10. In the present chapter, we discuss several issues in defining the base of a VAT – the treatment of real property and land, the treatment of public sector and nonprofit activities, and the treatment of financial services. These three issues have proved troublesome in practice and not easy to resolve in theory.

Of course, many other design issues are also often troublesome in developing and transitional countries – for example, the treatment of agriculture and the treatment of tourism – but are not discussed in this book.[2] Other

---

[1] An exception occurs when inflation is as rapid as in Argentina in the late 1980s: VAT payments were indexed in an attempt to reduce the real revenue loss because payments took place a month after transactions. Similarly, Chile in the late 1970s required VAT advance payments every 15 days and adjusted credits carried forward by a price index. Casanegra de Jantscher, Coelho, and Fernandez (1992) discuss some aspects of the effects of inflation on VAT payments and administration.

[2] We make a brief comment on the taxation of agriculture in Chapter 7. For some thoughts on tourism issues see Edmiston and Bird (2004) and, for a more analytical treatment, Gooroochurn (2004) and Gooroochurn and Sinclair (2003). Interestingly, Weekes (2005) notes that Barbados is currently considering eliminating its present reduced rate of 7.5% on tourist-related activities. On the other hand, both Mexico and Uruguay are currently considering measures to facilitate 'tourist refunds' of VAT, a feature that currently exists in a number of countries. Canada announced in 2006 that it will end such tourist refunds: as one would expect, the tourism industry immediately began to produce estimates of the number of jobs that would be lost as a result. Such issues need more analysis than they seem to have received in most countries.

interesting and sometimes important issues we do not discuss include the treatment of gambling, a number of issues related to VAT and services (especially cross-border services),[3] and many aspects of VAT administration (including penalties, issues related to imports [uplifts, post-import control, etc.], and tax 'offsets'). It would take a much longer book than this to do justice to all aspects of VAT.[4]

TAXING REAL PROPERTY

Real estate is tangible: it consists of land, land improvements, buildings, and building improvements. It is highly durable, so its services may be consumed over a long period. In contrast, "real property represents the individual legal rights associated with ownership of the tangible real estate. Since all legal rights are intangible, real property is intangible" (Reilly and Schweis 1999, 16–17). Services associated with real property include construction and renovations. All aspects of this complex set of goods and services need to be considered carefully in setting up a VAT.

In principle, there is no reason to treat durable consumption goods such as housing differently than nondurable consumption goods or services. In practice, however, the appropriate and equitable treatment of housing and housing services remains one of the more difficult areas in VAT. The politically most difficult aspect – one that, unsurprisingly, as yet no country in the world has dared to tackle – is the taxation of the imputed consumption services provided by owner-occupied housing.[5]

How is real property treated under VAT? OECD (2004, 30) lists "supply of land and buildings" and "letting of immovable property" as 'standard' VAT exemptions. However, there are many exceptions to this rule:

- Australia taxes supplies of land (except certain farm land), commercial property, and new residential property.
- Austria imposes tax on letting (renting or leasing) of private housing.
- Canada taxes both the supply and the leasing of commercial land and buildings.
- Finland and Sweden have an optional system for taxing the letting of commercial building in certain cases.

---

[3] We comment briefly on some aspects of this difficult issue in Chapter 8.

[4] Readers interested in these and other VAT issues not discussed here will often find some relevant discussion in Ebrill et al. (2001) and Schenk and Oldman (2007).

[5] Of course it would be difficult to establish a fair tax base for such consumption in the absence of market transactions (Conrad 1990).

- France has a similar optional provision in some cases (letting land and buildings for agricultural use, and certain cases of letting of undeveloped immovable property for professional use), although its general rule is to tax the letting not only of immovable property but also of developed land for professional use.
- Hungary normally taxes the supply of buildings and land not used for housing purposes and taxes nonhousing letting of immovable property.
- Ireland, for variety, taxes only 'long-term' letting of commercial property, along with the supply of land and buildings.
- Italy taxes the supply and letting of commercial property at the standard rate but only taxes residential housing when let by enterprises (and at a favorable rate of 10%).
- Japan taxes only the supply of land.
- Korea goes the other way and taxes only the rental and supply of commercial buildings.
- Mexico, however, taxes only the letting of commercial buildings.
- The Netherlands does the same, although it will tax the supply of immovable property if such taxation is requested by both buyer and seller.
- New Zealand taxes the letting of nonresidential immovable property as well as the supply of land and buildings (unless they have been used for residential accommodation for five years or more).
- Poland taxes the rental or tenancy of immovable property used for commercial purposes.
- Turkey appears to tax all letting but only the sale of commercial buildings.
- The United Kingdom taxes freehold sales of new commercial buildings beginning three years from completion date and, as do a number of other countries already mentioned, provides an 'option to tax' other supplies of commercial buildings.

When 17 of 29 OECD countries follow another path, one wonders how 'standard' the real property exemption really is. We noted earlier that with respect to tax issues 'the devil is in the details.' As the preceding list makes clear, when it comes to VAT and real property, there are many details.

The dominant VAT treatment of real estate around the world is to exempt not only services from owner occupation but also commercial leasing or letting of residential property, presumably in order to prevent distorting the choice between house ownership and renting. Exemption of residential rentals may be justified on distributional grounds as home ownership is correlated with income. More surprisingly, however, in much of the world even most nonresidential property escapes VAT.

Under the Sixth Directive applicable in the European Union, although both sales and rentals of real estate are exempt, newly constructed buildings as well as improvements are taxable. Applying tax to new buildings amounts to charging a 'prepaid' VAT on future services (whether use or subsequent sale) at the time of purchase – the treatment generally applied to durable goods.[6] The result of applying this treatment to commercial (as well as residential) property is obviously that increases in the value of – and hence the services provided by – such property are not included in the tax base, thus violating productive efficiency (Cnossen 2003). In addition, if new buildings are taxed but land and old buildings are not, owners of the latter reap windfall gains (Conrad 1990). More complexity arises when, for example, an old building on a site is replaced by a new one, since the value of the property must then be divided into land value and building value.[7]

The original exemption of all but new real property in France and other EU countries was probably due to the fact that existing property was already subject to special taxes such as the registration tax in France. Most countries around the world subject land and real property to many taxes other than VAT (Bird and Slack 2004). Property transfers in particular are subject to various taxes and charges – land transfer taxes, stamp duties, notarial fees, registry charges, in some instances succession and gift taxes. Transfers of land and real property are treated quite differently under VAT in different countries. In Japan, for example, new construction is taxed at the standard VAT rate, while in Canada such construction is taxed at a lower rate. In Germany it is exempt but subject to an alternative tax and in the United Kingdom while residential construction is zero-rated, commercial buildings are taxed at the standard rate. Moreover, although the two EU member states

---

[6] Conrad (1990) suggested an extension of the prepayment method in the form of what he called a 'stock value-added tax' (S-VAT). Under this proposal, VAT would be paid on the sale of any type of real estate, new or old, improvements or constructions, with VAT registrants' receiving VAT credit on purchases but not on sales, and nontaxable sellers' being refunded the taxes paid by the purchaser. Rental payments would be taxed if the lessor were taxable.

[7] See van Steenwinckel and Theissen (2001) for a recent EU court case dealing with an analogous complication. As Bird and Slack (2004) note, for some tax purposes it may often make sense to distinguish land and building values. However, the point here is that since many countries do not normally do so (e.g., for purposes of real property taxation), requiring such a distinction for VAT purposes complicates matters. An additional complexity arising from the EU treatment is that a number of countries allow purchasers (or lessees) of commercial property an option to be taxable in order to recover VAT paid on inputs.

Table 6.1. *Canada: GST/HST and QST Refunds in Respect of Tax on Real Estate*

Percentage of Use in Commercial Activities	Registered Partnerships and Corporations	Registered Individuals	Public Sector[a]	Financial Institutions
≤10%	No	No	No	% of use
10% < x ≤ 50%	% of use	No[b]	No[c]	% of use
50% < x < 90%	% of use	% of use	100%	% of use
≥90%	100%	100%	100%	% of use

Note: Under the GST/HST system, Input Tax Credits (ITCs) are claimed, and under the QST system, Input Tax Refunds (ITRs) are claimed.

[a] Governments, nonprofit organizations, charities, municipalities, universities, schools, and hospitals.

[b] In rare cases, registered individuals may obtain an ITC according to the percentage of use.

[c] With the exception of governments, registrants in the public sector can elect to have property in this category treated case by case. ITCs and ITRs are determined according to each property's percentage of use in commercial activities.

just mentioned normally exempt sales of commercial property, Canada taxes such sales (though at a lower rate) and Japan does so at the standard rate (Cnossen 1996).

Taxes on the transfer of land and real property discourage the development and formalization of land markets. The fact that such taxes exist – often at surprisingly high rates – in so many countries around the world is presumably attributable primarily to the administrative ease of imposing them. The 'taxable event' (the recorded exchange of title) is readily visible, even if the true value of the transaction usually is not. Nonetheless, countries that wish to develop efficient markets would be well advised to consider lowering specific taxes on land transfers and perhaps making up revenue losses by, for instance, strengthening basic property taxes.[8]

In contrast to the EU approach, Canada and New Zealand treat both the sale and the rental of real estate as taxable under VAT and, in addition to owner-occupation, exempt only residential rents and rental values. Construction, alteration, and maintenance of all buildings are taxable, as is the rental of business accommodation. The sale of existing nonresidential buildings is also taxable. This approach has the virtue of keeping the VAT chain intact for more transactions. However, as Table 6.1 shows for the case of Canada, it is not without its own complexities.

Many other special rules also apply to real estate in Canada. For example, builders who rent or occupy a residential property that they have built must

---

[8] As Bird and Slack (2004) argue, the efficiency effects of taxes on property values, unlike those of taxes on property transfers, are almost entirely beneficial as a result of the more inelastic nature of the tax base.

generally pay GST (Canada's VAT) on the fair market value of the property. They may also claim input tax credits as appropriate. In addition, purchasers of new housing as well as home owners who build or substantially renovate their own home may claim a special GST rebate, with a maximum of 36% (of taxes paid) for units valued at less than C$350,000 being progressively reduced to no rebate if the unit is valued at over C$450,000. Any purchaser of new residential rental property may claim such a rebate provided that the residential units are subsequently leased on a long-term basis to individuals as their place of residence.[9] In effect, this rebate amounts to a reduction of the GST rate on such housing to around 3.8%. Such provisions obviously add considerable complexity to the system. Little is known about the overall economic impact of differing VAT treatments of real property (Bennett 1991).

What does this diverse experience suggest with respect to applying VAT to real property in developing and transitional countries? In many such countries, as Youngman (1996, 276) notes, a "certain degree of circularity accompanies the process of establishing public claims on land and building values through annual taxation in the early stages of a transition to a new regime of property rights." In other words, when property rights are not clearly established, it is difficult to impose a sensible real property tax even though the immovable nature of the tax base in principle makes it easier to enforce payment. Given the weak fiscal administration in most developing countries, in practice the only way to tax real property is likely to be some form of tax on sales (in effect, VAT prepayment as described earlier), for example, on nonresidential sales. Some consider even this approach to be either unworkable or undesirable because of the inadequate financial market and the liquidity problems buyers would face in meeting large 'up-front' tax demands. Of course, if VAT is applied to (some) property transfers, presumably the other special taxes so often imposed on such transfers should be correspondingly reduced; however, we are not aware that this has actually been done in many countries. As a minimum, countries should subject the value of such intermediation services as real estate commissions to VAT.

PUBLIC SECTOR, NONPROFIT, AND CHARITABLE ACTIVITIES

Most countries do not apply VAT to goods and services supplied by public sector bodies (including governments), nonprofit organizations, and

---

[9] Similar (complex) rules apply for the Québec Sales Tax (e.g., Québec 2005). Chown (2001) depicts some of the complexities arising in the United Kingdom's VAT treatment of buildings. See also Angermann (2000) on Germany.

charitable organizations – hereafter referred to as the PNC sector.[10] The main reasons seem to be concerns about social and distributional issues. Surprisingly little effort has been made to assess the distortions and compliance, and administrative costs that may arise from these provisions. While nonprofit and charitable activities are seldom critical issues in developing and transitional countries, these countries too are frequently concerned about impeding further development of these sectors.[11] Moreover, the role of the state sector is often critical in such countries: getting VAT right for the PNC sector matters everywhere.

The Way We Are

At present the PNC sector is treated in many different ways by VAT regimes around the world. As is true for any sector under a VAT, the goods and services supplied by the PNC sector may fall into one of four categories:

- *Taxable.* Seller is entitled to a refund of the VAT incurred on input purchases undertaken to make taxable sales ('supplies' in the usual language of the law).
- *Zero-rated.* Even though the seller does not collect VAT on zero-rated supplies, it is nonetheless entitled to a refund of the VAT incurred on input purchases. (Under the usual destination-based VAT system, exported supplies are zero-rated.)
- *Exempt.* Seller also does not collect tax when making an exempt supply. In contrast to the zero-rated case, however, it is not entitled to a refund of the VAT incurred on input purchases undertaken to make exempt supplies.
- *Nontaxable.* The economic effects of being outside the scope of the VAT and hence nontaxable are the same as for exempt supplies.[12]

---

[10] See Gendron (2005) for an extended treatment of the issues discussed in this section.

[11] Concern over creating tax barriers to the expansion of the 'civic society' was, for example, an issue of some concern in Ukraine a few years ago. A more important issue in many poor countries has been the insistence of most official aid donors and foreign nongovernmental organizations (NGOs) on the necessity of exempting aid-financed imports from VAT. Although we agree with Chambas (2005) that this position is both illogical and adverse to sound development policy, we think it is unlikely to be changed soon, and the issue is not further discussed here.

[12] This definition of 'nontaxable' is used in the EU under the Sixth VAT Directive. Terminology sometimes differs among countries. In New Zealand, for example, zero-rated supplies are called *nontaxable* supplies. In Australia, sales are said to be *taxable*, *GST-free* (zero-rated), and *input taxed* (exempt). The last of these terms is particularly useful and conveys the desired meaning much more clearly than the standard terminology, but we have nonetheless followed the latter in the present book.

In all countries much PNC activity is exempt under one label or another. In addition, in some countries special VAT refund schemes may apply to certain parts of the PNC sector.

Aujean, Jenkins, and Poddar (1999) group the activities of the PNC sector into the redistribution of income and wealth, the provision of public goods and services, and the provision of goods and services that are similar to those supplied by the private sector. Redistribution is a transfer and does not in itself create value added, although organizations involved in transfers inevitably incur some VAT on inputs. Although it is often feasible to measure consumption and to charge prices for such services as health care and education, whether provided by a public agency or otherwise, it is generally considered socially undesirable to do so presumably (though sometimes tenuously) on externality grounds or for distributional reasons.[13] Finally, many PNC activities are essentially similar to those of the private sector – electric and water utilities, postal services, radio and television broadcasting, organizing trade shows, providing recreation facilities, and so on. Even in these cases, however, many outputs are exempt, either for distributional reasons or sometimes because they are considered hard to tax for a variety of conceptual, compliance, and administrative reasons.

In principle, as Aujean, Jenkins, and Poddar (1999) note, it is wrong to treat the PNC sector as the final consumer of the goods and services it provides simply because it provides such services for free (or below cost). As with any exempt activity, some revenue is generated from inputs purchased by registered traders along the supply chain, but the revenue that would have been obtained from final sales (to nonregistered traders and consumers) is of course lost. Two distortions result. First, because the effective tax rate is lower than on other activities, demand patterns are influenced. Second, at the same time cascading – the charging of tax on tax (or multiple taxation of the same value-added) – may occur if downstream firms using exempt services increase prices to cover the cost increase due to the tax. Input choices are distorted because the exemption of components used as inputs makes VAT on some intermediate inputs irrecoverable. Producers further along the chain have an incentive to substitute away from those inputs. The net effect on revenue depends on the stage at which the exemption occurs. A particularly interesting example in the case of many developing countries is the common exemption from VAT of goods financed by international aid to developing countries, which both costs the country revenue and distorts the pattern of economic activities (Chambas 2005).[14]

---

[13] One of the authors explored these issues at some length in Bird (1976).

[14] See Barlow and Snyder (1994) for a case study of Niger that includes a discussion of aid.

The incentive to 'self-supply' is an extreme case of a distorted input choice. Whenever registered traders produce exempt supplies, they have an incentive to self-supply taxable goods and services rather than purchase taxable goods or services or outsource taxable services. The reason is that the input VAT on outside purchases of taxable goods and services is irrecoverable because the supplies that embody those inputs are exempt. This 'self-supply bias' is sometimes referred to as a distortion of competition. The impact of exempt status on the decision to contract out public services has received some attention in the EU recently.[15] Since PNC agencies that render exempt services face a disincentive to contract services out to the private sector, both outsourcing and in some instances privatization are penalized. None of these results is conducive to sound economic development.

The extent of self-supply bias is directly proportional to the VAT rate. The extent to which this bias affects choices depends on the degree of substitutability of self-supplied goods and their pretax prices relative to those of purchased goods. The pretax price advantage of outsourced services does not need to be very large to negate the incentive to self-supply (Edgar 2001). No doubt in most countries cultural, socioeconomic, and political factors constitute much greater barriers to the contracting out of public services than VAT. Still, the issue deserves more attention on both economic and administrative grounds than it has generally received.

Since the PNC sector often provides a mix of services that are taxable, zero-rated, and exempt, complexity arises from the need to apportion input VAT between taxable and exempt activities. Simple in theory, such apportionment is fraught with problems in practice. It is difficult both to track input use and to determine apportionment to reflect the extent of taxable and exempt activities. Conceptually, tracking may be based on actual use or on some allocation formula, but providing such a choice to taxpayers comes at compliance cost and may be a source of revenue uncertainty because taxpayers can manipulate the allocations. Small nonprofit organizations with some taxable sales bear especially high compliance burdens. The existence of VAT registrants that are partially exempt introduces significant complexity for both taxpayers and tax officials and creates opportunities for fraud.

The Way We Might Be

If the current exemption system for the PNC sector is unappealing, two alternatives may be considered: one might modify the exemption system or

---

[15] See, for example, Dijkgraaf and Gradus (2003), Wassenaar and Gradus (2004), and Gjems-Onstad (2004).

Table 6.2. *Rebate Rates under the Canadian GST/HST and Québec QST*

Type of Organization	GST Rebate Rate (%)	HST Rebate Rate (%)[a]	QST Rebate Rate (%)
Municipalities	100	0/57.14[b]	0
Universities or public colleges	67	0/67[c]	47
School authorities	68	0/68[d]	47
Hospital authorities	83[e]	0/83[f]	51.5
Charities and nonprofit organizations[h]	50	50	50[g]

[a] Applies to the provincial HST portion of 8%.
[b] Rate is 0% in Newfoundland and Labrador, and 57.14% in New Brunswick and Nova Scotia.
[c] Rate is 0% in New Brunswick and Newfoundland, and 67% in Nova Scotia.
[d] Rate is 0% in New Brunswick and Newfoundland, and 68% in Nova Scotia.
[e] Health Care Rebate applies to eligible organizations (e.g., charities, nonprofit organizations, and public institutions) that render services similar to those usually rendered by hospitals.
[f] Rate is 0% in New Brunswick and Newfoundland, and 83% in Nova Scotia. In New Brunswick, hospital and school authorities (see note *d*) that are part of the provincial government pay HST on their purchases, but the full amount of the tax is subsequently rebated to them.
[g] Other than public service bodies.
[h] Rebate applies to a nonprofit organization only if its public funding accounts for at least 40% of total funding.

replace it. One modification that might be considered in other countries would be to adopt what Gendron (2005) calls the "Canadian system." In this approach, all supplies made by organizations in the PNC sector are within the scope of the VAT.[16] However, some services are taxable, some are exempt, and some are zero-rated. Input taxes that such organizations incur to deliver taxable or zero-rated supplies are fully creditable. However, in the case of exempt supplies the Canadian VATs depart from the pure exemption model by granting rebates in whole or part of tax paid on inputs used to make exempt supplies, as shown in Table 6.2. Indeed, federal (GST) rebates were enhanced recently. In 2004 the GST rebate rate for municipalities was increased from 57.14% to 100%, and in 2005 the 83% GST rebate rate for hospitals was extended to eligible charities, nonprofit organizations, and public institutions that render services similar to those usually rendered by hospitals (the "GST/HST Health Care Rebate").[17] Interestingly, none of the

[16] In Canada, VAT encompasses three taxes – the federal Goods and Services Tax (GST); the Harmonized Sales Tax (HST) in operation in the provinces of New Brunswick, Newfoundland and Labrador, and Nova Scotia; and the Québec Sales Tax (QST) in operation in the province of Québec (see Table 8.2).
[17] As one would expect, once the doors of zero-rating were opened, the pressure to expand access to the central treasury rapidly increased. For example, within a few days of the initial

three HST provinces follows the federal GST rebate pattern fully. All these rebates are funded from general government revenues.

This system is simple, but as usual deeper consideration reveals some problems. For example, rates that vary by type of supplier are likely to result in nonneutral treatment of similar supplies and create at least a small incentive to choose some service-delivery methods over others. The new GST/HST health care rebate is particularly complex because it requires tax-payers to extend the necessary allocations of activities to one further activity.[18] Furthermore, in spite of the fact that the GST and QST are relatively well harmonized (see Chapter 8), the Québec rebate system is generally less generous and the different rates for the same supplier-activity combinations introduce additional compliance costs (Québec 2005). Under the Québec system, the apparently equal treatment of charitable and nonprofit organizations effectively penalizes charitable organizations since most of their supplies are exempt while most supplies made by nonprofit organizations are taxable. As a consequence, the latter recover a much larger fraction of the total QST paid on inputs.

Some European countries also have rebate systems that compensate public bodies for input VAT paid to make exempt or nontaxable supplies (Table 6.3).[19] In the EU, activities of public sector bodies in education and health are exempt while other activities of public sector bodies in their role as public authorities are nontaxable. An example is a local government that collects refuse. Both nontaxable and exempt activities are considered outside the scope of the VAT in the EU, although derogation of nontaxable status is possible in the event of a significant distortion of competition.[20] In practice, the EU regime for the PNC sector is highly complex and has given rise to conflicts between community law and national law as well as the occasional court case.[21]

---

federal announcement of a full rebate to municipalities, one of the authors saw a banner hung on a nearby elementary school saying, "Why Discriminate against Schools? Give Us the GST Rebate Also!"

[18] Some of the many complexities to which the rebate system has given rise, not least in the health area, are discussed in, for example, Kreklewetz and Seres (2005) and Diamant and McKinney (2005).

[19] Swinkels (2005) discusses some other aspects of PNC treatment under VAT. Yang (2005) notes that in China, where government purchases in principle bear VAT, 25% of the amounts paid by local governments are in effect refunded since local governments receive 25% of VAT collected in their jurisdiction.

[20] Norway has VAT exemptions for health and social services that are similar to those under the EU regime: see Bryne (2002) for a comparison of the VAT system in Norway with that in the EU.

[21] See Swinkels (2005a) on the VAT exemption for medical care.

Table 6.3. *Input VAT Compensation for Public-Sector Services in Europe*

Country	Compensation Scheme[a]	Suppliers	Funding of Scheme
Denmark	VAT refund, taxable activity (refuse collection)	Counties, municipalities, interauthority companies	Municipalities fund a "VAT Compensation Fund"
Finland	VAT refund	Municipalities, municipal federations	Municipalities fund the refund scheme
Netherlands	VAT refund	Municipalities, provinces	Through reduction in grants[b]
Norway	VAT refund, taxable activities (postal services, refuse collection, etc.)	Local governments	Through reduction in general grant to municipalities[b]
Sweden	VAT refund	Municipalities, country councils	Municipalities and country councils fund the refund scheme
United Kingdom	VAT refund	Local and police authorities	Central government revenues, no contribution by local authorities

[a] For further details including exceptions and exclusions, see Wassenaar and Gradus (2004).
[b] Extra VAT receipts from increased contracting out are added to the fund but that does not cover the drop in grants – for example, in Norway in 2000, the reduction in grants accounted for 80% of the funding. (Corresponding figures for the Netherlands are not available.)
Source: Compiled from Wassenaar and Gradus (2004).

The VAT refund schemes described in Table 6.3 in the specific context of refuse collection apply generally to nontaxable or exempt activities of local governments. The main aim is to compensate suppliers for VAT paid on inputs in order to level the playing field between government and private sector supplies. Although we do not have information on the specific refund rates, it seems likely that they are usually less than 100% and vary by activity.[22] The Netherlands provides refunds for VAT incurred in the Netherlands or in other EU member states. None of the other refund schemes mentioned in Table 6.3, however, covers VAT paid to other EU member states, a fact seemingly inconsistent with EU rules. With the exception of the UK refund scheme, which is funded by the central government, all these schemes in

[22] Wassenaar and Gradus (2004) specifically note that refunds vary by activity in Denmark.

effect require local authorities to pay for most refunds through reduced grants by the central government since increased VAT receipts are reportedly insufficient to pay for the refund schemes. Local public bodies may thus have to increase local property taxes or other local levies while central governments receive a small windfall.

A possible modification would be to permit some degree of departure from a pure exemption system, for example, by including goods and services that are otherwise outside the scope of VAT in the scope of the tax or by converting exempt goods and services into taxable or zero-rated goods and services. A variant would be to tax explicit fees charged for public sector outputs. This approach seems especially appropriate in cases when the fee represents the full consideration and is therefore equal to the market value of the supply, as is sometimes the case when goods and services compete directly with those supplied by the private sector (e.g., municipal golf courses in some countries).

A more drastic approach is simply to eliminate the prevalent exemption approach to the PNC sector.[23] Australia and New Zealand do this in a refreshingly simple way: all activities of public bodies and nonprofit organizations are within the scope of the VAT (David and Poddar 2004; Poddar 2005). The GST in Australia and New Zealand applies to organizations in the PNC sector in the same manner as to private sector organizations (New Zealand 2001).

Life is of course never quite this simple. For example, in Australia special rules apply to charities, gift-deductible entities, and government schools (Australia 2003).[24] To get the flavour of the way real-life VAT law often reads it may be worth spelling out these rules a bit. For example, sales of donated second-hand goods, raffles and bingos, and noncommercial sales of goods or services by these organizations are 'GST-free' (zero-rated) – *if* the amount charged for the good or service is less than 50% of the market value or less than 75% of the amount the organization paid for the goods or services. However, if they so choose, these organizations may also simplify their lives (if perhaps complicating those of their prospective customers and competitors) by electing to make sales at a fundraising event *input taxed* (exempt). Similarly, noncommercial supplies of accommodation are also zero-rated – *if* the amount charged is less than 75% of the market value or less than 75% of the cost to the organization of providing the accommodation.

---

[23] See Gendron (2005) for a more detailed comparison of the various approaches mentioned here.

[24] A 'gift-deductible entity' is one to which gifts are deductible for income tax purposes.

Table 6.4. *Requirements for Equality of Treatment under Full Taxation*

	Taxation of Private Goods	Taxation of Public Goods
Economic neutrality	Same treatment of supplies made by private businesses and PNC bodies	Apply to any consideration charged for supplies
Consideration	Apply VAT on amounts charged as consideration (price *plus* grants directly linked to supply)	Supplies made for nil consideration call for zero-rating
Input tax deduction	Full (once supplies become taxable)	Full
Revenue loss	None	None if government collecting VAT is the one making the supply
Distortion of competition	None	None since public goods are supplied by private businesses

Source: Poddar (2005).

Finally, nonprofit organizations that are members of the same nonprofit association can elect to form a 'GST group' if they make considerable sales and purchases amongst themselves.[25] With group treatment members do not have to pay GST on group transactions but of course can claim no credits. Even simple rules when examined carefully often turn out to be surprisingly complex, as indeed they may have to be to produce the desired results in a complex world.

Aujean, Jenkins, and Poddar (1999) make a coherent, convincing, and passionate case for the full taxation of the PNC sector. They begin by noting that the original VAT thinking on this issue was formalized in the EU at a time when there was little competition between the private and public sectors. Half a century later, however, exempting PNC activities is likely to be much more distorting because of the existing and potential competition between private and public sector provision of many goods and services. Moreover, the current system in practice can be quite complex. The economic advantages of full taxation and the reduction in complexity provide compelling motives for change. Table 6.4 sets out some ideas about ways supplies by organizations in the PNC sector might be included in the scope of the VAT.

---

[25] Similar 'grouping' rules – found in many VAT laws – usually apply to commercial activities also, of course, and can be equally complex to deal with there.

Wassenaar and Gradus (2004, 383) conclude that "such a thorough change of the European VAT legislation is not to be expected in the near future mainly because of some conceptual issues." In reality, however, it appears to be not conceptual but political difficulties that block action in the EU. Developing countries do not carry the specific political baggage of the EU.[26] But they too are unlikely to follow the Australian and New Zealand examples, for both political and administrative reasons. Problems other than the proper treatment of the PNC sector loom larger on the VAT policy horizon of most such countries. Nonetheless, more thought should be given to this question in countries such as Egypt and other present and prospective VAT countries in the Middle East and elsewhere in which the state sector constitutes a major component of the formal economy and hence of the potential VAT tax base.

For example, the 100% rebate to municipalities under the Canadian system is equivalent to zero-rating. Zero-rating is consistent with full taxation in the case of public services supplied for nil or nominal consideration.[27] But zero-rating is unlikely to be sensible in the context of most developing and transitional countries. First, it reduces revenue. Second, neutrality is violated if private goods supplied by PNC bodies are zero-rated while private goods supplied by the private sector are not. Third, choice between taxable and zero-rated goods is also distorted. Fourth, complexity costs are increased since rules defining the goods and services to be zero-rated must be designed and their implementation monitored. Finally, to reduce the refund problems we discuss in Chapter 10, developing countries should avoid any domestic zero-rating if at all possible. A special reduced tax rate for PNC activities has similar problems since zero-rating is simply the extreme case of reduced rates, although it costs less in revenue and, perhaps, may be more likely to be monitored carefully. As we discuss further in Chapter 7, reduced rates may thus in some instances provide an appropriate compromise between the Scylla of exemption and the Charybdis of zero-rating for developing and transitional countries – even though such a compromise solution inevitably has some of the defects of both extremes.

Developed countries should consider full taxation of the PNC sector. The case for the status quo is extremely weak. There is no good reason why countries with adequate administrations and modern economies should not

---

[26] As Sijbren Cnossen once put this point in a private comment: "History tends to restrain progress!"

[27] As mentioned earlier, pure transfers are not zero-rated but are rather simply not subject to VAT because they do not constitute consumption nor involve value added. (Presumably the services needed to arrange transfers are intermediation services that use up real resources and therefore create value added.)

follow the Australian-New Zealand model and treat all goods and services supplied by public sector bodies, nonprofit organizations, and charitable organizations as they do any supplies from the private sector. Such a system would be administratively simple, reducing compliance and administrative costs. The current self-supply bias benefits no one, so its removal would be a gain. If countries are not willing to go this far, something like the Canadian system described earlier may provide an acceptable compromise. At the very least, all countries should consider taxing explicit fees.

Should countries without well-developed and sophisticated tax administrations consider following similar paths? Once VAT becomes well established, we think that in some instances they should perhaps do so. As we stress in Chapter 9, no country is given a good VAT administration. It must 'grow' one over a (sometimes) long period. Much the same is true with respect to 'growing' a taxpayer base that makes the essentially 'self-assessed' VAT a feasible revenue source for any country. No tradition of voluntary compliance exists in most developing and transitional countries, 'tax morale' is low or nonexistent (Bird, Martinez-Vazquez, and Torgler 2006), and, as we discuss further in Chapter 12, self-assessment is essentially an alien concept. The illiteracy of small traders, widespread underreporting of tax liabilities, weaknesses in tax administration, and lack of taxpayer service compound the problem.

In such conditions, when might it make sense to extend VAT to the PNC sector? Experience suggests to many that one key to VAT sustainability in developing and transitional countries is to 'do it right, right away.' But does this mean beginning with full taxation of PNC? We think not. As Poddar (2003) argues with respect to financial services taxation (see later discussion), beginners are best advised to stick to tried and proven approaches. The NOSFA principle mentioned in Chapter 1 underlies much of the discussion in this book. But it does not mean that every country should try to build its own 'perfect' VAT from scratch. This approach worked amazingly well in New Zealand, and arguably the New Zealand approach to the PNC sector is simpler than the 'standard' approach. However, in the very different and considerably more difficult circumstances facing most developing and transitional countries, trying to do something simpler that is not 'normal' may produce more disasters than successes. On the whole, countries seem well advised not to build the ideal system for their circumstances but rather to combine 'off-the-shelf software' (in the form of tax policy and administration design components tested out elsewhere) in ways that fit their particular circumstances.

The key problem is to balance the objective of applying taxation to the PNC sector as a source of revenue with the prevention of distortions that arise under the exemption system. Since the income elasticity of the outputs of the PNC sector is positive and probably greater than 1.0, revenue-short countries should in principle apply VAT as widely as possible to goods and services provided by both public sector bodies and nonprofit organizations and charities, subject to the (important) public policy interest constraints noted earlier. In doing so, however, they should also avoid multiple rates, nonstandard exemptions, and excessive zero-rating. To implement such advice successfully, countries may employ any of the approaches set out earlier in this section. In practice, however, approaches like exemptions with rebates and zero-rating that create (rather than resolve) complexities are unpromising. Developing or transitional economies that wish to move in the direction of a better VAT would seem best advised to begin simply by taxing user fees for PNC services, and then perhaps gradually move in the direction of what we have called the Canadian system. Those that are able and willing to do more – or that do not yet have a VAT in place – might be best advised to consider the Australian-New Zealand approach. These countries do not have a perfect system, but it is probably about as close as any country is likely to get in practice.

FINANCIAL SERVICES

Even more than a method to tax the PNC sector, a method to tax financial services is in many ways the key 'frontier' issue for VAT in developed countries. No convincing conceptually correct *and* practical solution for capturing the bulk of financial services under the VAT has yet been developed anywhere. Developing and transitional countries face constraints that make the taxation of financial services a formidable challenge. Since even developed economies with sophisticated financial institutions and markets and capable tax administrations have opted with few exceptions to exempt such activities, it is not surprising that exemption also rules in almost all developing and transitional countries. While, as we discuss later, it may not be very difficult to collect at least some direct VAT from financial services even in such countries, it is not clear that developing countries would collect more or less than they now do indirectly (in the form of input taxes) by exempting such services.[28]

Current Practice

Under the system in most VAT countries the output of the financial sector – financial services – is untaxed, but input VAT incurred by suppliers

---

[28] For an extended discussion of this subject, see Gendron (2006).

of financial services is for the most part irrecoverable. The result is thus partial taxation. Two reasons are used to justify the exemption of financial services from VAT. First, some argue that the consumption of financial services should not be taxed in the first place. Secondly, identification and measurement problems may preclude taxing such services.

Contrary to the first argument, however, the basic logic of VAT is that household consumption of financial services *should* fall into the VAT net. The production of such services uses up real resources and hence creates value-added. Nonetheless, some have argued that financial intermediation services do not increase consumption per se but only change the intertemporal budget constraint facing consumers (Whalley 1992; Chia and Whalley 1999).[29] However, some who accept the lack of direct consumption benefits have nonetheless suggested that fixed fees charged for financial services should be taxed while implicit fees should be zero-rated (Jack 2000). Others, invoking different assumptions, assert that VAT on financial services to consumers should be at least as high as VAT on other consumer goods (Rousslang 2002).[30] Most recently, Boadway and Keen (2003), though arguing plausibly that the view that financial services purchased by consumers should not be taxed because they yield no utility is a fallacy, suggest that lower (but nonzero) tax rates on financial services may provide an appropriate solution to an optimal consumption tax problem. As Poddar (2003) rightly notes, however, this seems to imply that the 'correct' consumption base is not 'value-added,' whereas in his view "VAT is designed to be a tax consistently applied to all the inputs that contribute to value-added" (Poddar 2003, 360).

The second rationale for exempting financial services may be called the "hard to tax" argument. Output from financial services activity is argued to be so hard to tax for a variety of conceptual, administrative, and compliance reasons that it is preferable to settle for simply collecting some VAT revenues on inputs used by registered traders along the supply chain. The major difficulty usually mentioned is the problem of identifying the intermediation service element that is part of a margin or spread.

Whatever its rationale, the exemption approach has its own problems. VAT generates revenue from inputs purchased by registered traders along the supply chain, but it does not generate any revenue from final sales. The result is that the effective tax rate falls below the statutory rate and that

---

[29] Grubert and Mackie (2000) have argued similarly that financial services used by consumers should not be taxed under a consumption tax since such services do not enter consumer utility functions. The logic of this argument is hard to accept.

[30] Similarly, Auerbach and Gordon (2002) argue that VAT should apply to resources devoted to financial transactions as it does in other sectors.

cascading takes place along the chain to the extent downstream firms using exempt services increase prices to cover the cost increase due to the tax. Other things equal, registered traders unable to recover input VAT paid to produce exempt services would prefer to substitute taxable inputs for exempt inputs in order to maximize VAT recovery. In practice such substitution may be limited since any substitutes are likely to be at best imperfect, although only anecdotal evidence is available on the extent of the resulting distortion. For instance, Schatan (2003) reports serious problems in Mexico, where banks reportedly managed to shift inputs artificially away from exempt activity and towards taxable activities so as to maximize input VAT recovery.

The incentive to self-supply is closely related to the distortion of input choice. In the case of financial services, given the benefits of specialization in this field, it is perhaps unlikely that self-supply is a perfect substitute or that the pretax prices of self-supplies and purchased goods and services would be equal (Edgar 2001). Nonetheless, the exemption system may affect cross-border flows of goods and services. For instance, EU banks that export financial services outside the EU can claim VAT on inputs since such exports are zero-rated. In contrast, EU registered traders purchasing exempt financial services in the EU must bear some irrecoverable input VAT.[31] Moreover, registered traders have an incentive to import services that are zero-rated (in the exporting country) rather than purchase such services domestically from exempt suppliers and thus indirectly bear input VAT.

Partially exempt traders (like many in the financial sector) introduce significant complexity in the VAT system because of the need to apportion input VAT – and hence input use – between taxable and exempt activities.[32] Such apportionment may seem simple in theory but – as mentioned earlier with respect to the PNC sector – is fraught with problems in practice. Insufficient control by the tax authority over the apportionment process can lead to absurd results. For example, not only may partially exempt banks with significant shares of taxable and exempt activities recover most of their total input VAT, but some may even end up in a net credit position (Schatan 2003). It is not surprising that much of the work of VAT consultants in the EU reportedly arises with respect to the exemption for financial services, which requires a large number of organizations to account for both taxable and exempt supplies.

---

[31] Such problems may arise with any exemptions, not just those of financial services, although among all categories of services, cross-border flows of financial services are probably the hardest to track.

[32] Gale and Holtzblatt (2002) define the complexity of a tax system as the sum of compliance and administrative costs.

Much effort has been devoted to working out alternative approaches to applying VAT to financial services. Little empirical work has been done to quantify the economic distortions and costs that result from the exemption system. In the absence of such evidence, it is perhaps not unreasonable to conclude that such effects are probably not decisively important. If so, then the simplest advice one might give developing and transitional countries would seem to be to maintain the exemption system since at least it wrings some VAT revenue out of the financial sector by taxing inputs at the preretail stages.[33] We return to this point shortly.

Alternative Approaches

First, however, since considerable attention has been paid in recent years to possible alternatives to the exemption system, it is worth reviewing the main contenders here. Many types of financial services may be distinguished: (1) deposits, borrowing, and lending (banking operations, credit card operations); (2) purchase, sale, and issuance of financial securities (bonds, shares, options, guarantees, and foreign currencies; gold and precious metals); (3) insurance (life; property and casualty); (4) brokerage and other agent services (buying and selling of financial securities; underwriting and other transactions whereby agents act as principals); and (5) advisory, management, and data processing (asset management and investment advice; administrative and information services, incidental or supplementary to financial services).[34]

Many different approaches have been suggested to tax these various activities, and some are actually used to some extent in a few countries. The main approaches may be summarized as follows:[35]

- The *addition method* is an accounts-based method under which value added is calculated as the sum of wages and profits. Israel currently taxes

---

[33] Of course, some such countries (e.g., Malaysia) have highly developed financial systems and may reach a different conclusion. For interesting discussions of some of these issues in Hong Kong, see Mintz and Richardson (2002) and Hong Kong (2006).

[34] This classification follows Poddar (2003). Bakker and Chronican (1985) provide an early but excellent appraisal of tax options for different types of services. The taxation of life insurance is not discussed here. As Chen and Mintz (2001) show, property and casualty insurers in OECD countries face a combination of value-added taxes, sales taxes on premiums, premium taxes, property transfer taxes, property taxes, taxes on capital or assets, and income taxes. This pattern suggests significant taxation and, in all likelihood, a complex pattern of distortions. For further discussion, see Zee (2005, 2006), Schenk and Zee (2004), Ebrill et al. (2001), and European Commission (1997).

[35] A more detailed summary may be found in Gendron (2006).

financial services and nonlife insurance using this method. However, since the tax is administered outside the VAT system, those taxed cannot claim VAT paid on purchases.

- More conceptually appealing is a *cash flow VAT* under which all cash inflows from financial transactions are treated as taxable sales on which VAT must be remitted to the tax authorities and all cash outflows by financial institutions are treated as taxed purchases with entitlement for input VAT credit. This approach has two variants. The Tax Calculation Account (TCA) system is a tax suspension account for margin transactions that is handled by financial institutions. Tax or credit amounts credited to the TCA accrue interest until the TCA is closed and the net VAT remitted. The second variant is similar, except that business transactions are zero-rated. This method seems the conceptually correct way to apply the VAT to margin services, but it is obviously complex and has not yet been adopted anywhere.[36]

- An alternative approach suggested recently by Zee (2005) is called *modified reverse-charging*.[37] The proposal is intended to achieve the same results as TCA without its administrative complexity. However, since under this system consumers who borrow would be overtaxed, a complex system would still be needed to ensure "that, when borrowers are granted VAT credits, the credits are derived from deposits that have in fact been reverse-charged" (Zee 2005, 86). A related approach suggested earlier to reduce this problem would be to use only part of the interest as the tax base, adjusting the tax rate to cover only the proportion of the transaction that represents the service charge (the 'separate tax rates' approach of Bakker and Chronican 1985). To do this, one has to estimate the service charge. One reason for the development of the cash flow VAT was precisely to resolve the problem of identifying the service charge in the margin.

- A simple approach used to a limited extent in Mexico is simply to calculate VAT liability on the basis of *net operating income*. For an

---

[36] The cash-flow method is set out succinctly in Poddar and English (1997) and more comprehensively in European Commission (1997). An earlier method (suggested by, e.g., Bakker and Chronican [1985]), would have required an invoice setting out the full value of the transaction – its actual amount (such as fees and commissions) or its nominal amount (such as capital or income amounts from deposits, loans, withdrawals, and so on). The obvious problem with this method is that it may cause liquidity problems since it applies the tax to capital and income amounts in the case of margin services. The cash flow method prevents this problem.

[37] We discuss reverse charging in more general terms in Chapter 8.

institution the tax base consists of net interest, plus margins and fees received from other activities of the institution. For a specific activity the tax base is net income before other costs with tax calculated at the tax-inclusive.

- In Japan an almost equivalent system is applied. VAT is levied on an accounts-based measure of value added, with each business calculating value added as the difference between revenues and allowable purchases. While this *subtraction approach* is simple, complex rules – similar to those in the income tax – are needed to separate financial from nonfinancial businesses.

- Argentina applies another approach, which we may call the 'taxing gross interest' method. Under this system VAT applies to the interest on most loans. Although the measure was implemented outside the realm of tax policy – to curb borrowing in order to reduce inflation – the government allowed the interest on loans from certain institutions to be taxed at about half the standard VAT rate.[38] The fact that interest on deposits is exempt is consistent with the nontax policy objective.

- The Province of Québec (Canada) zero-rates financial services, imposing capital, payroll, and premium taxes on financial institutions to compensate for the revenue loss.

- As usual New Zealand has followed a different path. Prior to 2005 New Zealand exempted financial services with some exceptions. Non-life insurance other than creditor protection policies was taxable under something like the cash flow system since VAT was charged on premiums and recoverable by registered businesses.[39] Since 2005 financial services supplied between registered businesses or by a (registered) financial intermediary to a registered business have been *zero-rated.* This approach, which had earlier been pioneered in Québec, considerably reduces distortions and greatly reduces the complexity of the tax. It has two disadvantages, however. First, final consumers are taken out of the VAT net. Second, all revenue from taxation of inputs under the exemption system is lost. New Zealand does not zero-rate supplies from financial institutions to other financial institutions as the vast majority of such supplies consist of exempt services.

---

[38] See Schenk and Zee (2004) for a fuller description of the VAT treatment of financial services in Argentina. This approach in some ways is similar to the separate tax rate approach mentioned earlier.

[39] Australia, Singapore, and South Africa use a similar approach with claims paid grossed up by one plus the VAT rate because of deemed VAT paid.

- Although the Australian Goods and Services Tax (GST) essentially exempts financial services, it makes some important exceptions. For example, brokerage not undertaken by a principal, financial agency services, and nonlife insurance are all taxable. Moreover, to reduce the self-supply bias, a credit is allowed equal to 75% of GST paid on a specified list of eligible goods and services purchased to make exempt supplies.

- An *exemption system that permits full input credits* of course approximates zero-rating. In Singapore financial services are taxable if they are provided in return for a brokerage fee, commission, or similar consideration but are otherwise exempt. Input tax credits may be claimed using two methods. The first requires segregation of eligible sales and amounts to the zero-rating of services provided to registered businesses. The second method is based on recovery rates that depend on the type of financial institution. The aim is to reduce cascading and preserve the competitiveness of the financial sector.

- Under yet another approach, used in (at least) Belgium, France, and Germany, financial institutions may *elect to be taxable*. This option is appealing to financial institutions that deal mostly with business customers that can claim credit for VAT paid.

- South Africa taxes almost all *explicit fees* and nonlife insurance. However, it requires taxpayers to allocate input credits between the remaining exempt (margin) services and taxable fees. In Singapore taxable services include brokerage for executive transactions for the sale of securities on behalf of customers, brokerage for life or general insurance, general insurance premiums, and merchant banks' fees for corporate restructuring. Principal services are exempt (Poddar 2003). This approach is essentially a narrower variant of an approach – as yet not apparently in use anywhere – that would tax all explicit fees and commissions. In effect Australia, New Zealand, Singapore, and South Africa apply partial versions of the method, with each located at different points on the continuum between full exemption and full taxation of fees and commissions.

Much of the discussion of alternative approaches to VAT with respect to financial services has taken place in the EU, but surprisingly little has actually been done there. The reason may be that, presumably because of the relatively small size of inputs subject to VAT in the end – because of the partial input VAT recovery allowed under the exemption system by some EU governments – in effect "the current exemption system almost operates like a system where all banking services, supplied to businesses and households, are zero-rated" (Huizinga 2002, 516). Full zero-rating would be cleaner and more efficient, but the present system gives governments some revenue from the financial sector. Despite the numerous (but largely unquantified) shortcomings attributed to the exemption system, exemption continues to dominate, perhaps in part because no single alternative seems to have much appeal.

What Should Developing Countries Do?

Weak tax administration is the principal impediment to the successful implementation and use of sophisticated and diversified tax instruments in developing and transitional countries. Any method of dealing with financial services that imposes a heavy administrative burden must therefore be viewed with scepticism. As in the case of the PNC sector, perhaps the best advice for most such countries is simply that they should set aside such complex issues as the taxation of financial services as far as possible and concentrate on more essential aspects of VAT design and implementation such as those we discuss in Chapter 7.

Only two approaches to financial services seem potentially feasible in most developing countries – exemption and what may be called 'reduced exemption.' If a country already has an exemption system, it should probably stay with it. Some theoretical arguments support this position. For example, Edgar (2001) provides a detailed defence of exemption on the basis of what he sees as serious deficiencies and difficulties with both the major alternatives of zero-rating and cash flow taxation. Moreover, as Boadway and Keen (2003) note, making financial services fully taxable will not necessarily increase VAT revenues and may even reduce them. The reason is simply that only final consumers would pay VAT on such services in a full taxation regime. In the exempt regime, however, VAT is collected on business inputs, with some revenue leakage in the case of exports (which are zero-rated) and some revenue increases when taxable goods and services embodying financial services sell at a higher price to reflect input VAT. As Huizinga (2002) demonstrates, even EU countries seem to gain substantial revenue from this system – though this does not mean that it is desirable. Boadway and Keen (2003) properly note that this result should not simply be extrapolated to developing countries, because of their very different profiles with respect to, for example, the distribution and levels of consumer wealth and income, the sophistication of financial markets and final consumers, the income elasticity of demand for financial services, and attitudes towards risk.[40] Still, in view of the tight revenue constraint faced by most such governments, this aspect of exempting the financial sector is not unimportant.

If something else is to be done, perhaps the only real alternative in the context of most emerging economies is what may perhaps be called a 'hybrid' system. Such a system might (i) subject all fees and commissions to VAT and (ii) also subject all margin services to VAT using what were earlier called the 'separate tax rates' and 'taxing gross interest' methods.[41] This approach has several advantages. First, since all services are taxable, the scheme reduces the incentive to institutions to substitute margins for fees, the incentive for self-supply, and the import bias. Substitution of margins for fees will not reduce tax revenue unless services move to the informal sector or abroad. Second, it keeps the VAT chain intact all the way to nonregistered persons. Third, it provides full input VAT credits to all registered traders without the need for complex input allocation mechanisms and the attendant distortions. Fourth, the tax ultimately falls on final consumption, the intended base. And finally, it prevents liquidity problems since it does not apply VAT to capital amounts (e.g., deposit and loan amounts) themselves but rather to interest or margins.

Importantly, across the board application of this method might yield more revenue than taxing the true base. In most cases the value of the intermediation service is not known and is subject to estimation error.[42] The value of the service is clearly less than the full margin, which includes the pure time value of money, the risk premium, and the intermediation charge. In its pure form, the 'separate tax rates' component of the approach would apply VAT to a portion of the margin (or interest paid or received if margin

---

[40] Oddly, the literature emphasizes the price elasticity of demand in discussion of the taxation of financial services. Horror stories are usually based on estimates of price elasticity that seem too large to be plausible for financial services as a whole (since there are very few, if any, substitutes for financial services taken as a group). Since the end purpose of the VAT is to raise revenue, the income elasticity is more important and deserves more attention in future empirical work.

[41] This suggestion draws substantially on Bakker and Chronican (1985), who appraise separate tax rates and taxing gross interest for each of the following service groups: financial intermediation, trading in financial assets, fee and commission activity, and insurance services. As noted earlier, both elements of the hybrid system are clearly superseded by the cash-flow approach in theory. But if no one – and certainly no developing or transitional economy – can yet implement the cash-flow or the modified reverse-charging approaches, the hybrid approach appears to have some merit.

[42] Such errors arise, for example, from averaging borrowing and lending rates and averaging the proportion of margin that represents elements other than intermediation.

is not available) to acknowledge the fact that the intermediation charge is a fraction of the full margin. This is equivalent to applying a lower tax rate to the full margin. This method therefore corrects for excessive taxation at the full VAT rate so that no further adjustments would be needed in principle. The portion of the margin that represents the intermediation charge could be based upon transaction-specific data, but this method would be complex and costly. Alternatively, it could be based upon aggregate institutional data for the type of transaction involved, for instance, calculating the proportion of interest paid on consumer loans that represents intermediation. In either case, the method requires some approximations.[43]

Obviously, the compliance and administrative costs of such methods are not trivial. Financial institutions would need to provide data to the tax administration in order for the latter to arrive at the proper tax rate for the type of transaction involved. Banks, for instance, would be unwilling to reveal the composition of margins for competitive reasons. Some trade-off always exists between precise assessment (and hence neutrality) and high compliance costs and simple tax methods. Still, any country with a relatively developed financial sector and good tax administration could likely operate such a system if it wished to do so, perhaps coupled with some special administrative schemes such as zero-rating of transactions between registered traders to reduce compliance and administrative costs. When there are no exempt services, there is of course no need to 'ring-fence' zero-rating (New Zealand 2004).

Since few developing or transitional countries could reasonably operate even this simplified system, an alternative and simpler approach would be simply to tax gross interest or margins, as Argentina in effect does.[44] The resulting tax collection would be excessive, but, provided refunding worked properly – a significant qualification, as we discuss in Chapter 10 – this would pose little problem for registered traders since they would obtain full credit for VAT paid. If a country were concerned about excessive tax collections at the consumer level, it might perhaps follow something like the Canadian model of providing a refundable income tax credit to offset excess VAT paid on financial services based on a notional amount of excess VAT paid (in effect an ex post correction rather than the ex ante one used in the separate

---

[43] As noted earlier, a cash-flow VAT would of course obviate this approximation problem and thus supersede the separate tax rates method. Our premise here, however, is that the cash flow method is too complex for any developing country.

[44] Taxing gross interest is a special case of separate tax rates in which the full VAT rate is applied to gross interest. In this case, the problem of excess tax does not self-correct.

rates method).[45] In effect, this approach converts the transactional separate rate method to an aggregate (taxpayer level) method, substantially reducing compliance and administrative costs. In principle, it also has the advantage of encouraging overall compliance with respect to the overall tax system by creating an incentive to file an income tax return to receive credit and by linking indirect and direct tax systems.[46] Of course, this process too would also not be easy to apply in the many developing and transitional countries that do not have either broad personal income taxes or competent tax administrations. For such countries, exemption remains the policy of choice.

---

[45] The methods developed in European Commission (1997) and subsequent reports could provide useful guidance in preparing estimates of notional amounts. One way to ensure equity of treatment would be to develop and use the same guidelines for a certain period (say one or two years) and then revise them periodically to reflect innovations in services and other relevant changes in markets. Filers would need supporting documentation in the form of invoices or bank statements showing the name of the supplier; its VAT registration number; the description of the services; capital, interest, and other relevant amounts; and VAT paid.

[46] The government could use the notional refund rate as a mechanism to achieve a target amount of net revenue from the sector. This mechanism could of course also be implemented as part of the pure separate tax rates method. It would require selecting tax rates subject to a revenue constraint. However, the ex ante basis of the scheme and the requirement for separate implicit tax rates by type of transaction make the mechanism far more complex than the aggregate approach suggested in the text.

SEVEN

Key Issues in VAT Design

Once the base of a VAT is determined, several key design issues such as the level and structure of rates must be resolved. Many lessons for VAT design suggested by experience in developed countries are relevant everywhere, but some need to be reconsidered in developing and transitional countries, in which tax reality is even more dominated by administrative capacity and political necessity. As Laffont (2004) remarked in surveying another important policy issue (public utility regulation), not only do we have surprisingly little solid empirical knowledge about the critical factors determining what policy design is best for any particular country, but even the relevant economic theory remains rather sketchy. Moreover, outside experts often know even less about the relevant political economy context. In this chapter we consider some of the important aspects of VAT design that require close analysis of the country in question: rates, thresholds, exemptions, zero-rating, and excises.

RATES

Expert advice on VAT rates is simple: there should be only one rate. (Actually, this means that there should be two rates, since a zero rate should be imposed on exports.) The uniformity of this 'uniform' rate advice rests on the assumption that the administrative and compliance costs of rate differentiation outweigh efficiency and equity arguments that might be made for such differentiation. Administratively, more rates seem clearly to be associated with higher administrative and compliance costs and hence reduced VAT 'efficiency' in the terms discussed in Chapter 4 (Cnossen 2004). Economically, although the differential rates found in practice are also often associated with increased distortion of choice and hence welfare losses (Agha and Haughton 1996), a good theoretical case can of course be made in efficiency terms for imposing higher rates on goods and services for which demand is less elastic or that are closely associated with (untaxed) leisure (Ebrill et al. 2001). Moreover, as some evidence cited in Chapter 5 indicates, and as we discuss further later, a good equity case can sometimes also be made for rate differentiation. Indeed, when cross-border smuggling is a problem, as it is often is with luxury goods in many developing and transitional countries, even administrative considerations may sometimes suggest rate differentiation. It is not easy to strike the right balance in any country.[1]

One problem is that the efficiency, equity, and administrative arguments for differential rates may suggest very different, and contrary, patterns of rate differentiation. A more important problem is that the empirical evidence in support of all these arguments is shaky. On balance, most of the small band of VAT experts have been persuaded by the considerable anecdotal evidence suggesting both that the administrative argument against multiple rates is correct and that the rate differentiation found in practice seems often more likely to distort than to correct resource allocation decisions. Hence, the case for a single rate dominates in expert advice.

Not for the first time, however, the world does not seem to agree with the experts. Even countries that may appear to have simple 'uniform' VAT rate structures seldom have them in reality, as we discussed in Chapter 2 (Table 2.1). Jamaica, for example, is usually said to have a uniform VAT rate: in 2004, this rate was 15%. In reality, however, in 2004 Jamaica was also imposing a rate of only 12.5% on some construction inputs (cement, steel bars, etc.), rates varying between 0% and 157% on motor vehicles, a rate of 20% on some telecommunications services, and an effectively lower rate on tourist activities.[2] Indeed, one recent study even referred to Jamaica's "anarchy in tax rates" (Artana and Naranjo 2003, iii).

Despite the preponderance of expert advice favoring a single standard rate applied to all taxable transactions, most countries do not seem to be listening. The real 'standard' appears to be to have at least two (nonzero) rates (see Annex Table A.1), although it does appear, as International Tax Dialogue (2005) notes, that more recent VAT adopters are more likely to impose a single rate.

---

[1] As Kopczuk and Slemrod (2006) show, when administrative considerations are important, as they are in developing and transitional countries, they may outweigh the welfare cost created by distorting production patterns; see also Keen (2006a).

[2] Tourism is discussed briefly in Chapter 6. One might question on developmental grounds the apparent propensity in many developing countries to impose higher taxes on mobile phones than on other phone services (see, for example, Roller and Waverman [2001]), but this issue is not discussed further here.

The most important reason for the proliferation of multiple rate structures is that multiple rates are perceived to be more equitable. Experts commonly dispute this argument for several reasons:

- International experience suggests strongly that having more rates makes it somewhat harder to administer a sales tax, for example, by increasing the scope for misclassification of transactions (Ebrill et al. 2001, Cnossen 2004).
- Multiple rates may mean that a higher average rate is required to raise a given amount of revenue, thus increasing the economic costs of imposing the tax (Agha and Haughton 1996).[3]
- Higher sales tax rates on 'luxury' goods are an ineffective means of increasing progressivity. Not only are such levies usually poorly targeted, but any minute equity gain achieved in this fashion is unlikely to offset the costs in terms of reduced efficiency and effectiveness of the tax (Cnossen 2003).[4]
- Similarly, lower tax rates on 'necessities' are generally poorly targeted and ineffective. The rich may spend relatively less of their income on 'basic food,' but they are likely to spend absolutely more and hence receive more benefit than the poor from such concessions (Ebrill et al. 2001).

There is considerable merit in the last two points. Nonetheless, as we discussed in Chapter 5, the distributive impact of imposing a uniform VAT on the highly unequal income-consumption structure found in most developing countries needs to be taken explicitly into account in designing the rate structure of the tax. In particular, given the general inadvisability both of domestic zero-rating and widespread exemptions (as discussed later), a reduced rate for some items may prove to be the lesser of evils when political necessity or distributional policy objectives mandate a more explicitly progressive VAT.

An equally (or more) important question concerns the *level* of VAT rates. We shall comment briefly on only three aspects of this question. Is there a minimum VAT rate? Is there a maximum rate? And if there are two rates, is there some 'magic ratio' that should be maintained between them? Since

---

[3] On the other hand, as mentioned earlier, if the higher rate is imposed on goods and services for which demand is less elastic, the efficiency cost of raising a given amount of revenue should be lower.

[4] There may sometimes be a case for limited 'luxury' excises (e.g., on vehicles), but these should, as we discuss later, be imposed separately from the VAT and outside the VAT's rate structure.

little serious research appears to have been done on any of these questions, at this stage all we can do is to offer some preliminary thoughts based on specific country experience.

Minimum Rate

For years, conventional wisdom was that imposing a VAT with a standard rate less than 10% (Tait 1988) did not make sense. The reasoning underlying this conclusion appears to be simply that because VAT is a relatively complex and expensive tax to set up and administer, it is unlikely to be worth doing so unless it collects a good deal of revenue, and at a rate of 10% it will likely do so.[5] In the absence of serious study of administrative and compliance costs at different rate levels, this argument is not persuasive.[6] Moreover, it has not persuaded such countries as Japan, Taiwan, and Canada, all of which have standard rates well under 10%.[7] Indeed, the initial rate of the Japanese VAT was set at only 3%, although it was subsequently raised to 5%. A very few developing countries (e.g., Nigeria, Panama) also have rates less than 10% (Annex Table A.1).

In most developing countries, however, the need for revenue – and the failure of other taxes to produce sufficient revenue – have led to the imposition of rates of 10% or higher.[8] Indeed, in most transitional countries emerging from the former Soviet bloc, VAT rates were initially set at 28% (reflecting the former dominance of the turnover tax in the revenue structure),

---

[5] The requirement that member states of the EU must have a minimum standard VAT rate of 15% appears to be more related to concerns about cross-border trading (Chapter 8) and control of fraud (Chapter 10). It also reflects the very important role VAT revenues play in supporting the large government sectors in major EU countries.

[6] Warlters and Auriol (2005) present data on administrative costs (budgetary outlays as a percentage of revenue collected for 10 countries); some similar data may be found in Gallagher (2005). No one appears to have collected compliance cost information for VAT in developing and transitional countries. As Wu and Teng (2005) note, the only comparable 'compliance' data available on such countries appear to be the survey information reported in the Global Competitiveness Report; see <www.weforum.org>. This survey simply asks international business executives how much 'tax evasion' they think takes place in the different countries in which they operate. Unsurprisingly, the results are highly correlated to such other measures as estimated corruption and the extent of the 'underground economy.'

[7] In early 2006 Taiwan was reportedly considering raising its 5% rate to 10%. As noted earlier, Canada lowered its rate from 7% to 6% in mid-2006.

[8] We do not discuss here how to estimate the initial VAT rate needed to produce a given revenue target, which obviously depends both on the base chosen and on the estimated administrative effectiveness in reaching that base. Various approaches to this task are discussed in detail in Bird (1991). For other treatments, see Aguirre and Shome (1988), Mackenzie (1992), Shome (1995), Pellechio and Hill (1996), and Jenkins and Kuo (2000).

although most subsequently lowered their standard rates to closer to 20% when they adopted a more 'modern' form of VAT a few years later. In some transitional countries VAT remains highly unpopular and controversial. In Ukraine, for example, recent political discussion has canvassed alternatives ranging from going back to the turnover tax to altering VAT to what is essentially a retail sales tax to drastically lowering the standard VAT rate (currently 20%) to 12%.[9]

Maximum Rate

The lowest standard VAT rate that makes sense for any country in principle depends primarily on the marginal cost of raising public funds (MCPF) through a VAT compared to other possibilities. The MCPF in turn depends on factors such as the strength of behavioural responses, the marginal administrative cost of different taxes, the size of the informal sector, and the level of revenue required (Warlters and Auriol 2005). Presumably it should be possible to calculate such a 'minimum' rate for most countries, but it has not yet been done. Similar factors should govern the highest VAT rate feasible in a given country at a given time, but again we are not yet in a position to say what that rate might be. If one focuses solely on revenue, however, it is not difficult to estimate what the maximum VAT rate might be in at least some circumstances.

As tax rates rise, potential taxpayers seek to lower their tax liability through both legal and illegal means. The 'revenue maximizing tax rate' (RMTR) is the rate that would yield the most revenue. At rates lower than the RMTR, increases in the rate will increase revenue; once the RMTR is reached, however, more revenue would be raised by *lowering* the rate, as Laffer and Seymour (1979) argued was true with respect to U.S. income taxes in the 1970s, for example. Although this argument was shown to be empirically invalid with respect to U.S. taxes on wage income at the time (Fullerton 1982), much the same argument has frequently been made in other contexts – for example, with respect to all taxes (Scully 1991), with respect to capital taxes such as those on capital gains (Burman 1999), and perhaps most credibly with respect to particular excise taxes (Bird and Wallace 2005). For example, as the tax rate on beer increases, all else being held constant, consumers may shift to other forms of alcohol (smuggled or illicitly produced) or even to soft drinks, thus reducing the beer tax base. Depending upon the price

---

[9] The last of these options was suggested in September 2005 by a Presidential Task Force set up by the new government (Lanovy 2005).

elasticity of demand for beer and the efficiency of the revenue system, this base reduction may in time reduce beer tax revenue.[10]

Can similar thinking be applied to a general consumption tax such as VAT? When incomes are low, consumption can probably be expected to grow at around the same pace as economic activity in general. Over time, however, as income levels rise, savings will tend to expand at the expense of consumption. In addition, experience suggests that over time the tax base will tend to erode as a result of both 'exemption creep' and persistent evasion. As we discuss further in Chapter 11, periodic rate increases (or base expansions) are thus often necessary simply in order to maintain consumption tax revenues.

In the case of Jamaica, for example, a 1993 rate increase to a standard rate of 12.5% – a 25% increase – yielded a substantial increase in revenues, of 99% in nominal terms and 53% in real terms. A few years later, however, a similar increase in the standard rate of 2.5 percentage points (to 15%) yielded a much more modest increase in revenues, 45% in nominal and 16% in real terms. On the basis of this experience, and assuming that the tax continued to be administered in the same way and at the same level of efficiency as in the past, Edmiston and Bird (2004) estimated that RMTR for the GCT in Jamaica was 18%. An estimate based on only two previous rate changes is clearly suspect. Nonetheless, absent major changes in either the base or the administration of the tax or both, one might suspect that there may not be much room left in Jamaica for further exploitation of the VAT as a revenue source.[11] An earlier investigation of the relation between changes in VAT rates and VAT revenues also found for a number of developed countries that increases in VAT rates tend to produce diminishing increases in revenues (Silvani and Wakefield 2002).[12] No developing country, however, seems as

---

[10] If there is only one good to consider, the RMTR is equal to $-1/2\eta$, where η is the own price elasticity of demand for the taxed good. More generally, the revenue maximizing rate is a more complicated function of demand and supply elasticities. Moreover, since taxes are not costless, both the administrative and compliance costs associated with particular tax rates should also be taken into account when computing the RMTR (Bird and Wallace 2005).

[11] In 2006, Jamaica increased its standard VAT rate to 16.5%.

[12] Silvani and Wakefield (2002) examined 22 cases of changes in standard VAT rates (ranging from a cut of 4 percentage points in Chile to an increase of 7 percentage points in Costa Rica) in 21 countries, mostly in Latin America and Europe. Interestingly, Jamaica was one of only four countries in their sample in which 'productivity' [(VAT revenue/GDP)/VAT rate] increased when rates were increased. Matthews and Lloyd-Williams (2000) undertake a related exercise with respect to VAT in a number of developed countries and suggest that the RMTR for VAT is about 20%. Note that these studies focus only on VAT revenue, unlike the studies of VAT impact on total revenue by Ebrill et al. (2001) and Baunsgaard and Keen (2005) discussed in Chapter 4.

yet to be at the RMTR for VAT. As a rule, increasing VAT rates will therefore yield more VAT revenue in absolute terms and cutting rates will reduce revenue. While the welfare-maximizing rate is presumably lower than the RMTR, in many developing countries increasing VAT rates may thus be the best way to raise additional revenues – assuming, of course, that action has first been taken to eliminate as many of the unwarranted exemptions and concessions usually found in all taxes as the political economy of tax policy (Chapter 11) will permit.

The Range of Rates

We suggest later in this chapter that there is a strong case for at least one reduced VAT rate in some developing and transitional countries. Can anything be said about precisely how 'reduced' such a rate should be relative to the standard rate? As we discuss in Chapter 10, refunds create serious problems in developing and transitional countries. It is thus important to keep domestic zero-rating to a minimum. Indeed, the best amount of (non-export) zero-rating is probably zero. If so, any reduced rate should clearly be sufficiently above zero to minimize the need for refunds.[13] One might, for example, argue that a reduced rate no less than, say, 40% of the standard rate may serve the purpose. One way to establish just how low such a rate might be in any particular country may perhaps be to inspect the input-output table (if one is available) to ensure that industries producing goods to be taxed at a reduced rate do not purchase too high a proportion of inputs taxed at the standard rate.[14]

On the other hand, when it comes to rates (or exemptions or zero-rating) one must always think of what might be called the 'slippery slope' argument. Perhaps a persuasive case can be made in some instances to have a reduced as well as a standard VAT rate. Once this first step is taken, however, some might argue that it may perhaps become all too easy to make a case for yet another rate (or exemption, or zero-rating) for this or that reason that seems persuasive to some groups.[15] Whatever one thinks of this argument,

---

[13] Some countries have followed the French 'butoir' rule and simply limited or prohibited refunds. As Emini (2000) shows for the case of Cameroon, although such 'imperfections' in VAT may in some instances be welfare improving in the short run, they are likely welfare reducing when capital is mobile.

[14] We owe this suggestion to Carlos Silvani.

[15] As Cornford (1908) put the point in a different context, one must be aware of 'The Principle of the Wedge': in a bureaucratic-political context, a good reason for not doing a good thing may be that it will open the door to doing a lot of other things, many of which may not be so good.

in the real world in which tax policies are formed, it may often be good 'gamesmanship' for those who are willing to end up with two rates to begin by insisting on the virtues, indeed necessity, of a single rate.

THRESHOLDS

In most countries, a surprisingly small number of VAT registrants, sometimes less than a few dozen, account for 80% or 90% of VAT collections.[16] One must of course keep a close eye on such fiscal 'whales' (Baer, Benon, and Toro Rivera 2002). However, what has proved to be a considerably more troublesome problem in VATs around the world is the way to deal with the many 'minnows' in the system – the small taxpayers who constitute the majority of VAT taxpayers. We discuss this issue more fully in Chapter 10, but we consider one important aspect here: where should the threshold – the point at which firms must register as VAT taxpayers – be set?

When VAT came into the world the usual expert advice was to set this entry point, which is usually defined in terms of annual turnover, as low as possible. The idea was essentially to ensure that all potentially taxable transactions were caught in the fiscal net by having the VAT base as wide as possible. From this perspective, which implicitly assumes that administrative and compliance costs are zero, the ideal VAT threshold was zero. As time went on, however, and more experience with the difficulties of imposing general sales taxes in fragmented economies with large informal sectors was accumulated, conventional wisdom changed. It now suggests that the threshold should be set considerably higher in most countries – say, at a level of U.S.$100,000.[17]

---

[16] In Egypt, for example, 10% of registrants account for over 90% of Goods and Services Tax (GST) collections. In Jamaica, the largest 100 taxpayers account for two-thirds of domestic GCT collections.

[17] Keen and Mintz (2004) show that the 'optimal' threshold is determined by balancing collection costs against the marginal value of additional tax revenues (the amount of which naturally depends on the tax rate and the tax base). Cnossen (1994) reports average VAT administration costs of U.S.$100 per registrant and compliance costs of U.S.$500. Using this figure Ebrill et al. (2001, 119) estimate that with a VAT rate of 15%, a ratio of value-added to sales of 40%, and an estimated marginal value per dollar of tax revenue, a threshold of U.S.$52,000 would be indicated. Since the relevant costs are those related to marginal taxpayers, they are likely to be higher, as Ebrill et al. (2001) note. Allowing for inflation since 1994, one can reasonably adjust the 1994 cost figures to, say, U.S.$150 and U.S.$650, thereby increasing the threshold estimate to about U.S.$68,000. Since the relevant costs are those applicable to the marginal taxpayer, they are likely to be higher than average costs, so in view of the rough nature of the other assumptions made, the round number given in the text seems not unreasonable as a reference point.

Developed countries with good tax administrations may be found at both ends of this spectrum, from countries like Sweden with thresholds of zero – everybody in the VAT pool! – to Singapore (U.S.$600,000) at the other extreme (Table 7.1).[18] Similar variety may be found in developing countries. In the Middle East, for example, thresholds range from EUR 18,000 in Morocco and Pakistan to a high of EUR100,000 in Lebanon, the most recent (2002) VAT adopter in the region (Crandall and Bodin 2005).

The argument for a higher VAT threshold is elegantly made by Keen and Mintz (2004). Even if some revenue is forgone by dropping many small tax-payers, in most countries any revenue loss could likely soon be recouped if the administrative effort freed from processing numerous low-return taxpayers were shifted to the medium and large taxpayers who universally account for most VAT revenue.[19] As International Tax Dialogue (2005) notes, it is a bit puzzling that most developing countries establish and maintain low thresh-olds for VAT registration, thus encumbering their already overburdened administrations with a large amount of essentially useless work.

To some extent, this result may occur simply as the result of inflation. As Table 7.2 shows for the case of Jamaica, even a low rate of inflation soon erodes the real value of any threshold level. Although Jamaica's threshold was increased substantially in 2003, it remained only a fraction of that initially implemented in 1991. To be constant in real terms, the threshold in 2003 should have been closer to J$1.4 million than its actual level of J$300,000. As Table 7.3 shows, even higher thresholds would have had small direct effects on revenue. Indeed, imposing a threshold closer to the U.S.$100,000 mentioned earlier would have eliminated 75% of existing VAT taxpayers but resulted in a revenue loss of less than 4%. Similar stories can be told in many other countries.

Several arguments may be made for low thresholds. For example, since good tax administration rests on information, it is obviously advantageous in principle to include as large a share of economic activity in the tax base as possible in order to be sure to capture as much information as possible.

---

[18] We discuss later some of the special schemes to deal with small taxpayers that are mentioned in Table 7.1.

[19] Keen and Mintz (2004) note that a good case can be made for a lower threshold for service firms where value-added presumably constitutes a larger share of turnover. As Table 7.1 shows, differential thresholds do exist in a number of countries. On the whole, however, to preclude imposing an additional classification burden on the system, we think that in practice most developing countries should impose a uniform threshold. (Perhaps it should be mentioned that there is of course no need to require all importers to be VAT registrants since all taxable items should be taxed at import regardless of whether they are imported by a VAT registrant or not.)

Table 7.1. *VAT Thresholds: Selected Countries*

Country	Standard Threshold (in local currency)[a]	Threshold In U.S.$[b]	Special Rules
Argentina	144,00	47,255	Lump-sum scheme (covering VAT and income tax) for small business
Australia	50,000	36,684	Businesses <A$1million are on cash basis
Austria	22,000	26,049	Must register if turnover >EUR7,500, but sales only taxable if exceeds EUR22,000; thresholds for nonprofits is EUR100,000
Belgium	Zero	Zero	Only taxable (and have to file) above EUR5,580. Flat rate scheme if turnover <EUR500,000 – need not issue invoices
Bulgaria	50,000		
Canada	30,000	25,731	Simplified scheme if <C$200,000. Threshold for nonprofits is C$50,000
Chile	Zero	Zero	
China	24,000– 60,000	2,974– 7,436	Threshold varies from RMB2,000–5,000/month for taxable sales, RMB1,500–3,000/month for taxable services
Cyprus	9,000	25,867	Special scheme for farmers and retailers
Czech Republic	1 million	40,681	Based on last 12 calendar months
Denmark	50,000	7,934	
Estonia	250,000	16,106	Special schemes for travel agents, lumber sales, and second-hand goods
Finland	8,500	8,926	If turnover is <EUR20,000, a decreasing portion of the first EUR8,500 is exempt
France	76,300	90,344	EUR27,000 for services (other than provision of accommodation). Simplified schemes for prescribed businesses
Germany	17,500	20,721	Based on prior year turnover; <EUR125,000 can use cash basis
Greece	9,000	10,657	EUR4,000 for services. Flat rate scheme for, e.g., farming, fishing
Hungary	Zero	Zero	
Iceland	220,000	2,724	
Ireland	51,000	60,387	EUR25,500 for services. Apportionment scheme for retailers and flat rates, e.g., for farming
Italy	Zero	Zero	Special schemes for some categories of businesses
Japan	10 million	84,793	
Korea	Zero	Zero	Simplified scheme for small business
Latvia	10,000	15,493	
Lithuania	35,000	29,197	Firms with turnover >EUR2,896 have the option to register. Flat rate scheme for farmers
Luxembourg	10,000	11,841	

(continued)

Table 7.1 *(continued)*

Country	Standard Threshold (in local currency)[a]	Threshold In U.S.$[b]	Special Rules
Malta	10,000	11,841	EUR23,364 for services with low value added, and EUR14,018 for other services. In all cases, figures quoted are those at which exempt status is lost even though to qualify for such status the thresholds are lower (e.g., EUR28,037 in the standard case)
Mexico	Zero	Zero	On cash-flow basis
Netherlands	Zero	Zero	Noncorporate registrants that owe less than EUR1,883 in a calendar year can get a reduction in liability that cancels it at the level indicated and then diminishes to nil at EUR1,883. Simplified method optional for some traders
New Zealand	40,000	27,340	Small businesses may use cash method
Norway	50,000	7,411	>NOK140,000 for nonprofits
Poland	10,000	11,8421	Three years after losing the exemption because of exceeding the threshold in the previous year, firms may again qualify for the exemption
Portugal	Zero	Zero	However, there are an effective exemption of EUR12,470 for those under the simplified regime and a 'standard' exemption of EUR9,975 for taxpayers (other than those engaged in foreign trade) who do not have to keep standard accounting records
Romania	1.7 billion	43,928	
Russia	4 million	139,189	Based on quarterly turnover (RUR1 Million). Cash and accruals
Singapore	1 million	601,252	
Slovak Republic	1.5 million	46,934	The reference period is the previous three months
Slovenia	5 million	24,723	Accruals or cash
South Africa	300,000	47,320	Cash if <R2.5 million
Spain	Zero	Zero	Simplified scheme for unincorporated businesses
Sweden	Zero	Zero	But specific activities (e.g., provision of food by natural persons to employees) may be exempt if <EUR3,315
Switzerland	75,000	56,988	Cash basis on request. Flat rate scheme for prescribed traders; >CHF150,000 for nonprofits
Turkey	Zero	Zero	
United Kingdom	61,000	104,828	<£600,000 can use cash basis. Simplified flat rate schemes for retailers and farmers

[a] Most data refer to 2005 or 2006, but some may apply to earlier years.
[b] Converted: by the authors using January 1, 2006, rates, where possible.
Sources: Annacondia and van der Corput (2003); OECD (2004, 2004a, 2006).

Table 7.2. *Jamaica: Threshold Required to Maintain 1991 Level, Allowing for Inflation*

Year	Actual Threshold	Maintenance Threshold
1991	144,000	144,000
1992	144,000	259,488
1993	144,000	363,802
1994	144,000	473,307
1995	144,000	600,626
1996	144,000	753,786
1997	144,000	872,884
1998	144,000	953,189
1999	144,000	1,028,491
2000	144,000	1,090,201
2001	144,000	1,156,703
2002	144,000	1,244,612
2003	300,000	1,335,469

Source: Edmiston and Bird (2004).

Table 7.3. *Jamaica: Revenue Losses from Alternative Thresholds*

Share of Taxpayers Dropped	Threshold (in J$)	Revenue Collected (2002) (in J$million)	Revenue Loss (2002)	Revenue Loss (%) (2002)
	144,000	14,0504		
48.37	1,000,000	14,032.3	J$18,174,493	0.13
50.00	1,109,376	14,019.6	J$30,845,348	0.22
71.72	5,000,000	13,632.0	J$418,421,158	2.98
75.00	6,571,948	13,499.4	J$551,142,355	3.92

Source: Edmiston and Bird (2004).

Such an explanation would be more convincing if there were evidence that anyone had really put such information to good use.[20] On the contrary, it is often countries with the lowest thresholds that fail to administer VAT effectively or that provide many thus caught in the VAT net with legal escape routes through simplified systems like those noted in Table 7.1. Indeed, a cynic might suggest that one rationale in some countries for establishing and maintaining a low threshold may perhaps be the resulting increased demand

[20] If (as in Egypt) the level of staff is not increased when the threshold is lowered, the result is presumably a decrease in the amount of administrative effort devoted to the larger taxpayers who pay most of the VAT.

for large numbers of low-qualified staff (or even the increased opportunities for corruption). Another possible rationale for a low threshold may be that the deep distrust of taxpayers prevalent in many tax administrations induces policymakers to dip as deeply as possible into the pool of potential taxpayers in order to try to catch some 'hidden whales.' No matter what the rationale, the outcome of an unduly low threshold in a developing country is unlikely to be positive. It does not make sense for most countries to apply VAT as widely as their laws require, and it is puzzling that so many developing and transitional countries persist in (nominally) attempting to do so.

Wherever the threshold is set, compliance costs seem always and everywhere to be relatively more burdensome for smaller firms (Cnossen 1994). A second question is therefore what, if anything, should be done to 'simplify' VAT procedures for small registrants. Many countries have tried to lessen the blow in different ways, ranging from providing some form of simplified accounting such as a 'cash' basis to subjecting small registrants to something that is called a VAT but is really a flat-rate turnover tax. Such schemes are found in many of the countries shown in Table 7.1, though sometimes on an optional basis and sometimes for selected sectors such as agriculture. Similar systems are found in other developing and transitional countries. For example, Jamaica provides three distinct 'simplified' systems (Edmiston and Bird 2004). Whatever the approach taken, the effect of applying some form of turnover or presumptive levy to firms below a (usually self-reported) threshold is essentially to remove from VAT many of the firms drawn in by a low threshold in the first place.

While such simplified approaches have the virtue of allowing new and potentially growing firms to escape from often arbitrary tax administrative practices (Engelschalk 2004), they generally add new complexities to the tax system as a whole, as we discuss in Chapter 10. Not nearly enough attention has been paid in most countries to the appropriate design and implementation of such 'supplementary' or 'complementary' (depending on the way one views them) levies as part of a VAT system.[21] Much useful research remains to be done on such matters.

---

[21] A separate issue, important in some countries, is the way such levies relate to the similar turnover-based local business taxes (Bird 2003). For further discussion of this issue, see, for example, World Bank (2003) on Ukraine, Yang and Jin (2000) on China, and Kaplan (2005) on Argentina. Another question relates to the voluntary registration schemes found in some countries, under which firms below the normal threshold may apply for registration. Firms might wish to do this because they sell primarily to registered firms and their customers would like to be able to deduct input VAT legally, or perhaps because they themselves are purchasing many inputs from registered firms and would like to deduct VAT on such purchases. Abstracting from administrative costs and fraud, voluntary registration is obviously an appealing idea: it levels the competitive playing field and widens the tax

EXEMPTIONS

A recent OECD (2004) publication sets out what it calls the 'standard exemptions' found in VAT systems in OECD member countries: postal services; transport of sick/injured persons; hospital and medical care; human blood, tissues, and organs; dental care; charitable work; education; noncommercial activities of non-profit-making organizations; sporting services; cultural services (except radio and television broadcasting); insurance and reinsurance; letting of immovable property; financial services; betting, lotteries, and gambling; supply of land and buildings; certain fund-raising events, and others. We discussed some of these activities in Chapter 6. Others, such as sporting and cultural services, may to some extent also be pushed into our 'PNC' category. The point we want to emphasize here, however, is that without exception every single OECD country departs to some extent from this 'standard' list.

New Zealand is at one extreme: not only does it not grant any 'nonstandard' exemptions, but it actually taxes almost all of the 'standard' exemptions. More commonly, however, countries exempt all of these and add some of their own favorites to the list. Portugal exempts agriculture, as does Poland; Belgium exempts legal services, as does Greece, which also exempts 'author rights' and 'artist services'; many countries exempt burials (Korea, Netherlands, United Kingdom, Italy, etc.) and public transport (Denmark, Iceland, Ireland, etc.); Australia exempts specific basic foods and cars for use by people who have disabilities, while Finland exempts 'certain transactions by blind people' and Japan does the same for 'certain kinds of equipment for the physically handicapped'; and so on and on. Developing and transitional countries are no different. They too generally have extensive and somewhat idiosyncratic lists of exemptions, as illustrated by the very partial lists shown for a few countries in Table 7.4.

Any exemption system produces myriad economic effects, some quite complex. Ebrill et al. (2001) identify the most important problems: revenue effects, distortions of input choices, incentive to self-supply, import bias and undermining of the destination principle, compliance costs, and further distortions due to partially exempt traders. To some extent, such effects are inevitable with any VAT since none covers all 'value added' in the economy. New Zealand comes closest to including most final consumption in the tax

net. In developing and transitional countries, however, one cannot abstract from the very real problems that overextension of the VAT net might cause for effective administration. Again, there seems to be little useful evidence in most such countries on which to base judgment on such matters.

Table 7.4. *Examples of VAT Exemptions in Selected Countries*

Class	Jamaica	Ukraine	Egypt
Food items	Infant formula, bakery items, cooking oil, canned fish, etc.	Processing of milk and meat	
Other goods	School uniforms, school bags	Books, periodicals; goods for disabled; imports of cars and parts; critical imports for domestic production	
Structures	Residential and agricultural rentals and leases	Housing for veterans; housing construction in general	Renting immovable property
Utilities	Water, electricity, postal		Postal service
Social	Red Cross, Boy Scouts, and other approved organizations		Noncommercial activities of nonprofit organizations
Medical	Includes dental, optical, nursing	Includes health resorts and children's recreational facilities	Basic medical and dental care
Education	Most, including training	Yes	Basic educational services
Other services	Undertakers, international travel, contracts with government	Meals for school children and patients; within penitentiary system; burial services; passenger transport	Cultural services; lotteries

Note: This table is based on information obtained in the countries mentioned. The lists are not necessarily up to date and are in any case far from complete. (For a complete listing for Jamaica, as an example, see Edmiston and Bird [2004].) The aim of the table is simply to illustrate the sort of wording found in the different countries as well as some aspects of nature and variety of the kinds of exemptions found in different countries. For more comprehensive reviews, see Ebrill et al. (2001) and Tait (1988).

base, but in general VATs in developed countries usually reach no more than 50% to 60% of consumption, while in many developing and transitional countries little more than 30% of the theoretical consumption tax base is reached.[22]

---

[22] As Ebrill et al. (2001, 41) show, the proportion of private consumption reached by VAT is actually highest (83% on average) for small island countries where most goods are imported. Apart from this case, regions range between 38% for sub-Saharan Africa to 64% for the European Union.

The broader the base of a VAT the better, for two reasons: First, with a broader base the rate required to achieve any revenue goal is lower; that means that the efficiency cost of raising revenue is correspondingly lower.[23] Second, administration is simpler with a broader base both because there are fewer avenues of escape and because a larger proportion of all activities are encompassed in the tax net. Nonetheless, not only does no country succeed in taxing all consumption, but none really wants to do so, for several reasons.[24]

Not Worth Taxing

One reason for exemption is simply that some consumption cannot realistically be put within the scope of VAT in most countries for a combination of political and administrative reasons. An important example everywhere is 'home-produced' consumption, such as the consumption services provided by such durable assets as houses and vehicles. In developing countries home-produced food provides another important example. In theory consumption services from durable goods could be in effect taxed in advance by taxing the acquisition of the asset – the 'prepayment' approach we discussed in Chapter 6 with respect to real property. As we noted there, however, this approach is not promising in developing and transitional countries, where it is difficult enough to get a VAT up and running without saddling it with tasks that most developed countries have not yet resolved adequately. We said much the same about the theoretically feasible and economically sensible possibilities of taxing the PNC sector and financial services. Many poorer countries have reached the same conclusion when it comes to the agricultural sector, which accounts for much of economic activity: they exempt it.

Some consumption should not be taxed because it is either economically inadvisable to do so or because, even if it may be economically sensible to tax it, there may be no net revenue gain from doing so. For such reasons, as we discussed in Chapter 6, most countries simply exempt public sector activities in general and education and health in particular. This practice obviously leaves a lot of consumption out of the tax base. It also creates both economic inefficiencies and administrative complexities and is being increasingly called into question on these grounds.[25] Nonetheless, as we said

---

[23] In the simplest case of a single VAT rate, the 'excess burden' (distortionary cost) of taxation increases with the square of the tax rate.

[24] To be completely exempt from VAT, zero-rating is required. So much of the discussion here applies also to the discussion of zero-rating later – although of course zero-rating (like a reduced rate) is consistent with the logic of VAT in a way exemption is not.

[25] As Due and Mikesell (1994) note, similar problems arise with retail sales taxes.

earlier, developing and transitional countries should not try to pioneer in these areas.

Exempting sectors – and thus subjecting them to VAT on their inputs – is probably about all that most such countries can or should do. To be true to VAT's internal logic and introduce zero-rating may, as we discuss later, invite administrative disaster. To follow the equally logical, but opposite, path of subjecting such sectors to the full rate would be unenforceable in most countries and might constitute political suicide. Several potential half-measures have been adopted in some countries, especially with respect to agriculture – for example, by applying special favorable rates, excluding many farmers through appropriate thresholds, and subjecting those in the VAT regime to simplified (and usually favorable) treatment in various ways.

In Ukraine, for example, as in a number of other transitional countries, most agriculture is included within the scope of VAT. There is no reason in principle why this should not be done, and some developed countries with important agricultural sectors (such as New Zealand) do the same. In practice, however, even countries with excellent administrations collect little or no net revenue from agriculture. This outcome was especially predictable in Ukraine because of two features of its VAT: First, a reduced rate (10%) is applied to the agricultural sector (which includes agricultural processing). Secondly, and more importantly, agricultural taxpayers required to charge VAT (and hence entitled also to claim input credits) are not required to remit the VAT they collect on sales to the government. They keep it. This is even better than zero-rating. With zero-rating you get to eat some cake in the form of input tax credits, but you do not also get to keep it in the form of output taxes that are charged to your customers but not remitted to government. Ukraine's special reduced rate for agriculture was eliminated in 2006, so the output tax on the sector rose to the normal 20%. But producers were still permitted to keep the proceeds; therefore, if they are able to pass the tax fully forward, they may actually have been made better off by being subjected to higher rates. In Ukraine, VAT on agriculture thus subsidizes rather than taxes the sector – as is presumably the aim of the policy. Certainly, taxing agriculture under this system produces no net revenue, although it does impose both administrative and compliance costs.

Political, economic, and administrative circumstances in Ukraine all suggest that any conceivably acceptable reforms of this system in the near future are unlikely to improve matters much. It would probably have been better, and certainly simpler, to have exempted agriculture in the first place. Exemption under VAT is the equivalent to partial taxation and gives rise to some economic and administrative complexities. But it would likely have been a better starting point for a country like Ukraine than the present 'pretend-tax' subsidy scheme administered through the VAT.[26] For example, it would no longer be necessary to devote considerable administrative resources to the futile attempt to extract revenue from this sector. Even some developed countries largely exempt agriculture from VAT. Arguably, they should not do so. In the circumstances of many developing and transitional countries, however, it is far from clear that attempting to subject agriculture to VAT should be given very high priority.[27]

Even when exemptions may make sense or at least be necessary for political or administrative reasons, they also raise the danger of what has been called 'exemption creep' (Gauthier and Gersovitz 1997). Once any activity or product or use is exempted from a tax, taxing it often becomes exceedingly difficult. Moreover, since exemption involves drawing 'lines' between what is exempt and what is not exempt, there is always pressure from near-substitutes or competitors to extend rather than reduce exemptions.

Exemptions may take various forms in addition to the sectoral exemptions (and the threshold exclusion by firm size) already discussed. Items may be excluded or exempted from VAT for three distinct reasons. Sometimes *products* (for example, basketballs) are exempt, sometimes *purchasers* (e.g., education institutions) are exempt, and sometimes *uses* (use of basketballs for organized youth sport) are exempt. Almost every conceivable combination of these three approaches can be found in some countries: some users are exempted with respect to certain uses of some items, some specific items are exempted only if used for certain purposes by certain users, and so on. Most such specific exemptions complicate administration considerably and increase economic distortions while generally serving no significant equity or other policy purpose.

---

[26] Exempting agriculture once it has been taxed can also create problems, of course. In Peru, for example, maize was subjected to tax. Since most domestic producers were small, they did not pay VAT. Nonetheless the larger producers (of chicken, pork, etc.) who used maize as an input claimed VAT credits. To reduce this abuse, maize was exempted. The result, however, was that the price chicken producers and other maize buyers were willing to pay for domestic maize fell to the lower international level so maize producers strongly protested the exemption. In effect, the (illegal) credit generated by the taxable status of maize had been acting as a protective duty for domestic producers. No one likes to lose benefits bestowed, even unintentionally, by government policy – or, in this case, government's inability to administer VAT effectively.

[27] Schemes such as the 'presumptive credit' (subjecting output to a tax assumed to be equal to the input taxes) used in the EU to 'wash out' the input tax in agriculture are obviously even less practical in developing and transitional countries. Such schemes may also provide yet another opportunity for hidden subsidies to agriculture.

Only Fair to Exempt It

One case in which specific exemptions may make sense sometimes, however, is with respect to some of the second class of exemptions found in many VATs around the world: exemptions for equity reasons. Certain food items are by far the most common form of equity exemption. In some instances (e.g., Canada) 'basic' food, or a list of specific items, is exempted on such grounds, although the precise rationale for selecting particular items is seldom clear.[28] In South Africa, for example, such basic food items as maize meal, dried beans, rice, and unprocessed vegetables and fruit are exempted (Go et al. 2005).[29] Similar exemptions are commonly found in many countries with VAT (or other forms of sales tax).[30] In the United States, for example, food exemptions have been estimated to cost up to 25% of potential retail sales tax revenue in most states. Due and Mikesell (1994, 79) argue that this "food exemption is perhaps the largest mistake the states have made in their sales tax structures, costing substantial revenue, adding administrative and compliance problems, and deviating from the basic rule of uniformity of treatment of all consumption expenditures. Large volumes of expenditure of persons above the lowest income levels are freed from tax for no justification whatsoever." Exactly the same can be said about exempting food under VAT.

There is wide (though not universal) agreement among experts that a better approach to any perceived regressivity resulting from the taxation of

[28] Bird and Miller (1989) attempted to provide at least a limited rationale at the time Jamaica adopted a VAT, using household survey data to select a small number of items consumed predominantly by the poor. By the time the tax took force, however, this list had been extended considerably, and it has since continued to grow.

[29] South Africa also exempts paraffin (a fuel used by many poor households). As Hughes (1987) shows, certain fuels tend to be used extensively by lower-income groups, for example, for cooking. The impact of taxing (or exempting) such fuels may vary substantially from country to country, depending upon the degree of substitutability of different fuels for different purposes and the structure of the fuel market. In Indonesia and Tunisia, for example, the tax on kerosene was found to be quite regressive, while in Thailand – in part because fuel prices in general were much less distorted by taxes, so that expenditure patterns had not been seriously altered as a result – it was not.

[30] Kreklewetz (2004), for example, tells the story of the food exemption from the retail sales tax currently imposed in Ontario (Canada). An attempt in the 1990s to withdraw a long-standing exemption of 'prepared food' (e.g., take-out meals) valued at less than C$4 was quickly killed by popular outcry. Interestingly, while most tax policy analysts would argue that there is no case for such exemptions in developed countries such as Canada, Kreklewetz (2004) draws the opposite conclusion and argues that food, whether take-out or not, should not only be exempt from retail sales tax but also zero-rated for VAT. When even well-informed tax experts in developed countries with good welfare systems feel comfortable in making such arguments, it is hardly surprising to find food exemptions everywhere.

food is through some form of income-related credit (such as one based on income tax returns or added to welfare payments). In other cases, one might perhaps conceive of a less direct offset through, for instance, expanding health or educational services available to the poor. When such offsets are both technically feasible and politically perceived to be acceptable offsets, this view is persuasive. But when such options are not available – and we think they are not in many lower-income developing countries – a good case can sometimes be made for exempting food (and perhaps a few other 'basic' items depending on local consumption patterns) on equity grounds.

Many exemptions found in developing and transitional countries, however, have no plausible equity or other rationale that can possibly justify the cost and complexity of administering and complying with them. Consider, for example, some of the exemptions found in Jamaica: school bags and noodle soups in aluminum sachets. Edmiston and Bird (2004) estimate that in total 44% of the potential VAT base was exempted in Jamaica. Even more questionable sales tax exemptions on equity grounds – for example, vehicles used by veterans or production by firms employing a certain proportion of disabled workers – are found in other countries. Provisions that exempt certain items (e.g., notebooks) when used by certain people (e.g., students) for certain purposes (e.g., schoolwork) – even if (or perhaps especially when), as is sometimes the case, some other official agency (e.g., the Ministry of Education) is supposed to certify compliance – are always a bad idea. Tax departments have enough trouble administering simple general consumption taxes. They should not be burdened with such complex and ultimately unachievable tasks as trying to administer a hodgepodge of trivial exemptions.

Exemptions as an Incentive Mechanism

Much the same can be said in even stronger terms when it comes to the use of VAT concessions for 'incentive' purposes. In Ukraine, for example, many such exemptions exist. World Bank (2003) reports that in 1999, 14% of registered enterprises were effectively exempted and in 2000 VAT concessions amounted to over 27% of VAT revenues – that is, over 21% of potential VAT revenue was forgone for these purposes. Many of these exemptions – such as that of imports of cars and parts – represent inappropriate industrial policies and have no place in a good VAT system. World Bank (2003) suggests that about three-quarters of VAT exemptions in Ukraine could advantageously be eliminated with no cost to equity and with gains to efficiency and administration.

Interestingly, Ukraine's initial VAT law of 1997 did not contain many of these questionable exemptions. But the process of base erosion started almost immediately with 10 amendments to the law in 1998, followed by many more in later years. Although a 1999 reform reduced the revenue loss from exemptions, that loss remains substantial. Such widespread tax concessions facilitate both evasion and corruption. Sometimes, once concessions enter the system, they subsequently become surreptitiously enlarged without quick response from the tax administration. In effect at least this part of VAT becomes a 'self-assessment' system – though one without the necessary administrative systems and safeguards or approaches to support such a system.[31] In the context of Ukraine tax concessions create opportunities for abuse and expand the prevalent system of 'audit by checking' to the detriment of more strategic approaches to collection and compliance.[32] Moreover, exemption creep is a problem: concessions feed on themselves, encouraging taxpayers to lobby for still more concessions just as they also have an incentive to defer payment in anticipation of future tax amnesties.[33]

Tax economists as a rule do not favor tax incentives, for good reasons (McLure 1999). Either they are redundant and ineffective, forgoing revenue and complicating the tax system without adding to capital formation, or they are distorting and inefficient, directing investment into less than optimal channels. In view of the difficulty of assessing the effectiveness of tax concessions and the ease with which they may be perverted to benefit special interests, even the best-designed tax incentive is likely to prove a useful tool of public policy only when a country has both a stable macroeconomic environment and a stable political and administrative system. Many countries that clearly do not satisfy these conditions continue to have recourse to such incentives for investment in part because many seem to think tax incentives are costless. They are not.

Consider, for instance, the case of the special territorial tax concessions Ukraine established during the 1990s in 20 special zones (11 "Free Zones"

---

[31] As Ebrill et al. (2001) stress, in an important sense the essence of a modern VAT is that it is a 'self-assessed' tax. However, Ukraine is hardly the only country in which the administrative, political, economic, and political context is not yet up to supporting a self-assessment system (Bird 2005). We return to this issue in Chapter 12.

[32] For discussion of the lack of any real tax audit in many 'post-Soviet' economies, in which what is called 'audit' is usually simply numerical verification (adding up the numbers on the return and the like), see Bird (1999).

[33] Edmiston and Bird (2004) tell much the same tale in Jamaica, for example. For an excellent analysis of the detrimental effects of tax amnesties in general, see Das-Gupta and Mookerjhee (1998).

and 9 "Territories of Priority Development").[34] Among other concessions, enterprises established in such zones were freed from all VAT on raw materials, equipment, and spare parts for own needs for up to five years. This provision amounted to an estimated 3% of VAT revenues in 2001, when 16 zones were in operation, with the major beneficiaries being located in the Donetsk basin (World Bank 2003). The concession was apparently put in place to provide support to the older industrial enterprises located in this region. However, there is little evidence that such policies are effective in attracting investment to less favored regions in any country while there is considerable evidence that such discretionary and nontransparent policies are conducive both to corruption and to substantial reduction of the effectiveness of tax administration in general.

Creating such 'on-shore tax havens' in a country in which there is already a huge underground economy inevitably adds to the difficulty of enforcing taxes fairly and effectively. The import of tax-free foods into the special zones and their subsequent resale, for example, soon became such a problem in Ukraine that the government attempted to limit imports of raw materials used to produce foodstuffs and created a special commission to investigate the legality of import operations in the zones.[35] In such ways fiscal favoritism may result first in abuses and then, as attempts are made to cope with the resulting problems, increased complexity and administrative costs. The net results are usually few demonstrable offsetting beneficial effects and clear negative effects on revenue.

The territorial concessions were finally abolished in Ukraine at the end of 2004. Unfortunately, since the underlying reasons they were created still exist, they may well pop up again in some other guise soon. As we note in Chapter 11, VAT design inevitably reflects to a considerable extent the political economy reality underlying tax policy and tax administration in any country. The problem in Ukraine is not so much that the design of its VAT is defective. It is rather that political institutions have demonstrated a strong preference for using the tax system as an important means of managing their constituencies. Somewhat similar forces seem to have been at work in a decidedly nondemocratic 'transitional' economy, China.

As Li (2005) discusses, in many ways the VAT in China is not 'normal' in several important ways. First, because credits are generally not allowed

---

[34] These 'zones' are not 'export zones' like those found in many countries. We do not discuss the latter here.

[35] In part, the need to take such measures reflects the fact that, as we note in Chapter 10, the credit-refund system has never worked properly in Ukraine.

for capital assets, the VAT is essentially a tax on production rather than consumption.[36] Second, China's VAT is also unique in that it does not zero-rate exports but rather permits fixed rates of export rebate on a presumptive basis with different rates for different classes of products. This practice obviously lends itself to discretionary policy and has been of substantial concern with respect to China's accession to the WTO. It is clear, for example, that for a period China deliberately subsidized the semiconductor chip industry through its VAT (specifically, by imposing VAT at 17% on such chips but then refunding up to 14% to companies that designed and made chips in China). China agreed to halt this practice in 2005 (Li 2005). China has also used VAT reduction or exemption as a tax incentive in other instances, for example, with respect to attracting investors to develop certain industries in the western region of the county.[37] In 2006, China appeared to be moving towards a more conventional consumption VAT, albeit in a very selective fashion, specifically by permitting input rebates in several poor northeastern provinces in large part to stimulate growth in these regions (Yu 2004).

Limiting the Damage

Base erosion (whether through exemptions or the zero-rating discussed later) is a potential time bomb in many VATs. Excessive use of such so-called tax expenditures (Bruce 1990) damages the integrity of the tax system. Tax expenditures complicate administration and facilitate evasion and corruption. Once created, such concessions are hard to remove and may easily be enlarged at the initiative of taxpayers, who may lobby for more concessions or simply redefine existing concessions in unforeseen and evidently undesired ways. Existence of too many concessions, special cases, and exemptions makes it difficult to administer VAT effectively. The level of discretion of tax auditors is increased and bargaining situations – and hence the risk of corrupt arrangements – created. Such hidden costs of concessions are a major hindrance to efforts to improve and strengthen tax administration in many countries.

No quick solution to such problems seems likely in countries in which tax incentives are seen as an important means of managing political constituencies (e.g., Ukraine) or achieving specific economic objectives (e.g., China).

---

[36] The principal reason given for disallowing such credits is to restrain 'excess demand' for investment goods – in other words, to provide some offset for the perceived biases of financial markets. Revenue concerns have also been a factor, however (Yu 2004).

[37] We are grateful to Duanjie Chen for calling to our attention the item "Tax Preferential Treatment for Developing Western Regions," in Tax Yearbook of China 2002 [*in Chinese*].

One approach is to have a periodic 'clean-up' reform every decade or so in order to clear the deck of at least some of the accumulated debris of years of erosion. This was done in Jamaica in 2003, for example. Unfortunately, in the absence of more fundamental changes in the political and administrative environment, the process of erosion is all too likely to resume the next day. One small but important step towards tackling the more basic problems may simply be to do more to promote awareness of the problems and dynamics of tax expenditures both within the government and more widely. Specifically, to maximize the likelihood of beneficial results from tax concessions and to reduce the damage that may be caused by poorly designed and implemented incentives, countries should at the very least stick to three simple rules (Bird 2000):

Keep It Simple. The more concessions there are and the more complex they are, the less likely they are to produce desirable results at reasonable cost and the more likely they are to be conducive to evasion and corruption. Concessions should therefore be as few in number and as simple in structure as possible. When it comes to VAT, as we suggest elsewhere, perhaps reduced rates may be a lesser evil than either exemptions or zero-rating. Similarly, concessions linked to specific products are simpler to deal with than concessions granted only when such products are purchased by specific users or for specific uses or, even worse, specific uses by specific users.

Keep Records. Whatever concessions exist, consistent records should be kept as to who receives what concessions and at what cost in revenue forgone. If a concession is intended to achieve a particular result, such as encouraging investment in a particular region, then results in terms of investment, employment, and so on, should be systematically reported publicly. In the absence of such information, government is simply throwing money away. Poor countries can least afford to do so.

Evaluate the Results. As we discuss in Chapter 9, it is not enough just to gather potentially useful numbers. Such numbers must be used to be of any value. Ideally, at regular intervals – say, annually or at most every three or five years – data on each tax concession should be examined carefully to assess whether the concession is achieving results worth its estimated cost. If not, it should be eliminated. Since if VAT works properly as a tax on final consumption it is hard to see how any form of tax concession can be an effective production incentive, the first such evaluation may be enough – in a transparent world – to kill such bad ideas. Other 'tax expenditures' may have sufficient rationale on administrative or equity grounds to persist, but even then it is clearly good practice to reexamine their budgetary implications periodically.

Of course, few countries at any level of development follow such pre-scriptions. One result is that too often tax expenditures are seen as costless because their costs are not recorded anywhere. Ideally, not only should the fiscal cost of tax expenditures be reported annually, but it should done as part of the annual budgetary process – a so-called tax expenditure budget. Many developed countries now do this, and the result, though not dramatic, has at least been to call attention to the existence and cost of tax conces-sions and perhaps to reduce their number and scope to at least some extent (Surrey and McDaniel 1985). Some have called for similar tax expenditure exercises in developing countries (Maktouf and Surrey 1983; Swift 2003), and a few such studies have been done, for example, for Guatemala (Mann and Burke 2002). A recent report (World Bank 2003) suggested that perhaps countries might consider imposing a ceiling on the combined effect of tax expenditures – for example, providing that all tax expenditures combined cannot reduce taxes by more than $x\%$ – although we are not aware that any country has followed this approach with respect to VAT.[38]

ZERO-RATING

Under a VAT, an item is only truly nontaxable when it is 'zero-rated,' that is, subject to a rate of zero so that VAT imposed on previous transactions is rebated at the time of final sale. Both exemption and zero-rating com-plicate administration. Exemption requires that registrants making both exempt and taxable sales prorate their input tax credits. The easiest form of exemption to deal with under a VAT is to exempt some activities (e.g., financial services) from collecting VAT on their sales but to subject them to tax on their purchases. Exemptions of particular products – for exam-ple, for distributional reasons – give rise to the prorating problem. So do exemptions of purchases by particular users (e.g., schools). As mentioned earlier, exemptions of particular products when used by particular users for particular purposes (e.g., vehicles when purchased by educational institu-tions to be used for school purposes) add the problem of verifying use. All

---

[38] Such an 'alternative minimum tax' is of course not uncommon with respect to income taxes. This approach obviously raises more problems when applied to indirect taxes. Nonetheless, it is in effect what is done when, as discussed in Chapter 10, a system of VAT 'withholding' is applied or any of the many 'simplified' systems that constitute part of the VAT structure in many countries is used.

such exemptions are subject to potential abuse and require careful policing to protect the tax base. The costs of such enforcement probably exceed the revenue benefits.

To prevent such problems, sectors such as finance and agriculture that are often exempt from tax on their sales are normally not exempt from tax on their purchases. But of course this means that all these good things are taxed to some extent. The obvious response to this problem is to zero-rate such items on the grounds that an 'exemption' should really be nontaxable and that, with VAT, means it should be zero-rated. Even some developing and transitional countries such as Jamaica (see Table 7.5) provide surprisingly extensive zero-rating.

Unfortunately, zero-rating confronts such countries with two major problems. First, the tax administration may have to refund tax to hundreds, perhaps thousands, of nonexporters. In 2002, for example, Jamaica was liable to refund about J$2 billion in 'negative GCT payable.' In some countries (such as Ukraine) one result has been the accumulation of substantial arrears of VAT refunds, as we discuss further in Chapter 10. Given the weak tax administrations found in many countries, the problem of fraud may become uncontrollable. In one country when VAT was established it was alleged that more VAT invoices were printed on official presses at night than during working hours, and the illegally printed ones sold out the back door to buyers eager to have 'proof' of purchases to support their claims for refunds.[39]

In most countries VAT invoices are issued directly by suppliers without prior government involvement. While this practice makes good sense, it also means that private firms are, so to speak, 'printing (potential) money' or 'writing checks on the government' since a VAT invoice may at some point constitute a legal claim on public funds. We return to this critical issue in Chapter 10. To anticipate our conclusion, the combination of the fraud problem with refunds and the high administrative cost of dealing with many nontaxable or negative returns should, we think, simply rule out any (nonexport) zero-rating in most developing and transitional countries. Zero zero-rating should be the goal.

---

[39] As originally set up, the system in this (deliberately unidentified) country required that a separate official numbered VAT invoice be obtained from the government by suppliers and then issued to registered purchasers. Quite apart from the illicit supplement this practice provided to the income of some officials, this approach – still used in some countries – is not a good idea. In effect it creates a new problem: in addition to verifying that credits claimed relate to legitimate inputs, the administration must also now verify that the official invoices are valid. Two problems, no solutions.

Table 7.5. *Jamaica: Zero-Rating, 2004*

Category	Items
Agriculture	Animal feeds, except pet food; machetes; farm forks; planting material; agricultural chemicals; insecticides; coverings and containers designed for the packaging of agricultural goods
Health	Most drugs; contraceptives; orthopedic appliances; laboratory appliances; invalid carriages; goods acquired on behalf of Jamaican branch of the Red Cross, St. John's Ambulance Brigade, or the University Hospital of the West Indies or any private hospital necessary for their functioning
Government and diplomatic and international organizations	Goods and services for the personal or official use of nonservice staff of missions and international organizations, trade commissions, and consular officers; goods and services for a ministry or department of government or a statutory body or authority (with some exceptions)
Exports	Exported goods and services other than used goods
Places of worship	Nonconsumable goods used as vestments, furnishings, or decorations in a place of worship; altar bread and wine; offertory envelopes
Education	School books; school buses; items for use in an examination on behalf of examination bodies approved by the minister of education; goods and services acquired by the University of the West Indies and the Council of Legal Education; exercise books
Motor vehicles	Motor vehicles for numerous categories of persons, mostly people in political positions or higher government offices, people recruited by the government from overseas; or people employed by educational institutions
Items under certain enactments	Exemptions from customs duty due to the Bauxite and Alumina Industries (Encouragement) Act; the Export Industry Encouragement Act; the Hotels (Incentives) Act; the Industrial Incentives Act; the Industrial Incentives (Factory Construction) Act; the Jamaica Export Free Zones Act; the Motion Picture Industry (Encouragement) Act; the Petroleum Act; the Petroleum Refining Industry (Encouragement) Act; the Resort Cottages (Incentives) Act; goods used in the Modernization Programme
Other items	Coins and currency imported by the Bank of Jamaica; equipment and materials used solely in a research and development program

Source: Edmiston and Bird (2004).

The efficiency and possible equity costs of partial taxation through exemption or, perhaps better, reduced rates seem as a rule to be better choices for most countries than the theoretically preferable solution of zero-rating. Reduced rates (at a high enough level, as discussed earlier) have at least two advantages over exemptions. First, since they do not require prorating of inputs between exempt and taxable inputs they are less costly in terms of administration and compliance. Second, they may make it easier to move towards taxing a broader base at a uniform rate since taxing 'favoured' items at reduced rates finesses what might be the politically intractable problem of taxing something that was previously exempt.[40] That the item should be taxed is already accepted. With the reduced rate approach all that is under discussion is the appropriate rate, not the principle of whether it should be taxed or not.

An additional reason for reduced rates in some instances may be to combat evasion. For example, when the tax on meat products was reduced to 10.5% from the previous level of 21% in Argentina, revenues actually increased. The reason appears to be that many such products were exported by a few large firms (not by mainly small producers, who in reality hardly ever pay tax); therefore, when this tax was reduced, these firms claimed lower refunds. Something similar may have happened in Turkey when inputs to the textile industry were taxed at a reduced rate, although as is all too often the case when one begins to look into the details of precisely how VAT works in a particular country it is hard to find clear evidence one way or the other. Of course, as we note in Chapter 10, the real problem in all these cases is likely inadequate VAT auditing – though again we note that no one has any solid empirical evidence upon which to base such judgments. Instead, as is so often true when it comes to VAT, all we can do is rely on our assessment of experience in a number of countries, which suggests that reduced rates may often be the lesser of the three administrative 'evils' of exemption, zero rating, and multiple rates.

VAT AND EXCISES

Selective taxes on consumption – excises – produce a surprising amount of revenue in most countries – often almost as much as general consumption taxes like VAT (see Table 2.4). An important question in designing a VAT is therefore what to do with the excise taxes. As Cnossen (2006) discusses, only alcohol, tobacco, motor vehicles, and fuel yield enough revenue to

[40] We owe this point to Duanjie Chen.

deserve special consideration.[41] In principle, such items, whether imported or produced domestically, should generally be taxed on a specific rather than ad valorem basis at levels that are set not only to yield revenue but also to offset externalities arising from their consumption, with rates periodically adjusted to offset the effects of inflation.[42]

Goods subject to excise taxes in any form should also be subject to general consumption tax at the normal rate. That is, the base of the sales tax should include any special excise (or import) levy. This treatment is especially important with VAT because otherwise firms producing excise goods would not be able to credit input taxes and this sector of the economy would be relatively disadvantaged. If the resulting combined rate of tax is considered 'too high,' the excise rate, not the VAT rate, can be adjusted downward. On the other hand, if the rates of excise taxes are set correctly to offset externalities arising from consumption of, for example, petroleum products, there is no reason for making any adjustment to these rates. Interestingly, however, the almost universal reaction to recent increases in fuel prices in Canada was to urge that the VAT, not the excise, on gasoline be reduced. While this recommendation makes little sense for many reasons, it is striking that absolutely no one taking part in the discussion made the obvious point that if the excise tax is correctly set in economic terms – as is of course always arguable – then, unless VAT is applied at the same rate as on other goods, consumption patterns will be distorted, and that is presumably an undesirable result.[43]

Many countries do not honor the rule of setting the excise tax and then subjecting the price-cum-excise tax to the normal VAT rate. Indeed, sometimes not even import duties are included in the base of the sales tax applied to imports.[44] VAT can be significantly complicated by incorporating what

---

[41] Environmental taxes and gambling are also discussed in Cnossen (2005) but seem unlikely to be major revenue sources in most developing countries. For a review of major excises in developing countries, see Cnossen (2006). We do not discuss the potentially important area of energy taxes other than those on motor fuels. Soft drinks are sometimes included in the 'basic' excise list, but as Bahl, Bird, and Walker (2003) argue, this is not a particularly good idea.

[42] For a detailed discussion of methods to tax alcohol, for example, see Bird and Wallace (2006).

[43] Note, however, that if excises are higher than warranted by social costs, imposing VAT on the 'excess' excise amounts to a differential VAT rate, which is equally questionable (Cnossen 2005a).

[44] In 2005, for example, this was the case with Liberia's limited VAT, applied only on imports and manufacturing. In a variant of this problem, although Guatemala in 1985 applied its sales tax correctly to import values including customs and excise duties, it nonetheless grossly undertaxed imports because these values were converted to domestic currency for purposes of applying the sales tax not at the current exchange rate but at a pre-devaluation rate.

are really excise taxes. In Egypt, for example, a wide variety of selective taxes at both specific and ad valorem rates are included in the VAT law although, since the items in question can neither claim or give rise to input credits, they are not really in the VAT system. In Jamaica, although the system is more logical in subjecting only a few items to selective taxes, matters are again complicated because some excise goods are subject to VAT and some are not. Moreover, over the years, the inclusion of differential taxes on motor vehicles in the VAT structure has complicated the system substantially.

The most logical treatment is to confine selective excise taxes to a few items and to subject these items to VAT, including excise tax and customs duties in the VAT base. VAT taxpayers who buy such goods (for trading purposes, not personal consumption) would then be entitled to credit VAT (but not excises or customs duties) against VAT due on their own sales. Enterprises subject to excise tax would be similarly entitled to deduct their own input VAT from VAT due on their sales.

Finally, many countries impose restrictions on the extent to which VAT imposed on excise goods is creditable. The idea is to reduce the obvious potential for abuse, for example, when businesses buy vehicles that are used essentially for personal purposes. The simplest form of such restrictions is to prohibit VAT input credits for certain goods such as tobacco or alcohol (unless purchased by distributors of such products). Tax provisions favoring motor vehicles that can be used as private cars – for example, SUVs, jeeps, high-end pickups, diesel-powered or 'hybrid' vehicles – are especially prone to abuse. Countries with tax administrations vulnerable to fraud would seem well advised to have rules limiting input credits on such 'dual-use' items even if the result is, as it will be, to impose some tax on legitimate business inputs.

EIGHT

New Issues in VAT Design

In recent years, two important new issues have been added to the list of problems facing VAT designers and administrators everywhere – the taxation of electronic commerce and the increasing interest in the possible use of VAT in some form at the subnational level of government. As we noted in Chapter 6 with respect to financial services, what most developing and transitional countries need to do is to get their VATs working properly before they begin to worry about the first of these problems. The second issue – subnational VAT – while of concern mainly to a few large countries (e.g., Brazil and India) is sufficiently important there to warrant close attention.

VAT AND THE DIGITAL ECONOMY

Governments, international organizations, and pundits have over the last few years poured forth reams of paper on how sales taxes should be applied to 'digital' sales (or 'electronic commerce,' hereafter 'e-commerce'). The general line most OECD countries have taken on this issue is simple, reasonable, and persuasive: taxation should be neutral and equitable for all forms of commerce, electronic or otherwise, simultaneously minimizing both compliance and administrative costs and the potential for tax evasion and avoidance (Li 2003). But what does the growth of e-commerce imply for VAT in developing and transitional countries?[1]

VAT Is a Partial Solution

To begin with, simply adopting a VAT (compared to any other form of consumption tax) offers a partial solution to the problems posed by digital

---

[1] For a useful overview of this issue, see McLure (2003). Much of the present section follows Bird (2005a).

commerce. No special problems arise under VAT when it comes to the business-to-business (B2B) sales that constitute the majority of all e-commerce transactions.[2] Such sales are handled simply through what in the European Union (EU) is called the 'reverse charge' mechanism (Doernberg et al. 2001). What this means is simply that such services (e.g., telecommunications services) are deemed to have been supplied where they are received so that the *buyer* is liable for the tax. With respect to the most troubling electronic sales from a tax perspective – sales of digitized products that take place across international borders – the way this system works is simple: since no tax is imposed on the import of services, there is no input tax credit against subsequent output taxes. Buyers are thus taxed indirectly on their purchases because they ultimately pay the tax on both the value added by these (nontaxed) purchases and that added by their own subsequent taxable sales.

From an administrative perspective, ideally sellers would have information on the location and VAT identification of the buyer (if he or she has one) and would include this information on their invoice. Such information might be available electronically, for example, through an online real-time central registry of all VAT taxpayers – a system that has existed in Singapore for some time, for example (Bird and Oldman 2000). The EU's VAT Information Exchange System (VIES) serves essentially this purpose for VAT registrants in the EU.[3] How well such a system works, however, ultimately depends on the efficacy of tax audit – always the weakest point of tax administration in developing and transitional countries. Since the reverse charge mechanism depends on buyers' not falsely claiming input credits and the ability of tax administration to verify the validity of such claims, VAT may not work well in many countries even in taxing B2B e-commerce. Indeed, it is unlikely to be any more effective in practice than the similar 'use tax' often imposed as part of a retail sales tax.[4]

Even in countries with excellent VAT administrations it is hard to deal with sales of digitized services to nonregistered taxpayers – so-called B2C (business-to-consumer) transactions. No country has had much success in inducing nonresident sellers of such items to register or buyers to report their

---

[2] For example, B2B sales accounted for over 70% of e-commerce sales in Canada in 2002 (Bird 2003a).

[3] See the discussion in Ligthart (2004) as well as OECD (2005). The compliance costs that the VIES imposes on VAT registrants are significant, according to Verwaal and Cnossen (2002), although most of these costs arise from the required eight-digit product classification code and not the particulars of the VAT transaction.

[4] See Due and Mikesell (1994) on the very limited efficacy of the use tax in the United States.

purchases. Since 2003, for example, the EU has required non-EU vendors that have EU Internet sales over EUR100,000 to register for VAT in the EU and to collect and remit the tax. But where do they register and what tax do they pay? There are now 25 EU Member States, with different VATs. If a 'remote seller' is already 'established' in one of the EU Member States, it is supposed to apply the VAT of that Member State. If it is established in more than one EU Member State, however, it can apparently choose which rate to apply. If a seller has no EU establishment, it is required, first, to determine whether its EU customer is a consumer or a business.[5] If it determines that the purchaser is a consumer, the online seller must then register in an EU Member State and file and pay VAT to that country, a procedure that is obviously difficult to verify or enforce. Under the so-called simplified scheme vendors have the choice of registering in *any* Member State they choose and paying tax (if applicable) to that Member State. That country is then supposed to remit the revenue to the country of consumption – information on which must presumably also be supplied by the seller. In contrast to this complexity, an EU online seller simply applies the home country's VAT to all sales within the EU.

This way of dealing with B2C cross-border sales seems complex and difficult to enforce and may not be sustainable. In effect, what it amounts to is that within the EU such sales are taxed on an origin basis, that is, by the country of the seller. Suppliers outside the EU, however, are in effect taxed on a residence basis (country of the consumer) and are hence (if they comply) faced with higher compliance costs since they have to remit to all such countries. It would not be very surprising to find that EU Member States (or regions) with lower VAT rates will prove particularly attractive to new non-EU vendors that are considering establishing an EU subsidiary or branch and thus putting themselves in a position to be treated as EU sellers.[6] The effect of such tax planning would of course be to shift revenues to those regions.

No doubt the EU will in time work out some viable solution to such problems, for example, simply by setting the minimum tax due on all such sales made to EU purchasers at 15%. However, the likelihood that a developing or transitional country facing similar problems in dealing with cross-border

---

[5] One way to facilitate this would be to permit free public access to the VIES system (Ligthart 2004).

[6] For example, Heredia and Fernandes (2003) noted that the autonomous region of Madeira in Portugal had the lowest VAT rate in the EU (13%). This rate was subsequently increased to 15%, but as we discuss in Chapter 3, several regions in the EU continue to have lower rates.

services will be able to do much about them in the near future seems low. The best that OECD countries have come up with so far, for example, is to recommend a simplified registration system, requiring nonresident suppliers who sell more than a specified amount into a jurisdiction to register as sales taxpayers in that jurisdiction and preferably taxing them on a simplified 'turnover' (gross receipts) basis (OECD 2003). Still, one way or another, as we suggest later, developed countries are likely to work out some way to deal with B2C sales before the problem seriously undermines their revenue systems. Most developing and transitional countries are better advised to concentrate on first establishing an appropriate VAT and then running it effectively before worrying unduly about the looming problems electronic commerce poses for VAT.

Lessons from History

Taxation has always been the art of the possible. Changes in tax policy and tax structure usually reflect changes in administrative realities as much as or more than they do changes in policy objectives. Early tax systems in all countries depended mainly on levying taxes on items subject to physical control, count, and verification such as land and excise taxes and customs duties. The rise of mass industry and the development of the financial system led to the dominance first of withholding at source with respect to the income tax and then to the consumption tax equivalent of withholding – the VAT. Digital fiscal pessimists argue (or assume) that the digital revolution has overthrown the administrative and informational underpinnings of the present system: "What may be a sound rule from a tax policy perspective may be totally unworkable in light of available technology (e.g., the ability to make anonymous, untraceable electronic cash payments or the ability to locate a server anywhere)."[7]

The digital revolution is by no means the first such revolution to affect the flow of commerce and hence the actual and potential tax base: "In 1831 a British member of Parliament asked Michael Faraday, a pioneer of electrical theory, what use his discovery might be. Mr. Faraday replied that he did not know, but that he was sure governments would one day tax it. The Internet may be rather harder to tax, but someone, somewhere will find a way."[8] What lessons might countries confronting the growing reality of digital commerce learn from fiscal history?

[7] Abrams and Doernberg, quoted by McLure (1997, 298).
[8] "The End of Taxes?" *The Economist*, 23 September 2000, at 30.

The two critical problems in taxation are first to identify the tax base and then to enforce the tax. The anonymity and mobility associated with electronic commerce make both of these tasks difficult. But every cloud has a silver lining. In the case of the cloud cast over taxation by the rise of digital commerce, the silver lining is that the new information-driven world simultaneously makes it easier to improve services and reduce costs in tax administration. The new technology may also make it easier to maintain and even extend the reach of the tax net. Technological revolution includes not just problems but potential technological solutions. Many writers on this subject, for example, seem to take as an article of faith that the Internet is a borderless technology. In reality, however, given the interests of not only governments but also businesses in knowing where customers live, 'borders' are being constructed in cyberspace every day in various ways.

There is no quick fix for the problems digital commerce raises for VAT, but if necessity is indeed the mother of invention, a workable technological solution to at least some of the fiscal problems arising from the new technology may loom in the not too distant future (Ainsworth 2005). One such solution, for example, might simply be to require that, in order to be legally valid, a transaction must be geographically coded with the physical location of both buyer and seller. No wall is perfect, but one can certainly be built to enclose much of the existing tax base – provided always that the will to do so is present in enough jurisdictions. In effect, the VAT already essentially does this for B2B transactions by shifting the onus for compliance to the purchaser, who is more visibly tied to a particular jurisdiction and hence more easily accessible to audit and enforcement actions.

The advent of the digital economy may even strengthen the government's role as tax collector. The more tax authorities are driven to share information across borders and to promote technology that reveals the location of buyers and sellers, the more effective will taxation become not just with respect to electronic commerce but for all transactions. From this perspective the real danger from the growth of e-commerce may lie not so much in the erosion of the tax base as in the erosion of privacy as governments take defensive action to protect their revenues (Cockfield 2002). More transparency in this respect may simply be another price we have to pay for living in a complex modern society (Brin 1998).

A quite different response might be for countries, as it were, to go 'backwards' to the future by relying more heavily on such old and traditional tax handles as excises and property taxes (Bishop 2000). In the long run, as governments struggle to maintain their revenues in the face of new pressures tending to expand the underground economy and tax evasion, some reassignment of revenues may take place (e.g., in federal countries, perhaps shifting more taxes on employment income to lower-level governments and more corporate and sales taxes to the central government). Reliance on payroll and consumption taxes in general may also increase.[9] In the short run, however, changes seem more likely to take the form of minor 'fixes' here and there than such major swings in tax mix. For example, the provincial consumption taxes in Canada (some of which are VATs, as discussed later in this chapter) may move (as in the EU) towards a single registration system, a change that seems both feasible and in the interests of all jurisdictions involved. Moves in this direction would be facilitated if all Canadian provinces moved to VATs. Such a move is in any case desirable (Bird and Wilson 2004) and is likely to be encouraged by the rise of digital commerce.[10]

Coupled with new information requirements, such measures may stem the tide for a while. In the longer run, however, if the state is not to be downsized, the result of the pressure exerted by e-commerce on the tax system in all countries may well have to be a stronger cartel – as some might call it – against the taxpayer. Some argue that no approach except continued efforts to develop more coherent international tax standards and policies holds much promise (McLure 2003). Progress in this direction is unlikely to occur quickly, or uniformly, especially in developing and transitional economies (Keen and Ligthart 2004). Nonetheless, continued and expanded coordination, cooperation, and convergence (voluntary harmonization) among governments almost certainly lie somewhere in everyone's fiscal future. Such cooperation will not occur simply or quickly, but it will, experience suggests, eventually occur (Bird and Mintz 2003). Crises are often the mothers of solutions.

Such mild conclusions with respect to the big questions posed for VAT – and indeed taxation in general – by the 'digital revolution' may not be very exciting. Lasting solutions to these problems will in all likelihood eventually require both major revisions in policies and a great deal of hard, detailed, and persistent effort on all sides. In the end no completely satisfactory solutions to the problems posed for VAT and other taxes by electronic commerce – or, more precisely, by the increased strain that such commerce places on existing weak aspects of those systems – seem likely to emerge. About the best that can be done is for all involved to try to be as reasonable and consistent as possible. The endless negotiation and compromise on tax matters needed across jurisdictions may be more intensive than before but not be different in

---

[9] See, for example, the extended discussion of taxation and the underground economy in Alm, Martinez-Vazquez, and Schneider (2004).

[10] Such a solution seems much less likely in the U.S. context, however, where the much less ambitious multistate approach to a 'streamlined' RST seems about the best that can be hoped for at present (Hellerstein 2005).

kind. Tax policy, as Ken Messere (1999, 342) reminds us, "is about trade-offs, not truths." The process through which we develop the needed trade-offs, both nationally and internationally, in the end will largely determine the way VAT and other taxes are reshaped over time – and they must be reshaped in response to the rise of international commerce in all forms and not just the increasing share of these cross-border flows that takes the form of e-commerce. Developing and transitional countries should stay alert in this area and learn from the experiences of others. But there is no need for them to lead the way.

SUBNATIONAL VATS

Independent VATs applied simultaneously by two different and overlapping jurisdictions were long considered to be either undesirable or infeasible (Bird 1993). Some emphasized the high administrative and compliance costs of imposing two sales taxes on the same base. Others stressed that divided jurisdiction over such an important tax base might unduly limit the scope of central macroeconomic policy. Still others simply noted that central governments are obviously most reluctant to allow others to share this attractive tax base. However, the major technical problems that have been emphasized in the literature arise from cross-border trade.

Traditionally, it has been asserted that the only way in which subnational units can effectively levy a VAT was on an origin basis (as in Brazil).[11] Unless they did so at uniform rates, however, the results would be highly distortionary (Neumark Report 1963). Acceptable origin-based subnational VATs could thus only be achieved by giving up the subnational fiscal autonomy (and accountability) that such taxes might otherwise help to achieve.[12] On the other hand, it was believed that a destination-basis consumption VAT imposed through the generally used invoice-credit method could not be successfully implemented without physical border controls. In the absence of borders, the only feasible approach was thought to be some form of 'clearinghouse' mechanism in which transaction-based input tax credits and tax liabilities could be netted against each other, with any remaining balance settled by interstate payments.[13]

---

[11] See Guérard (1973) on the development of VAT in Brazil; for an update, see Afonso and de Mello (2000).

[12] For a detailed argument on the desirability of such accountability, see Bird (2001).

[13] See, for example, the discussions of these problems by McLure (1980), Cnossen and Shoup (1987), OECD (1988), and Poddar (1990). An interesting example of a clearinghouse arrangement exists between Israel and the West Bank–Gaza, although the flow of revenues has proved to be vulnerable to political factors.

Many federal countries avoid such problems simply by keeping all VAT at the central level. If the central government wishes to share a certain percentage of VAT revenues with subnational governments, it can do so either by using a formula (as in Germany) or by using consumption statistics, as was recommended for the EU a few years ago (European Commission 1996). If, as was true in the Russian Federation at one point, a nationally uniform VAT was administered by subnational authorities and the revenues were shared on the basis of origin, much the same undesirable and distortionary incentives were created as in the case of nonuniform subnational origin-based VATs (Baer, Summers, and Sunley 1996).[14]

The principal reason VAT was originally adopted as the required form of general sales taxation in the European Common Market (now the EU) was its advantage in implementing the destination principle with respect to cross-border trade. Only with the value-added form of sales tax could member countries be sure that imports were treated fairly in comparison to domestic products, and that exports were not subsidized by overgenerous rebates at the border.[15] Ironically, the best means to apply VAT to cross-border trade *within* the EU has not yet been fully determined. From the Neumark Report (1963), with its recommendation for the eventual adoption of the origin principle for intra-EU trade, to the proposals of the European Commission (1996) and since, numerous experts have proposed a variety of solutions to the perceived problems. As yet, however, none has gained full acceptance in the European context.

Although some interesting arguments have been made in favour of the origin principle of applying a VAT within a country (or economic union), we think that the destination principle clearly wins the day.[16] The conditions of wage and exchange rate flexibility needed to prevent substantial distortions in production efficiency when different jurisdictions levy different rates under the origin principle seem most unlikely to be satisfied in most federal states (let alone in the EU, even after the move to the Euro). The destination principle is both more compatible with independent taxation of consumption and, in practice, seemingly less likely to result in important economic distortions (Keen and Smith 1996).

---

[14] For later developments in Russia, see Mikesell (1999).

[15] The question of export subsidization arose again recently with respect to China's export rebate system (Li 2005), as we mentioned in Chapter 7.

[16] For a useful outline of the various ways in which "destination" and "origin" have been defined over the years in GATT and EU discussions of sales and excise taxes, see Messere (1994). We do not discuss the theoretical debate about the relevant merits of origin and destination principles and the effects of switching from one to the other; see, for example, Lockwood (1993); Lockwood, de Meza, and Myles (1994, 1995); Bovenberg (1994); López-Garcia (1996); and Genser (1996).

At present, the EU applies the destination principle using what is called the 'deferred-payment' method (Cnossen and Shoup 1987). Exports by firms in one member country to registered traders in other member countries are zero-rated by the selling country without requiring border clearance. Such sales are thus treated just as sales to non-EU countries are. In contrast to imports from non-EU countries, however, imports by registered traders from firms in other EU member countries are *not* taxed at the border. Instead, importers in effect pay the VAT on imports (at their own country's rates) on their own sales since they have no input tax credits to offset against the tax due. As we described earlier with respect to cross-border digital sales, the system works on a self-assessment basis. Importers are supposed to declare their imports from other EU countries, compute the VAT that would be due (at their own country's rates), and claim credit for that VAT, all in one return. The net result is that VAT is collected on imports by registered businesses only when they are resold or incorporated into goods sold by the importing firm since imported inputs, unlike domestic inputs, will not generate offsetting input tax credits at that time. As an aid to enforcement, exporters that zero-rate sales to other EU member states are required to quote the VAT registration number of the buyer (Keen and Smith 1996).

This system of zero-rating intra-EU trade may be contrasted with the 'clearinghouse' method under which VAT would be charged on exports by the exporting state, with a credit allowed for this VAT by the importing state (as for any other input VAT, but at the tax rate imposed by the *exporting* state).[17] Revenue accounts would then be balanced between states either on a transaction basis or in accordance with consumption statistics. In practice, the deferred payment system – which in effect relies on private sector accounting subject to VAT audits – long appeared to work as well as or better than the alternative explicit public sector offsetting of accounts required in the clearinghouse approach. Nonetheless, as discussed earlier, some recent EU measures with respect to digital commerce have in effect instituted a kind of clearinghouse system with respect to certain cross-border sales.[18]

The deferred-payment system is not without problems, particularly with respect to the possible revenue loss from cross-border sales to final users. In addition to the new rules with respect to taxing digital commerce mentioned,

---

[17] This is essentially the way the 'common' system proposed in European Commission (1996) would work.

[18] As we discuss later, in Canada a sort of clearinghouse system is used with respect to the Harmonized Sales Tax (HST) and the deferred payment approach with respect to the Québec Sales Tax (QST).

other special rules have long been in place within the EU to cope with this problem. For example, vehicles (which are subject to high taxes) are subject to tax in the country in which they are registered, and firms that would otherwise be exempt from VAT are subject to VAT on the destination basis once their imports exceed a specified threshold (Keen and Smith 1996). Similar provisions apply with respect to subnational VATs in Canada and have been recommended to deal with problems of interstate trade under the state retail sales taxes in the United States (McLure 1997a). However, no one has yet found any simple and uniform way to deal with *all* cross-border shopping problems under any destination-based sales tax. In practice, such special provisions appear to have kept serious problems in check so far in both the EU and Canada, although evidence of increasing export-related fraud in the EU has led some European experts to consider new approaches, as we discuss further in Chapter 10.

Current Situation in Federal Countries

As Table 8.1 shows, the current situation with respect to subnational sales taxation in federal countries around the world is diverse.[19] Indeed, at first glance international experience appears to suggest that no one has managed to work out an acceptable system for taxing sales at two levels of government.[20] Although at least five possible methods for dealing with the problems potentially arising from two-level sales tax exist – and each may be found to some extent in one country or another – none is entirely satisfactory.

Sales tax may be collected *only* at the regional level either as VAT or as retail sales tax (RST). In the EU, for example, only the Member States and not the union impose VAT. Among federal countries, only the United States

---

[19] To some extent, similar systems apply in some nonfederal countries. In Japan, for example, there is a local consumption tax at the prefectural (regional) level that is 20% of the national VAT – in effect a 1% VAT. This tax is collected by the National Tax Administration in each prefecture and the local portion is paid to the prefecture (which pays tax collection costs of 0.35% of collections for national transactions and 0.55% for imported goods to the national government). The total is distributed among the prefectures by the following formula: 75% in proportion to retail sales in the prefecture (as shown in official statistics), 12.5% according to population, and 12.5% by the prefectural share of the number of employees. Any surplus or deficit is cleared between prefectures by direct payments. In addition, each prefecture transfers half of its VAT revenue to municipalities (50% according to population, and 50% on number of employees). Obviously, local governments have no autonomy with respect to VAT in this system.

[20] Bird (1993) says essentially this. For a more recent, and different, take on this question, see Bird (2005b). As someone once said when accused by a critic of changing his mind on some issue: "When circumstances change, sir, I change my mind. What do you do?"

Table 8.1. *Sales Taxes in Federal Countries*

Country	Federal VAT	State Sales Taxes	Type of State Tax
Australia	Yes	No	All VAT revenue goes to states
Canada	Yes	Yes	Some provinces have VATs; some have RSTs
Germany, Austria	Yes	No	States share in VAT revenue
Switzerland, Belgium	Yes	No	None
United States	No	Yes	Most have RSTs
Argentina	Yes	Yes	Gross receipts taxes[a]
Brazil	Yes (limited)	Yes	VAT (origin base)[a]
India	Not really (so-called CENVAT)	Yes	States moving from (generally) taxes at producer level to VAT

[a] States also receive a share of federal VAT revenues.

currently follows this path (with RSTs). The situation is considerably more complex in neighboring Canada, as shown in Table 8.2.[21]

In contrast, sales taxes are often levied only at the central level. Germany, for example, has a single VAT levied at the national level, although a proportion of VAT revenue is shared on the basis of a formula with the states.[22] Similarly, in Austria, the länder receive 18.557% of VAT revenue with another 12.373% going to municipalities (Genser 2000). Among other federal countries, Australia (since 2000), Belgium, and Switzerland also have a VAT only at the central level. In Australia, however, all the revenues from the new Australian VAT (called the GST or Goods and Services Tax) go to the states and are distributed in exactly the same way as the long-established equalization system. In fact, since other funding for equalization was cut correspondingly, in effect "all the GST does is to ensure the source for the equalization payments" (Greenbaum, 1999, 1744)."[23]

---

[21] Even in the United States, in which subnational VATs have usually been considered as replacements for business taxes, rather than sales taxes, some have recently suggested that VATs should now be considered also to replace retail sales taxes (Fox 2000; Capehart 2000; Ebel and Kalambokidis 2005). For further discussion, see Bird, Mintz, and Wilson (2006).

[22] Although the state share is supposed to be 50.5%, in fact this proportion is applied only after deducting several other earmarked shares from total VAT revenues. In 1999, for example, the states (länder) received about 47% of VAT revenues. Another 2.2% went to local governments, 5.63% to the federal public pension fund, and the balance to the federal government (Genser 2000).

[23] As part of the readjustment of federal-state fiscal relations accompanying the GST, it was originally expected that many state taxes, notably stamp duties, would be abolished in exchange for increased transfers, but the reduced base for the GST that finally passed meant that some of these duties continue to be levied (Cooper 2001).

Many have argued that the German solution of a centralized VAT with some of the revenue shared with states on a formula basis is probably the best approach in a federal country (Tait 1988). For example, some proposals for reform in both Brazil (Silvani and dos Santos 1996) and the European Union (Smith 1997) have essentially taken this tack. This approach is clearly feasible and has substantial advantages in terms of administrative and compliance costs. Even if all or some of the proceeds of the tax are to be distributed to the states, either on the basis of estimated consumption or on some formula basis, a single central VAT has substantial advantages and prevents many problems. This approach may indeed be the best way to finance regional governments in the context of many developing and transitional countries.[24]

Such so-called tax sharing is in reality simply an alternative form of inter-governmental fiscal transfer. The total to be transferred is determined by the designated share of VAT collections, and the amount to be allocated to each state is determined by a formula established by the central government. In some instances, as in China, allocations are determined on the basis of the 'source' or 'origin' of the revenues. This practice not only recreates some of the problems of origin-based state sales taxes (as long deplored in the case of Brazil, for example) but also opens a potential Pandora's box of complexity in attributing source as well as the possibility of inequity, as when all revenues are attributed to the location in which a firm files its tax return. Such revenues are not really regional (or local) taxes in any meaningful sense since the jurisdictions that receive the revenue are not politically responsible for raising that revenue.

In federal countries in which regional governments are strong, it is by no means obvious why either the central or the regional governments would be willing to accept such a system. On the other hand, even in such countries, weaker regions – those most dependent on central transfers – might indeed prefer such transfers to the right to tax a base that they do not really have. For this reason, asymmetrical regional tax systems like that now existing in Canada may over time become a more prominent feature in such countries as Spain and Belgium as well as, perhaps, some developing countries – particularly so-called conflict countries emerging from regional civil wars (Bird and Ebel 2007).

An example of such a country is Bosnia-Herzegovina, in which originally each of the two 'entities' created under the Dayton Accord was given almost complete autonomy in taxation (Fox and Wallich 2001). In 2003, however,

---

[24] In general, however, it is preferable not to base subnational transfers on the yield of any one tax since doing so is likely to bias national tax policy choices (Bird and Smart 2002).

indirect taxation was shifted upward to the central level (confusingly known as 'the State' in Bosnia-Herzegovina). The VAT introduced in 2006 is thus to be administered centrally. Nonetheless, the revenue is supposed to be shared between the two subnational 'entities' on the basis of final consumption – not estimated final consumption but actual final consumption as revealed on VAT returns. VAT taxpayers must thus distinguish sales to other registrants from sales to final consumers. Presumably this could be done by requiring buyers to supply their VAT identification number and providing some way in which sellers can verify this information. Whether such a sophisticated system will actually work in the conditions of Bosnia-Herzegovina remains to be seen.

To some extent, Spain has moved in the other direction. Initially Spain followed the German model with respect to VAT, with 35% of VAT revenues 'ceded' to the states ('autonomous communities') and distributed on the basis of estimated consumption. However, the communities can, and do, impose their own tax rates for property transfer taxes and stamp duties. Transfers of existing immovable property are not normally subject to VAT in Spain, but taxpayers have the option, under certain conditions, of waiving this exemption and paying VAT instead of the property transfer tax. They may choose to do so, for example, to claim input tax credits. Of course, when they do so, they reduce community revenue. Some communities have tried to discourage such behavior by lowering the property transfer tax if a person who has the option to waive the VAT exemption does not do so and by increasing the stamp duty (which applies to transactions subject to VAT) if the option is exercised (Ruiz Almendral 2003). In Spain as elsewhere, VAT and intergovernmental fiscal relations are related in ways that are not always obvious.[25]

If neither a completely central nor a completely regional VAT fills the bill, there remain three systems under which both levels of government might levy sales taxes. First, although the VAT may be the best of all possible sales taxes in some general sense, an argument can be made for maintaining two distinct sales tax bases in a federal state in which both levels of government tax sales (Piffano 2005). Such a solution is obviously untidy and may be costly, but it may be argued that such costs should simply be seen as part of the price paid for a federal system, which presumably has such offsetting virtues as respecting local preferences (Bird 1993). As shown in Table 8.2, Canada provides an example of this approach (five provinces have RSTs).

---

[25] For example, see Yang and Jin (2000) and Wong and Bird (2005) for detailed discussions of the connections between VAT and intergovernmental fiscal relations in China.

Table 8.2. *Sales Taxes in Canada, 2006*

Jurisdiction	Name of Tax	Type of Tax	Rate	Administration	Comments
Canada	GST/HST	VAT	6%/14%	Federal except in Québec, where it is provincial	GST rate (federal) is 6% and applied throughout the country; HST rate is 14% and applied only in the three HST provinces
Newfoundland and Labrador	HST	VAT	8%	Federal	Provincial share of HST is 8%, with revenues distributed to provinces based on estimated taxable consumption
Nova Scotia	HST	VAT	8%	Federal	Same as for Newfoundland
New Brunswick	HST	VAT	8%	Federal	Same as for Newfoundland
Prince Edward Island	PST	RST	10%	Provincial	Applied to retail sales price including GST
Québec	QST	VAT	7.5%	Provincial	Applied to GST base, including GST
Ontario	PST	RST	8%	Provincial	Applied to retail sales price, excluding GST
Manitoba	PST	RST	7%	Provincial	Same as Ontario
Saskatchewan	PST	RST	5%	Provincial	Same as Ontario
British Columbia	PST	RST	7%	Provincial	Same as Ontario

Note: The remaining province, Alberta, and the three northern territories (Yukon, Northwest Territories, Nunavut) have no sales tax. Alberta does levy a 5% hotel accommodation tax. As discussed later, the base of the QST is slightly different from that of the GST/HST. Goods and Services Tax/Harmonized Sales Tax is the official name of the current federal VAT: The HST applies in the three provinces shown, and the GST in the rest of the country. Each of the RST provinces has its own tax base, generally with considerable taxation of business inputs and with limited coverage of services. The formal name of the RST in most provinces is Provincial Sales Tax (PST). Although two provinces, Manitoba and British Columbia, permit some (very limited) municipal access to sales taxes, there are essentially no local sales taxes in Canada.

Brazil, India, and Argentina (as well as the Russian Federation) also have distinct taxes on sales at both state and federal levels.

Alternatively, both levels of government could maintain independent dual VATs, perhaps reducing compliance and administrative costs by harmonizing bases and to some extent rates. In principle it is possible to retain a substantial degree of state fiscal autonomy while still reducing substantially the economic and administrative costs of levying two independent and totally uncoordinated VATs at different levels of government (Poddar 1990). The Canadian province of Québec provides an example of such a system: it levies its own VAT, the Québec Sales Tax (QST).

A final alternative is that the VAT may be a joint or concurrent federal-state tax. Each government could set its own rate to a jointly determined base, and the tax might be administered by either level of government. From the point of view of fiscal accountability, this solution seems clearly preferable to the German approach. A variant of this approach is now used in three provinces of Canada (Table 8.2), as we discuss later.

Approaches to Regional VATs

Four possible approaches to state VATs in federal countries are set out in Table 8.3.[26] One is that the two levels of governments have completely independent VATs. Brazil comes close to this, although its states do not have complete rate autonomy. A second approach is that each level of government may have an independent VAT – 'dual' VATs – in which all levels set their rates independently but on similar bases and there is a high level of administrative cooperation (as in Canada's GST-QST system). Thirdly, there may be a single 'joint' VAT – essentially a central VAT with some of the revenue flowing to the states either in accordance with estimated consumption (as in Canada's HST) or with a distributive formula (as in Germany). Finally, there may be what McLure (2000) has called a 'compensating VAT' (CVAT). Of these four possibilities, only the second (dual VAT) and fourth (CVAT) seem worth further consideration if any importance is to be attached to state rate autonomy and administrative feasibility.[27] Essentially, as Table 8.3

---

[26] Much of this section is based on Bird and Gendron (1998, 2001). See also Schenk and Oldman (2007) for a review of some of the issues discussed here. Many important questions – for example, the treatment of exempt sellers – are not considered here. Varsano (2000) discusses some of these matters.

[27] Cnossen (2002) argues that the CVAT is functionally identical to the present deferred payment system in the EU combined with VIES (see earlier discussion).

Table 8.3. *Features of Alternative 'Federal' VAT Models*

Feature	Independent VATs	Dual VATS	Joint VATs	CVAT
Rate autonomy	Yes	Yes	No	Some
Collection incentive	Strong	Strong	Unknown	Unknown
Administrative requirements	High	High	Lower	Moderate
Administrative costs	High	Depend on how it is applied	Low	Moderate to high
Need for central administration	No	No, but lower cost	No, but probable	Probably
Need for single administration	No	No	Yes	No
Need for interstate administrative cooperation	High	Limited	No	No
Need for central state cooperation	No	Yes	Complete	Yes
Revenue distribution	Independent	Independent	Formula	Essentially independent
Need for clearing of some credits	No	No	No	Yes
Potential for interstate evasion	High	Restricted	No	Restricted
Cross-border shopping a problem	Yes	Yes	No	Yes

suggests, the dual VAT approach appears to rate higher in terms of autonomy but lower in terms of administrative feasibility. One's assessment of these alternatives hinges largely on the relative weight attached to each of these characteristics.[28]

The Dual VAT Approach. What lessons might Canadian experience with the 'dual VAT' GST-QST system, which handles the cross-border issue essentially

---

[28] An alternative VIVAT ('viable integrated VAT') proposal has been put forth by Keen and Smith (1996), Keen (2000), and Keen and Smith (2000). Although this proposal has some merits with respect to the EU case for which it was developed, for reasons set out elsewhere (Bird and Gendron 2000), we do not think it is very applicable in developing countries and hence do not discuss this alternative further here. (See also Genser [2000] for further discussion.)

on the same 'deferred payment' basis as in the EU, offer for developing federal countries such as Brazil, Argentina, and India?[29] One important lesson is that the best basis for a subnational VAT system is a well-designed and comprehensive national VAT. A second lesson, perhaps equally difficult to apply in most developing countries, is that such a system works best when there is an adequate degree of (justified) mutual trust by the subnational and central governments in each other's competence. That the system works between two such strong political opponents as the government of Canada and the government of Québec suggests that the required level of trust – or, perhaps more appropriately, respect – may not be all that high. Nonetheless, it is probably asking too much to expect an equivalent relationship (or quality of administration) soon in most developing and transitional countries.

Presumably, a single central administration and a common base (as largely prevails in Canada's personal income tax system) would also be ideal, but this degree of convergence appears to be neither essential nor necessarily desirable. What Canadian experience does suggest *is* critical is either a system of joint or unified audits or at least a high level of information exchange to make the system work well, combined with having each taxing government able independently to determine its own VAT rate in order to create the right incentives.[30]

The CVAT Approach. In many developing and transitional countries there may be little realistic prospect of good tax administration in the near future, especially at the subnational level. A potentially promising approach in these circumstances originally developed in Brazil (Varsano 1995) may be to impose what is in effect a supplemental central VAT – the compensating VAT or CVAT.[31] This proposal reduces the risk that households (and unregistered traders) in any state may dodge that state's VAT by pretending to be registered traders located in other states.[32]

How might such a CVAT work? Briefly, assuming that states can levy independent VAT rates – a key requirement for accountability – a CVAT would be imposed by the central government on sales between states at

---

[29] The same question – what lessons does Canadian experience with two-tier sales taxation offer – is considered with respect to the United States in Bird, Mintz, and Wilson (2006).

[30] The details of the Canadian system can be very complicated and may vary (e.g., with respect to the extent to which nonresident vendors are required to collect provincial sales taxes) considerably from province to province (Poore 2004).

[31] For further discussion, see Varsano (2000) and McLure (2000).

[32] Of course a sufficiently competent tax administration could curb such abuse by issuing VAT refunds only for taxes actually collected by VAT registrants and only when exports are legitimate. But few developing and transitional countries have such an administration.

some appropriate rate such as the weighted average of state rates (McLure 2000). States would zero-rate both international and interstate sales, but the latter would be subject to the central CVAT (as well as any central VAT, of course). Domestic sales would thus be subject to central VAT and either state VAT or central CVAT. There would be no need for any state to deal explicitly with any other state; nor, generally, would there be any need for interstate clearing of tax credits.[33] Registered purchasers in the other state would be able to credit CVAT against central VAT. The central government, which first levies CVAT and then credits it, would gain no net revenue from it.[34] More importantly, the state VAT applied to the resale by the purchaser would be that of the destination state. In other words, the results are exactly the same as in the GST-QST case – a destination subnational VAT is applied – but the CVAT now acts to protect state revenues to some extent from fraud.

If one does not have either a good central VAT or reliable administration, a system along these lines may perhaps make subnational VATs feasible and potentially attractive in large developing federal countries like Brazil and India in which states have major expenditure roles, the VAT is the principal source of actual and potential revenue, and tax administration is not solid.[35] More homogeneous or smaller countries would seem better advised on the whole to follow the German or HST approach to sharing VAT revenues, if they must do so, rather than attempting to introduce an inevitably complex system of subnational VATs.[36]

CVAT versus Dual VAT. The CVAT approach is inherently more centralizing than the dual VAT. In the dual VAT system (the GST-QST system in Canada)

---

[33] This assumes that the state VAT rates are lower than the central rate. If, as in Brazil, the state rates are substantially higher, there might be some residual need for a clearinghouse – though on an aggregate, not transaction basis – but this is not a problem if, as would seem generally advisable in developing and transitional countries, there is central administration of state VATs. For detailed exploration of the vices and virtues of separate local tax administrations, see Mikesell (2007).

[34] As in Canada, the central government might receive an agreed fee for its services.

[35] A question that requires further exploration is whether there is a minimal size of government that can levy an independent VAT surcharge. While cross-border shopping would obviously limit rate variability in metropolitan areas, this question is important in less developed countries – for example, some in Africa – in which expenditure functions such as education are being decentralized even to quite small rural governments that have no access to significant local revenues.

[36] Recall that the German approach is essentially a revenue-sharing approach, with a share of VAT allocated among subnational jurisdictions in accordance with a centrally determined formula. The HST approach, which in principle (though not in Canadian reality) would permit regions to set different rates on a uniform national base, allocates revenue on the basis of consumption statistics, that is, on an (approximate) destination basis.

the only VAT rate set centrally is that of the central government itself. There is no need for any central edict with respect to state taxes applied to interstate trade since no such taxes are applied. But countries in which the qualities of administrative competence and intergovernmental trust emphasized in Bird and Gendron (1998) are inadequately developed may be prepared to pay the price of a smaller degree of fiscal autonomy to implement successful regional VATs.

The dual VAT system may also be superior to the CVAT proposal in terms of administrative simplicity and cost (as a share of revenue). Neither CVAT nor the dual VAT requires traders to identify the state of destination.[37] In addition, neither requires any procedures to track and clear individual tax credits. While even a dual VAT system may conceivably produce 'excess' credits, it seems much less likely to do so than the CVAT precisely because of the overarching central VAT (McLure 2000). In addition, unlike CVAT (which is a final tax for unregistered purchasers but a creditable tax for traders), the dual VAT does not require any distinction to be made between purchasers other than determining whether they are nonresidents or not.[38] The other side of this coin (and an important consideration in countries with weak tax administrations) is that since CVAT is charged on all sales, a state's revenue is less at risk than under the dual VAT approach, which places a heavier burden on the tax administration to ensure that those who should pay actually do so. Finally, an interesting feature of the dual VAT system as applied in Canada is that the inclusion of the central VAT in the tax base of the subnational VAT provides a direct financial incentive for subnational administrators of such a system to pay close attention to the proper application of the central tax.

The CVAT approach may not provide sufficient room to permit the implementation of the many compromises that are likely needed in order to move

---

[37] Both approaches do of course require a distinction between 'out-of-state' and 'in-state' sales. Although Bird and Gendron (1998) mentioned approvingly both the EU practice of requiring that the registration number of registered purchasers be quoted on the invoice and the possible desirability of including in this number some indication of the location of the purchaser, neither feature is strictly essential to the functioning of a dual VAT, as Canadian practice demonstrates. Given the weaker tax administrations in most developing countries, however, such additional features might make any subnational VAT more feasible. For example, the new Bosnian VAT will apparently require such purchaser identification. OECD (2005) provides a recent summary of current thought on this question.

[38] Of course, CVAT can do without this distinction also if taxes on sales to unregistered traders are divided among jurisdictions in accordance with some formula. While the treatment of such sales is not discussed further here, this approach would move the system closer to a revenue-sharing scheme.

from the low-level fiscal equilibrium (poorly designed and poorly run tax systems) that now prevails in many developing and transitional countries to a more workable system in two important senses. First, the tax system needs to deliver the goods in the sense of generating adequate revenues for necessary public expenditures. Second, as we discuss further in Chapter 11, how taxes are levied and by whom may play a critical role in establishing the needed "Wicksellian connection" (Breton 1996) between revenues and expenditures at each level needed for good fiscal management in a multi-tiered government structure. This link is more transparent with the dual VAT system.

A final advantage of the dual VAT approach is that, as Canadian experience demonstrates, the system can accommodate even states that do not levy VAT (such as the province of Alberta) as well as some degree of difference in VAT bases with respect both to zero-rating final services and to crediting input taxes (as in Québec). Conceptual purists may not like the effects on efficiency of such policy flexibility. But real-world politics may require such flexibility if such major policy reforms as the introduction of subnational VATs are to be implemented. On the whole, the dual VAT approach seems more suitable to accommodating such compromises because of its greater tolerance for variation and the need for less-than-perfect agreement amongst the various governments concerned.[39]

Developing Federal Countries

Table 8.4 summarizes the situation in early 2006 in India, Brazil, and Argentina, contrasting these countries with the GST-QST system in Canada, on one hand, and the HST system, on the other. On the whole, moving to a decent VAT system with two levels of government applying independent VATs appears to require two preconditions in countries without strong tax administrations.[40] The first is a way to implement the destination principle on interstate trade. As we discussed earlier, this problem appears technically resolvable when there are a high enough degree of intergovernmental trust and cooperation and relatively competent administrations. The difficulty is that these conditions are hard to satisfy in most developing countries.

---

[39] Note that even under the more uniform HST approach in Canada, provinces can deviate substantially from federal policy in some respects, for example, with respect to the PNC rebates shown in Table 6.2.

[40] Bird and Gendron (2001) discuss each of these cases in more detail. For updates and additional useful discussion see, for example, Piffano (2005) on Argentina, and Bagchi (2005) and Rao and Rao (2005) on India.

Table 8.4. *Comparison of Some Federal Sales Tax Regimes*

	Canada: GST-QST[a]	Canada: HST[b]	Brazil	Argentina	India
Comprehensive federal VAT	Yes	Yes	No[c]	Yes	No[c]
Federal VAT revenue to states	No[d]	No, revenues from provincial portion of HST are distributed on basis of taxable consumption	Yes, by revenue-sharing formula	Yes, as part of general revenue sharing	No
Subnational taxes on destination basis	Yes[e]	Yes	No	No	Supposed to move in this direction with new VATs[f]
Subnational rate setting autonomous	Yes	No (but note that federal rate also cannot be changed without consent of HST provinces)	Yes (except for interstate trade)	Yes	Yes (except for so-called Central Sales Tax imposed on interstate trade that is supposed to be abolished over time)
Strong administration	Yes	Yes	No	No	No
Good cooperation between central and subnational governments	Yes	Yes	No	No	No

[a] GST refers to the federal goods and services tax and QST to the Québec sales tax. As discussed elsewhere, these are both VATs.

[b] HST refers to the 'Harmonized Sales Tax,' which is, as discussed elsewhere, a joint federal-provincial VAT.

[c] Brazil and India have federal taxes that are VATS in that they provide some credit for input taxes but essentially apply only to imports and manufactured goods.

[d] Canada's general equalization system does provide for federal transfers to compensate provinces with lower than average tax bases.

[e] As we note elsewhere, five provinces in Canada still have RSTs.

[f] In India 21 states now have VATs, but these taxes are currently operating in effect as origin-based taxes (as in Brazil) rather than destination-based taxes.

158

The second precondition is some means of compensating states for revenue losses implied by the transition. Interestingly, this problem did not receive much attention in Canada, the only developed country with a dual VAT.[41]

The debate on how best to design and implement a subnational VAT is far from settled. The final answer may turn out to be – as we have so often suggested in this book – that once again different contexts call for different solutions. What a country can, should, and will do obviously depends on many factors. Trade patterns, the location and size of the country and its subnational jurisdictions, the relative importance of B2B versus B2C transactions in the tax base, the quality of administration, the degree of trust and feasible coordination, the desire for local autonomy, the tolerance for asymmetry, the offsetting nature of equalization, the extent and nature of revenue shifts, and, not least, the existing sales tax structure – all these conditions will determine what happens. The road to feasible subnational VATs may be long and winding in many countries. However, as has often been noted, even the longest journey starts with a single step and, with respect to subnational VATs, the three large developing countries discussed here are already much further down this path than the first step.[42]

In striking contrast to the way the fiscal world saw matters until very recently, the question of subnational VATs is now definitely on the policy table around the globe.[43] We still have much to learn about this subject;

---

[41] The issue of compensation might well arise if other provinces moved to introduce VAT as, for example, Bird and Wilson (2004) urge. As Bird and Gendron (1998) note, the federal government did pay a relatively small 'compensation' to the three small HST provinces, but it refused to match this in the case of Québec on the grounds that Québec, in contrast to the other provinces, did not actually lose revenue – in part because it did not have to reduce its rates and in part because it gained revenue by imposing the QST on GST-inclusive prices. (Actually, the rate reductions required in the HST system are not an essential element of that system.)

[42] Another interesting case not discussed further here is Mexico, long a federation in form but increasingly becoming a federation in fiscal fact also: see, for example, Webb (2001) and Díaz-Cayeros and McLure (2000).

[43] We have not considered here another possible use of a VAT-like tax as a local business tax. As Bird (2003) discusses, this approach may be particularly suitable for regional and local governments in nonfederal or small countries in which it is inadvisable to fragment the national VAT. Since subnational governments around the world do, and probably always will, tax business, doing so through an income-type origin-based VAT – a quite different tax from the destination-based consumption VAT discussed in this book – would be considerably less distorting than most other possible local business taxes and is hence an attractive option. Such taxes exist in Italy, Japan, and some U.S. states and are under consideration in, for example, Colombia and South Africa. Indeed, Bird and McKenzie (2001) argue in the context of Canada that such a tax – which they call a Business Value Tax – would also be preferable to provincial taxes on corporate income.

one lesson that has already clearly emerged over the last decade is that a sustainable answer in any country will be one that is carefully customized for local circumstances. It remains to be seen whether such taxes can work satisfactorily in countries like India in which states have some genuine fiscal autonomy but both central and state governments face severe administrative constraints.

NINE

Administering VAT

VAT is as VAT does. The way VAT is administered determines its effects. A full discussion of all aspects of VAT administration would require a separate book. All we can do in this and the next chapter is to highlight a few issues that experience suggests are important in developing and transitional countries. In Chapter 3 we asked whether every country needed a VAT. We almost – though not quite – answered *yes* to this question. It thus seems appropriate to begin the discussion of VAT administration by saying a few words about the way a country that previously has not had a VAT should launch one.

LAUNCHING VAT

Experts tell us that a preparatory period of between 18 and 24 months is necessary to set up a VAT (Tait 1988). Experience confirms that this advice is reasonable. Some countries that have tried to move to a VAT more quickly have paid a substantial price for their haste and have found it difficult subsequently to get it right. On the other hand, experience also suggests that too long a preparation period may sometimes be costly. Since the window of opportunity to introduce major tax changes may be open only for a short time, countries adopting a VAT must sometimes take what may be called the 'big bang' approach. VATs introduced too quickly have not always worked out well, of course, and that is why experts so often emphasize the desirability of following the normal schedule mentioned. But if you do not have a choice, you do not have a choice. Waiting until you are ready may mean not doing it at all. Making the choice between doing the right thing in the wrong way (and hence messing it up) or not doing it until it can be done right (and running the risk of not doing it all) is the reason we have political institutions and policymakers. Let the expert without fault cast stones in such cases. We shall not.

What we stress here is a rather different lesson suggested by experience in many countries: what matters is not just the 'pre-implementation' planning phase but the critical 'postimplementation' phase. Even two years is not nearly long enough to get a good (or even an acceptable) VAT system up and running well. Ten years is more realistic. Developing and transitional countries cannot simply be 'given' a good VAT administration. They need to 'grow' one, and this process may take a long time. A modern VAT is a preeminent example of a 'self-assessed' tax (Ebrill et al. 2001). But what are the prior conditions that need to be satisfied before such a tax can be successfully implemented? Ebrill et al. (2001, 141) tell us that the conditions include simple, clear, stable tax laws; adequate service and support to taxpayers in complying with tax obligations; simple procedures for registration, filing, payment, and refund; effective collection enforcement; reasonable audit coverage; strict application of penalties; and provision for independent review. Very few developing or transitional countries can meet all or even most of these conditions.

The conditions needed for the successful functioning of a self-assessed tax like VAT can thus often not be taken as given; instead, they must somehow be created. Doing so is likely to prove a difficult and lengthy process.[1] Many countries are caught in the throes of a difficult dilemma when it comes to VAT (or indeed any major tax reform). If it is to be done at all, it must generally be done quickly, when the time to act is right. To be done well, however, it must be done carefully, deliberately, and with a good deal of planning and preparation. The important question is thus often the following: if it has to be done quickly or not at all, what *really* has to be done, and in what order?

Countries need clear guidance with respect to which of the many steps normally laid out in the 'complete' (ideal) preparation process are critical and any necessary sequence such steps must follow. Decisions must, for example, be made with respect to the key design issues we discussed in Chapter 7 and the key administrative steps we discuss later in the present chapter. But do all countries really need to work out in detail all 82 pre-implementation steps that Tait (1988, 409–15) sets out as sine qua non for preparation before launching a VAT? Obviously not, since so many of them fall far short of satisfying such conditions. Unfortunately, there have not been enough careful case studies of actual launches for us to be able to state which steps are really critical in terms of determining outcomes.

---

[1] See Kramer (1994) for early recognition of this point with respect to VAT in transition countries.

This question is important not simply with respect to countries launching a new VAT but also in the many countries that can and should improve their VATs. The path from an imperfect present VAT to a better one is unlikely to be a straight or smooth one. Policy innovation often follows a sort of logistic path, beginning with an initial leap forward at the time of creation when attention levels and reward expectations are high. Next is a subsequent period of letdown and perhaps even regression as those 'present at the creation' move on to pastures new. Finally, if all goes well, the process concludes with a prolonged incremental period of gradually settling into the normal bureaucratic pattern. One implication of this line of thought is that some aspects of both the sequencing and the time scale of the normal VAT launch schedule need reconsideration.

Which elements in the initial VAT design are most critical in the sense that if they are not in place, the tax simply will not function? Which are most urgent in the sense that if they are not done, other critical elements cannot be implemented? How much time and effort is needed in the circumstances of particular countries to make these critical and urgent steps as distinct from the many steps that would be eventually desirable?

It is of little use to tell those who have nothing that they must do everything before they can have something. Where does a country with almost no elements of a decent tax administration – or, to put it another way, a country that satisfies none of the conditions of self-assessment – begin when it comes to VAT? How does it proceed towards a more enlightened VAT once it has begun, however badly? No one has yet studied these critical issues carefully. To work out what one really has to know about a country in order to devise the 'right' implementation schedule for VAT in its particular circumstances – to determine what matters most and in what ways – would require a systematic set of detailed case studies within a uniform analytical framework. Is the critical factor the size distribution of the potential tax base? Or the relative importance of 'key' components (such as imports and excise goods) of the base and the degree of administrative control that can realistically be expected with respect to those components? Or the detailed industry-by-industry flow of 'VAT-able' items among different sectors and different sized firms? Or the level of accounting skills in the potential taxpayer population? Or the capacity of tax officials to administer an accounts-based tax and, in particular, the attention devoted to auditing such a tax? Or, perhaps most fundamentally, the degree of existing 'trust' between officials and taxpayers and how quickly (and in what ways) that trust can be built up sufficiently to support a self-assessment system? Or is it all of the foregoing and more?

No one can give definitive answers to such questions. But what experience does make clear is that simply transferring VAT experience from developed country settings to countries that have much more fragmented economies, larger informal sectors, lower tax morale, rampant evasion, and total distrust between tax administrators and taxpayers is not a recipe for success. The research agenda that needs to be completed with respect to VAT administration in developing and transitional countries is larger and more important than the similar agenda with respect to VAT design in such countries discussed earlier in this book. For example, if the extent and behavior of the informal sector depend largely on the interaction between formal institutions such as the tax administration and the prevalent norms and customs in a country (Gerhanxi 2004), the 'best' VAT design and implementation are likely to be different from those suggested by experience to date in the EU or developed countries more generally. The best VAT in many poor countries is likely to be a much simpler tax than that dreamt of in Brussels, Wellington, or Tokyo.[2]

All we can do here other than 'signposting' the need for more research is to provide a simple example: China. China is of course an incredibly complicated example – but, then, if one really explores countries, so are they all. China began to experiment with VAT in 1979 only with respect to two industries (machinery and agricultural tools) and three products (bicycles, sewing machines, and electric fans) in a number of specific cities such as Shanghai and X'ian (Yang and Jin 2000). At first glance, introducing such a narrowly based VAT may seem weird. Actually, however, it is not, since all VATs are limited in their coverage, although admittedly seldom as drastically and usually more by force of circumstances than as a matter of design. From this small beginning China moved in 1984 to a nationwide VAT. However, its VAT was still far from 'normal.' The base was narrow, many different tax rates were applied, and (as in some other transitional countries beginning to adopt more 'market-based' systems) the accounting and administrative system was inconvenient and complicated. Another major tax reform in 1994 removed many of these problems as China finally established what at first glance looks like a more or less standard VAT system.

But China's VAT is still far from standard for a number of reasons. For example, it excludes a considerable share of the service sector, which is instead subjected to a local business tax levied on a gross rather than value-added basis. Of course, many countries have similar local business taxes

---

[2] See the discussion of the EU, New Zealand, and Japanese 'models' in Chapter 2.

(Bird 2003). Moreover, as we discuss in Chapter 10, many countries also in effect impose similar taxes at the national level for small business though usually as part of their VAT systems rather than as a separate tax. What is both more important and more unusual is that China does not permit the crediting of input taxes in general. The major reason appears to be to discourage 'overinvestment,' an endemic problem in the Chinese economic system for a variety of reasons. Revenue has also been a concern.[3] Moreover, apparently largely for revenue reasons – but perhaps also for incentive reasons – China does not zero-rate exports but rather (as mentioned in Chapter 7) provides arbitrary presumptive credits for different classes of exports. Most recently, China has continued its process of gradually 'growing' into a more normal VAT by experimenting with granting credits for capital purchases in a few provinces.

In many ways China's gradualist approach to policy innovation seems commendable, although it can equally be argued that China may soon have to consider its fiscal problems more holistically if it is to continue to grow at its recent pace (Wong and Bird 2005). Not the least of these problems relates to its 'made-in-Beijing' VAT. The 'No One Size Fits All' (NOSFA) principle we stated in Chapter 1 does not imply as a corollary that the 'not invented here' (NIH) principle must hold. Countries can learn from each other, and it is perhaps time for China to take another close look at its VAT in light of worldwide experience.[4]

MAKING VAT WORK

The administration of any tax consists of a number of related but separable processes – registration, filing, payment, audit, and enforcement. Every process is important and is related to every other process. A defect anywhere in the administrative system can bring down the best-designed VAT. It is worth looking at this rather dry topic in a little more detail, not least because

---

[3] In other countries, Argentina's initial denial of investment credits and the continuing limitation on such credits for large businesses in Québec's QST (Gendron, Mintz, and Wilson 1996) seem to be revenue driven. For the history of the administrative arrangements between Québec's QST and Canada's GST that led to the 1996 agreement, see Mintz, Wilson, and Gendron (1994).

[4] One lesson such a look suggests is that 'gradualism' may be a more workable strategy for governments that do not have to be elected. In democratic countries, it is probably more important to get it right in the first place since rectifying initial policy errors is usually costly in political terms and power can quickly change hands. It is a lot easier to change policy if one need not either acknowledge prior errors publicly or persuade significant parts of the population that change is needed.

what is needed to make VAT work is much the same as what is needed to make any general tax, whether on income or consumption, work.[5]

Registration

Every person, sole proprietor, corporation, partnership, or legal entity that engages in an activity that is taxable under a VAT should be required to register for the tax.[6] The critical issue of the registration threshold has already been discussed in Chapter 7. A good registration process is central to a good VAT. The reality of applicants for new registration must be verified to prevent the creation of 'shell' companies that can be used as the basis for fraudulent credit claims. Those detected using fraudulent practices must be deregistered.[7]

On the other hand, it is essential not to make the already far too slow and complex process of establishing a new business in many developing and transitional countries more burdensome than it already is. New businesses need much better service and support from government than they now receive in most countries. Close attention must be paid to providing adequate taxpayer service – one-stop shopping, complete and accurate records, clear explanations, quick processing – if a VAT is to work satisfactorily. Those familiar with the way tax administrations actually function in many developing and transitional countries may find such advice too far removed from reality to be practicable. Nonetheless, unless tax administration and other 'interfaces' between the public and private sectors encourage rather than discourage the development of the formal economy, less developed countries are likely to remain less developed.[8]

Registrants should be required to keep at least minimal books – essentially records of sales and purchases. In a well-designed and adequately

---

[5] For this reason, many experts have urged that countries seize the occasion of launching a VAT to establish a 'model' administration in the expectation – or hope – that if this model succeeds, it will subsequently be emulated in other parts of the tax administration. The validity of this proposition, so far as we are aware, has not been examined in detail anywhere. Much of the discussion in the present section follows Edmiston and Bird (2004). Many important questions, for example, the organizational structure, the penalty system, and the question of joint audits of VAT and business income taxes, are not discussed here: see Bagchi, Bird, and Das-Gupta (1995) and Ebrill et al. (2001).

[6] Direct importers who are not otherwise registered need not be registered, however. Otherwise returning residents or individuals who make occasional purchases abroad become VAT registrants, and that is not a good idea.

[7] In the United Kingdom, for instance, about 1,000 VAT registrants a year (out of 1.4 million) are deregistered.

[8] See World Bank and International Finance Corporation (2006) on the need to reduce barriers to formalization.

administered VAT the incentive to register for most traders (the tax-free purchase of inputs) should be sufficiently great that it should not be necessary to undertake any extensive 'outreach' registration process. If a VAT is well designed and administratively credible, registrants who sell to those in the VAT systems will enter the system voluntarily since it will be so clearly in their interests to do so. If they do not, as we note elsewhere in discussing the informal sector, they will pay a fiscal penalty for their choice and the interests of both equity and competitive efficiency should thus be served to some extent.

Filing

Registrants are normally required to file returns on a monthly basis if their annual taxable sales exceed some specified limit, and smaller taxpayers to file bimonthly, quarterly, or even annually. Although no one seems to have studied the relative costs and benefits of such different filing periods, the practice is almost universal. Returns generally have to be filed within a month (or less) of the end of the relevant taxable period.[9] Some countries have different types of returns for different taxpayers, especially when some file on a 'simplified' or 'quick' basis and some are subject to special high-rate excise (or VAT) rates. In Jamaica, for example, there are both a general return used by all registered taxpayers who do not use the quick method and another return for quick method taxpayers. In addition, since in Jamaica (contrary to our advice in Chapter 7) excises are treated as part of the VAT system, there is still another return for those subjected to excises, as well as special returns for those engaged in tourism activity and for those dealing in general insurance. All this seems unnecessarily complicated. Even if the present special treatment of these sectors is retained, a policy that seems unnecessary (in the case of insurance and excise industries) or undesirable (tourism), such firms could simply file the basic return, supplemented as necessary by any additional information to support the special deductions allowed.[10]

---

[9] Of 45 countries with VAT, 32 require monthly filing for large firms (OECD 2006).

[10] An unduly neglected issue in many countries that we do not discuss here is the design of tax forms. The form (paper or electronic) is critical because it is both the major way in which information flows from taxpayers to administrators and the key way in which the administration informs taxpayers of what they want to know (Vázquez-Caro 2005). The VAT form plays a particularly important role in the whole system because the information it contains can and should be related to the information provided by the same (and other) taxpayers in relation to numerous other taxes – customs, excises, property transfer taxes, business income taxes, wage withholding, etc.

If a registered taxpayer fails to file a return on time, a failure to file notification should be issued automatically, and the delinquent filer charged an appropriate penalty (e.g., a fixed amount or a percentage of the tax due, whichever is greater).[11] For those who continue to be delinquent, an official assessment needs to be issued promptly. Such a pro forma assessment can be made, for example, by calculating the estimated tax payment as the average of recent returns or perhaps as a pro-rata share of estimated annual gross receipts. In some instances in Jamaica official assessments are even based on receipts as reported on an initial registration application submitted many years earlier, presumably on the dubious principle that a pittance is better than nothing.

Countries make trouble for themselves if they set up such administrative procedures incorrectly. A troublesome attribute of the estimated assessment program in Jamaica, for example, is that once any payment – even a negligible one – is made on an estimated assessment, the account is cleared, and in practice there appears to be no requirement that an actual return for the relevant period must subsequently be filed. With such rules, taxpayers who are assessed an amount (taking into account any penalty applied for nonfiling) that is less than they would have owed had they filed an accurate return thus have a strong incentive not to file a return at all. Why should they? Since over 10% of domestic (nonimport) VAT in Jamaica is calculated on an estimated basis, this is not a trivial issue.

Payment

All payments including those on estimated assessments should be accompanied by returns (Casanegra de Jantscher and Silvani 1991).[12] If payments are made without an associated return, either the taxpayer must indicate to which assessments the payments apply or some 'stacking rule' (such as e.g., delinquent principal first, then penalties, interest, and surcharges) must be applied. If an overpayment is made with a return for a particular period, a similar stacking rule may be used after the current tax due is covered. Alternatively, a taxpayer who overpays may receive either a credit (to be carried forward against future liabilities) or a refund. Even if government pays interest on such refunds (as it should but almost never does in developing or

---

[11] The design of an appropriate penalty structure (Oldman 1968) is another interesting and important subject that is not further discussed here.

[12] OECD (2006) shows that this is the practice in most, but not all, developed countries. In Italy, however, although large firms pay monthly, only annual returns are required, and in Korea although monthly returns are required from large firms, payments are quarterly.

transitional countries), most such taxpayers will probably request refunds, a subject we discuss in more detail in the next chapter. Of course, if tax due is not paid or paid only in part, appropriate penalties and interest must be promptly assessed, and enforced.

Tax payments may be made to recognized financial institutions such as banks, the revenue department itself, or both. Different countries have different systems. Countries that do not already make use of financial institutions both to receive payments and perhaps to do some initial processing of simple returns (those accompanied by full payment) should definitely explore this possibility further.[13] As a matter of good policy it seems best to keep the function of actually collecting and processing money out of the hands of the tax administration. Revenue officials should be more concerned with ensuring that the right people pay the right amounts than with spending their evenings adding up the day's proceeds. Not so incidentally, keeping the cash out of the tax office also reduces the opportunity for theft and corruption (Radian 1980).

Audit

Perhaps the safest statement that can be made about VAT in any developing or transitional country is that auditing procedures should be modernized and strengthened. Audit is the core of any tax system. This is especially true with respect to self-assessed taxes such as VAT. In most countries, the data needed to design sound audit design policies for those already in the tax net exist on the tax form.[14] In principle, audits should be done both randomly and on a more selective basis, taking into account the 'risk profile' of different types of taxpayers.

For example, since VAT is applied in effect to the difference between sales and purchases (or the 'gross margin,' as it is often called with respect to retailers), a critical factor is the reported markup coefficient – supplies as a ratio of inputs. When this ratio is equal to or less than 1.0, the taxpayer is, in effect, reporting that his or her sales are less than purchases. In other words, the taxpayer is claiming that the 'gross profit margin' (value-added) on such sales is negative. Taxpayers who have persistently very low markups (less than 0.5, for example) may sometimes have such reasonable explanations as substantial export sales. On the whole, however, as Silvani (1992, 286) notes:

---

[13] For a useful discussion of the issues involved, see Casanegra de Jantscher and Silvani (1991).

[14] The large relevant literature on audit design and implementation is not discussed here: for an earlier review see Bagchi, Bird, and Das-Gupta (1995).

"Experience has shown that taxpayers who report a low markup (under 1.10, for instance) have a strong likelihood of turning out to be tax evaders." Firms in particular lines of industry that report persistently lower markups than their competitors would seem to require close and automatic examination by tax auditors. Table 9.1 illustrates, for example, the situation in this respect in Jamaica with respect to the 81% of VAT taxpayers for which markups could be calculated.[15] About 13% of these taxpayers reported markups less than 1.0. Although this proportion does not appear to be particularly high in comparative terms,[16] what is striking in the Jamaican case is that over 100 of the largest firms (those in the top decile) also reported markups of less than 1.0, a result that appears to warrant further investigation.[17] Another way to use such data might be to compare the markup reported by a firm with the average markup for other firms in the same line of business.

Auditing is also the main way in which taxable activities hidden within the large informal sector found in many developing and transitional countries can be included in the tax net. Much better use can be made of the rich information already available in most countries not only to cross-check selected transactions within the universe of VAT registrants but also to follow the audit trail out into the vast unknown land of those who are not in the system but should be. To do so effectively, however, officials need both training in a range of accounting and investigative skills and clear direction and encouragement from above. Too often, they have neither.

A key tool in enforcing VAT compliance is to cross-check purchases of one taxpayer against sales recorded by others. Few countries, however, seem systematically to use such programs to detect underreporting, let alone outright fraud.[18] Some early attempts at widespread 'matching' of VAT invoices (e.g.,

---

[15] The remaining 19% mainly reported no taxable activity. Readers may perhaps wonder why Jamaican data are so often used to make a point in this book. The reasons are three: (1) the data are publicly available – as is definitely not the case in most developing and transitional countries; (2) one of us has worked extensively in Jamaica and is familiar with the data; and (3) unfortunately, a point that must be taken on faith, the evidence for Jamaica is consistent with our experience in a number of other developing and transitional countries.

[16] Silvani (1992) reports comparable proportions of 29% and 25% of taxpayers with markup ratios less than 1.0 in two cases he examines.

[17] Perhaps the most startling result shown in Table 9.1, however, is the large number of firms reporting very high markups in Jamaica. Business, it seems, is rather good for many firms subject to GCT (Jamaica's VAT). In contrast, in the two cases studied by Silvani (1992) – one in Latin America and one in Europe – only 18% and 23%, respectively, reported markups greater than 210%, or less than half the proportion found in Jamaica.

[18] In one country, the administration finally began systematic cross-checking only when a review of companies from which the administration itself bought services (on which it paid VAT) revealed that very few of these companies reported these sales on their VAT returns!

Table 9.1. *Jamaica: Markups Reported on GCT Returns, 2002*

Markup Range (%)	Number of Firms	Percentage of Total Number of Firms
<50	722	5.2
50–75	555	4.0
75–100	1,220	8.8
100–110	1,157	8.3
110–120	1,032	7.4
120–130	1,761	12.7
130–140	665	4.8
140–150	512	3.7
150–160	442	3.2
160–170	413	3.0
170–180	297	2.1
180–190	270	1.9
190–200	282	2.0
200–210	219	1.6
>210	5,455	39.2
Total	13,902	100.0

Source: Edmiston and Bird (2004).

in Korea) suggested that the results of this approach were not worth the effort (Choi 1990). Subsequent experience in some other countries (e.g., Taiwan and Singapore) using modern information technology to match invoices of buyers and sellers seems to have been more successful.[19] However, the widespread adoption of this approach cannot be recommended to the over-burdened tax administrations found in most developing and transitional countries. If such countries are ever to administer VAT at a satisfactory level, a higher priority is to adopt and implement such standard methods for improving audit practices as exchanging information between income tax audits (e.g., transfer pricing audits) and indirect tax audits. Without such back-up, even the fanciest computer-assisted techniques are unlikely to result in lasting gains.

For example, returns might initially be scanned to determine whether their markup ratios (or other parameters such as wage bills) fall within normal ranges for comparable firms. Those that fall outside these parameters should then be subjected to additional desk investigation (e.g., cross-checking information with customs and income tax for the period

---

[19] Ebrill et al. (2001, 148–50) present the usual case against relying on such matching. For a more positive appraisal, see Jenkins, Kuo, and Sun (2003, 179). See also Das-Gupta and Gang (2003).

in question). Although it is bad practice to focus audits on refund cases or to audit all those claiming refunds, initial refund claims by new businesses should have a high probability of being audited. When these or other 'issue' audits of any particular tax period (e.g., of sales of used automobiles between dealers, to mention the largest VAT fraud case uncovered to date in Canada) uncover potential problems, comprehensive audits of all taxpayers involved – preferably encompassing all taxes – should be undertaken for a period of several years. A quick 'pre-payment' audit may be useful with respect to refund applicants judged risky. More critical, however, are selective 'post-payment' audits on a (partially random) selection of all VAT registrants, large or small, refund claimants or not.

Developing and implementing a good tax audit system are not easy in any country. But such a system is essential to the achievement of sustainable good tax administration. Canada, for example, is generally considered to have a good tax administration. Indeed, a recent study of administrations in a number of developed countries concluded that in many ways Canada's administration was a 'north star' on which other countries might benchmark (Vázquez-Caro 2005). Nonetheless, a decade after Canada adopted a VAT the country's Auditor General (1999) still found it necessary to stress the need for the revenue agency to do more and better GST (VAT) audits because significant amounts of potential revenue were not being collected. Achieving a satisfactory level of tax administration is not a once-and-for-all task: every country must continually strive to maintain performance at a satisfactory level in the face of the constantly changing real world in which the tax system operates. Most developing and transitional countries have a very long way to go in this respect.

Enforcement

Arrears are a surprisingly important issue in some VATs. In Jamaica, for example, total GCT (VAT) arrears in June 2003 were J$37.8 billion, with roughly half of the total accounted for by only 93 taxpayers. Moreover, the level of outstanding arrears had been steadily increasing over time.[20] In principle, there should be no arrears at all with respect to imports, since all

---

[20] Some of the arrears (J$7.1 billion) were accounted for by 42 delinquent excise taxpayers. In principle, there should be no arrears on excise taxes since, under normal administrative practices for such high-rate excise taxes, tax should be paid before the goods are released for sale. This is not the case in Jamaica, however, where – partly because the excise tax has been bundled into the GCT law – excise firms seem to be treated as other VAT taxpayers are and hence are liable for tax only after sales are made.

taxes due at import should be paid before goods are released for sale.[21] If this treatment is considered unduly harsh for some exporters, consideration may be given to a limited 'deferral' scheme for a small number of bonded exporters.[22] For example, GCT might perhaps be suspended on imports by major exporters, defined as those for whom exports are more than 50% (or some higher proportion) of sales, who are in full compliance with all tax obligations, and who have posted a meaningful financial guarantee. While information on such imports will of course have to enter the system in order to facilitate compliance audits, since no tax will be imposed on such goods at the time of import, no refund will have to be paid at the time of export.

When penalties are assessed, they should be enforced rigorously and at once. If payment is not made in a timely fashion, there must be an immediate and credible sanction (such as interception of cash flows or seizure of property). If the penalties set in the law are considered to be too high to be properly enforced – a belief that obviously exists in many emerging economies, judging by the surprising number of waivers of penalties and interest and other relief that are granted to delinquent taxpayers – then they should be reduced. But if they exist, they should be enforced without exception. If this is not done, no tax, VAT or otherwise, can long withstand the constant erosion of the tax system as 'bad' taxpayers drive out 'good' ones.

VAT differs from most taxes, however, in that VAT delinquency is not simply a matter of tax collection but in effect the embezzlement of public funds. Firms liable for paying consumption taxes have for the most part themselves collected those taxes from others. If they do not remit the funds to the treasury in a timely fashion, they have, not to put too fine a point on it, stolen the money. Rigorous penalties for such an offense seem appropriate. At the very least, interest should be charged immediately when a payment is delinquent. Moreover, taxpayers should not have the option of objecting to assessments and hence delaying payment as they sometimes do. If they object, they can do so after reaching a satisfactory arrangement about payment. Such treatment may seem harsh. Again, however, it must be remembered that either the tax has already been collected from the public and is being improperly retained by the firm or, if the assessment objected to has been 'estimated,' it is, under the rules now applied in most countries, in all likelihood very much on the low side. In the extreme case, for example,

---

[21] When this is not done, as was the case in Ukraine for some years, the collection efficiency of VAT may be seriously impaired.
[22] See, for example, the Singapore system described in IRAS (2006); see also the discussion of refunds in Chapter 10.

as mentioned earlier with respect to Jamaica, a firm may be assessed on the basis of a fraction of the (self-assessed) turnover reported on its initial registration form!

Given the relatively strong incentives for taxpayers in many developing and transitional countries not to file and pay in a timely fashion, it is not very surprising that in practice some VAT liabilities are inevitably based on estimated rather than self-assessed assessments. Nor is it surprising that many such official assessments are also not paid in a timely fashion. The result is that often interest and penalties accumulate rapidly and soon exceed the initial (and usually low) assessment. In such circumstances taxpayers, when finally cornered, almost invariably appeal to have interest and penalties waived. Such appeals have no merit. Indeed, in principle there should be no waivers of VAT except in very exceptional cases of hardship. Again, it must be remembered that VAT collections in effect constitute treasury funds that are being temporarily held by a third party (the registrant). There should be no leniency when it comes to collecting from such agents what they have already collected from citizens.[23]

Nonetheless, when countries build up a considerable stock of accrued liabilities – once all efforts have been made to clear the most recent and largest accounts in arrear – very occasionally it may perhaps be worth considering a 'one-time' amnesty of accrued interest and penalties to clear the books of what are likely to be uncollectible debts. Should this be done, however, to prevent damaging the integrity of the tax system beyond repair, it is critical that any such amnesty should be accompanied and preferably preceded by clear and credible tightening of payment, audit, and enforcement procedures to preclude 'signalling' future leniency and hence building up the moral hazard problem once again (Das-Gupta and Mookherjee 1998).

To sum up, if someone is caught cheating on VAT, the tax administration must first act quickly to stop the practice and then impose civil penalties as appropriate. Such penalties might include such measures as intercepting income flows to delinquent taxpayers, seizing assets, and perhaps even temporarily closing businesses in the ways that have proved effective in some Latin American countries.[24] Finally, and only in especially serious cases, the administration has to be ready to proceed to the always lengthy and

[23] Of course, if what is at issue is a matter of law – for example, should VAT have been collected on a transaction on which in fact it was not charged? – treatment closer to that commonly applied to similar disputes about income tax would be appropriate (see Bagchi, Bird, and Das-Gupta [1995]).

[24] One must of course be careful not to put such sharp tools into the hands of corrupt tax officials who may all too easily employ them to harass and extort taxpayers.

difficult level of criminal prosecution.[25] A simpler way to build credibility for a penalty system without going to the extreme of launching a criminal case may sometimes simply be to publicize the administration of penalties, including the names of the people or organizations penalized, through the media.[26]

[25] In the United Kingdom, with 1.4 million registrants, only a few hundred cases a year go to prosecution. On average, it takes three to five years of detailed investigative work (and considerable resources) to bring a case to trial. Such costly tasks should not be undertaken lightly.

[26] For example, the province of Québec in Canada, which administers its own VAT (QST), as well as the federal GST in its own territory, now lists on its Web site the names of taxpayers who are under criminal investigation and the nature of the allegations using electronic Press Releases; see Revenu Québec page at: <http://www.revenu.gouv.qc.ca/eng/ministere/>. Since those charged with criminal offences in Canada are presumed innocent until found guilty in a court of law, some may think that this goes a bit too far.

TEN

Dealing with Difficulties

Even if attention has been paid to all the elements of good VAT administration we discussed in Chapter 9, tax administration remains a difficult task even at the best of times and in the best of places – conditions seldom met in developing or transitional countries. The way a tax system is administered affects its yield, its incidence, and its efficiency. It matters. Good tax administration is both inherently country-specific and surprisingly hard to quantify in terms of both outputs and inputs. The best tax administration is not simply that which collects the most revenues; facilitating tax compliance is not simply a matter of adequately penalizing noncompliance; tax administration depends as much as or more on private as on public actions (and reactions), and there are complex interactions among various environmental factors, the specifics of substantive and procedural tax law, and the outcome of a given administrative effort (Bird 2004a). All this makes the administration of a VAT complex. We discuss in this chapter two particular issues that have proved particularly difficult to deal with in many developing and transitional countries. One issue – the refund problem – relates to keeping those within the VAT system honest; the other – dealing with the small and shadowy – relates more to ensuring that those who should be within the VAT system actually are. As a filling between these two slices of VAT administrative problems, we also discuss some general ways in which VAT administration can be improved.

THE REFUND PROBLEM AND VAT FRAUD

Refunds are the Achilles heel of any VAT system. A VAT invoice constitutes a potential claim on the fiscal resources of the state. In the hands of a VAT registrant such an invoice may be used as a deduction against any output tax due and may become a direct claim for a refund. When refunds are due, they should be paid. Government cash flow problems should be dealt with directly and not 'managed' by improperly withholding funds legally due to taxpayers. In Jamaica, for example, the government is supposed to pay interest at a rate of $2\frac{1}{2}$% per month on refunds that are not paid after 90 days. In reality, however, the government seems often to have been slow in paying refunds as a result of lack of cash (Edmiston and Bird 2004). It has in effect been borrowing from taxpayers through what amount to 'forced loans.' Jamaica is hardly alone in this regard. Many developing countries occasionally or regularly operate in similar ways, spending what they have when they get it and getting what they can wherever they can (Caiden and Wildavsky 1980).

China has a particular version of this problem because all export rebates are paid from the national budget while 25% of VAT proceeds go to local budgets. The usual 'revenue pressure' argument for holding back on refund payments is exacerbated by this feature of the system, as well as by the reduced rates applied to numerous activities in China and the apparent prevalence of fraudulent returns (Chi 2003). China has attempted to cope with this problem more by scaling down the presumptive level of 'rebates' to exports than by simply accumulating refund arrears.

In Ukraine many VAT problems seem to arise from the refund system. But appearances can be deceiving. In 2004, for example, new refund claims in Ukraine amounted to 41% of collections. A recent study of refund levels in 28 countries for the 1998–2001 period found that 9 countries had refund-to-collection ratios in excess of 40%, with an average for the seven transition economies included in the study of 36.8%, so Ukraine's ratio does not seem out of line (Harrison and Krelove 2005).[1] Applying the regression equation of 'expected' refund levels estimated in this study for Ukraine in 2004, the predicted refund level is over 46%, or significantly more than the level actually observed.[2] Moreover, although exports – the major source of refund claims – substantially increased in the first half of 2005, the relative level of new refund claims was actually lower than it had been in the first half of 2004.

The annual level of refund claims in Ukraine in itself is not a problem. However, because of the marked accumulation of refund arrears from prior

---

[1] Interestingly, Ukraine, which was included in this study, had an average ratio of only 24% in this period.

[2] The estimated equation is Refunds = 0.16∗Exports + 0.75∗Growth + 0.19∗Literacy + 0.90∗Range, where exports is share of exports in GDP, growth is average GDP growth in period, literacy is literacy rate, and range is difference between lowest (nonzero) and highest VAT rates. The adjusted R square is 0.8826. (A number of dummy variables are included in the original equation, but none is applicable for Ukraine.)

years Ukraine definitely has a 'refund problem' in the sense that for years it did not pay refunds promptly, although much of this backlog has now been worked off.[3] One reason a huge backlog accumulated was simply that financially hard-pressed governments were reluctant to give money they had in hand back to taxpayers, however legitimate their claim. Another reason, however, was the widespread perception that some – perhaps many – refund claims, past and present, are fraudulent: the value of exports may be inflated, the exports may never have occurred, and the input taxes claimed on exports may be inflated or simply unreal. If such frauds exist, however – and they do – the problem is not with refunds per se but rather with the administration of the VAT in general.

There are many ways to cheat on any sales tax. As we discussed in Chapter 3, in principle – and with good administration in practice also – it is actually *more* difficult to cheat with a VAT than with other forms of (non-cascading) sales taxes. To the extent VAT fraud takes the form of obtaining illicit refunds, it may perhaps show up more explicitly in the budget than equivalent fraud with other forms of sales tax simply because it takes the form of explicit refunds rather than lower revenues as with other forms of evasion. But the net impact on the budget is the same in the end. Dealing with VAT refund fraud is no different from dealing with any other form of tax evasion. The correct treatment for VAT refunds is simply to pay legitimate claims promptly and not to pay fraudulent claims at all. The problem, of course, is the way to distinguish the good from the bad. The answer is to be found not so much in special treatment of refund claims as in better administration of all aspects of the VAT system.[4]

It is critical to ensure that refunds are justified not only in the sense of being related to legitimate business inputs but also in the sense that the taxes for which reimbursement is being claimed have actually been paid. Even in countries with well-established and experienced tax administrations such

---

[3] One should not confuse the payment of past debts (overdue accounts payable) with the relationship between current accounts receivable (VAT liabilities) and accounts payable (VAT refund claims) accrued during the year. In 2004, for example, Ukraine paid out 25.2 billion hryvnia (including so-called mutual settlements – 'offsets,' for example, against government expenditure liabilities of 11.3 billion hryvnia) in VAT refunds – or more than it collected in VAT during the year!

[4] In the particular case of Ukraine, many of the refund arrears accumulated arose from interenterprise arrears connected largely with the energy sector and arising in part at least from the persistent underpricing of energy (World Bank 2003). The solution to such problems lies in sensible energy policy, not in playing with the VAT refund system: for further discussion of the energy problem, see Shiells (2005) and Petri, Taube, and Tsyvinski (2002).

as Germany, so much fraud has been uncovered in the form of illegitimate invoices that it has recently been proposed that refunds should not be paid unless satisfactory proof is provided that the input taxes claimed have been received by government (Sinn, Gebauer, and Parsche 2004). Since 2002 Germany has made the buyer legally liable for tax not paid by the seller. However, this provision has had little effect because it is virtually impossible to prove that a buyer had any knowledge of a seller's intention not to pay the tax for which the buyer claims input tax credit.

Another common form of VAT fraud is to establish a bogus new firm that claims credits for inputs it does not actually buy and then disappears before it can be audited. Germany tried to deal with this fraud by demanding some form of guarantee from new firms. But this measure proved ineffective largely because firms were still able to make claims and declare bankruptcy before the authorities got around to acting. To prevent such problems, Sinn, Gebauer, and Parsche (2004) propose to ensure that all taxes claimed as input credits must actually have been paid. Their scheme would require banks to remit the tax directly to the government at the time of sale through the device of an intermediate 'trust' account. At the same time the bank would issue a receipt to the seller for VAT paid, to serve as proof of the input tax claim. Alternatively, for cash payments, sellers would be required to issue a tax receipt that demonstrates that the tax has been paid (in the form of either a verified credit card–like transfer to the government at the time of sale or a prepaid 'tax stamp').

The complexity of such schemes makes them inadvisable in the conditions prevailing in most developing and transitional countries.[5] Several alternative approaches might be considered to curb VAT refund fraud. For example, as we discussed earlier it is desirable to restrict zero-rating solely to exports to limit the potential range of legitimate refund claims. Similarly, any reduced rates should be high enough not to generate such claims except in highly unusual circumstances. Export sales against which input tax claims are made should be adequately supported by verified export declaration forms.[6] Other ways of limiting fraud that have been adopted in various countries range from making refunds to new registrants only after a mandatory six-month carry-forward of unused credits to limiting refunds only to firms in certain industries (as in China) or of a certain size (as is done in Québec with respect

---

[5] See the discussion of the somewhat similar scheme in Bulgaria in Harrison and Krelove (2005).

[6] Considerable attention has been paid to the question of integrating VAT and customs administration (Ebrill et al. 2001), but this continues to be a serious problem in many countries, not least with respect to refund claims by exporters.

to credits for capital goods, energy, and certain services).[7] Such methods may make fraud less likely or less attractive. Unfortunately, they both increase the degree of cascading in the tax and erect still more barriers to the creation of new formal-sector businesses (not least because interest is seldom paid on carried-forward or deferred credits). The 'first-best' approach to limiting fraud when administration is weak is to design VAT to limit opportunities for fraud, for example, by restricting zero-rating to exports. In the end, however, the only real solution to VAT fraud in any country is a stronger tax administration and in particular a strong audit program.

STRENGTHENING THE UNDERPINNINGS OF VAT ADMINISTRATION

One statement that can be made with certainty in any developing or transitional country is that its tax administration should be improved. As does much conventional wisdom, this one hides some deeper truths. One truth about VAT is that many countries do not meet the preconditions necessary to run a good self-assessment system (see Chapter 12). In addition, the degree of policymaker and even public support needed to improve VAT administration seldom exists. The few large formal-sector firms that account for most VAT revenues may support measures to extend the weight of the tax to their relatively untaxed competitors in the informal sector, but they react adversely to any measures that tighten the system as it applies to them. Small firms caught in the system complain both of the 'untaxed' competition and, often with justice, of the high compliance costs imposed by VAT. Those who are outside the VAT net are usually happy with their status. The public at large could not care less about the problems of the tax administration. Often, VAT has a bad name as being an unfair tax, and anything government does to improve it may be seen as being done to the people rather than for them.

The conditions for improving VAT administration in most developing and transitional countries are thus far from propitious. There is no magic formula for creating public support for better tax administration. At some basic level, what is really required is to strengthen the 'legitimacy' of the state (Chapter 11). This is not a process that happens overnight anywhere. Nonetheless, there are some promising experiences around the world and some feasible ways in which the critical and difficult job of collecting

---

[7] Harrison and Krelove (2005) provide a useful discussion of such methods. An important question that we do not discuss here is the potential for widespread VAT fraud to increase corruption in the revenue administration: see, for example, Li (1997) on China and Zuleta and Leyton (2006) on Bolivia. Fjeldstad (2005) provides an excellent review of the growing literature on corruption in tax administration.

adequate revenue for public purposes can be improved from within, as it were (Bird 2004a).

Before discussing methods to administer VAT better, however, we should make it clear that by saying that problems with VAT (or any mass modern tax) in any particular country are largely due to administrative weaknesses we do not necessarily mean to imply that the tax administration is either incompetent or corrupt. Both conclusions may be (and often are) true to some extent in many countries. However, the real problems are more fundamental. The creation and development of a modern tax administration are always and everywhere difficult and time-consuming tasks. It took centuries for Western countries to get to where they are today, and where they are is hardly fiscal nirvana. Improvements need not occur at a geological pace, however. The experience of a few countries, such as Chile, show that, when political conditions are right and the will to effect serious change exists, the process of putting into place a substantially better tax administration can be accomplished in a decade or so (Toro 2005).

Unfortunately, many countries – including most in sub-Saharan Africa – began their 'modern' tax systems with an unpromising legacy of state-private relations, with almost no trained officials, and in a very difficult political and economic setting. It is not surprising that there is still much to do in most such countries. Moreover, all too often developments over the years have made the task facing even the most motivated, competent, and honest tax administration difficult: the lack of consistent support from political leaders, constant changes in tax legislation, fundamental problems with the legal and judicial system, the rapidly shifting level and structure of private activity, and so on and on.[8] Nonetheless, there are always things that can be done to improve VAT administration.

One obvious but unduly neglected issue in most countries, for example, is that good administration of any tax requires serious analytical foundations based on sound information and intelligent analysis. One must understand a problem in order to solve it. Virtually without exception, major change and improvement in both tax policy and administration in any country require a solid analytical foundation in the form of a more systematic approach to assembling and analyzing data.[9] The beginning of wisdom is to identify the

---

[8] Vázquez-Caro, Reid, and Bird (1992) stress the importance of the 'environment' of tax administration.

[9] For a first-rate example of the kind of 'forward thinking' a good tax administration should conduct with respect to VAT, see Australia (2001). Of course, few if any developing or transitional countries have the resources to carry out such studies, but they can certainly learn much from this and the many other documents publicly available on Web sites such as <http://www.itdweb.org/>

size and nature of problems as carefully and fully as possible. Tax administrations in all countries operate within hard budget constraints: to get the most from what they have, they need to allocate resources as efficiently as possible. Efficiency is not a luxury in poor countries. It is an essential tool in the fight to become less poor. To administer VAT efficiently, one needs not only to estimate the 'VAT gap' but also to decompose that gap by both the sector of economy (energy, agriculture, services, etc.) and the nature of the problem (nonregistration, false registration, nonfiling, underreporting of sales, overreporting of purchases, nonpayment, etc.).[10]

Once the relative magnitude of the various problems facing VAT administration is better understood, the first and easiest step is to change the tax law to reduce the scope of these problems as much as possible, even at the expense of violating conceptual purity and economic logic. Examples are the suggestions for exempting agriculture and raising thresholds we discussed earlier in this book.

Few VAT problems can be solved by such containment measures, however. If studies such as those mentioned earlier are done on an industry basis (as they should be), they may help to establish industry norms (such as e.g., refund claim levels), deviations from which should give rise to further examination of such firms. Comparative information of this sort is essential in determining the risk profile (with respect to noncompliance) of taxpayers who are of different sizes, operate in different lines of business, and have different patterns of tax-relevant activity. Taxpayers in stable, well-established businesses with good compliance records are, by definition, much less likely to offend than those in new, variable businesses with no established record of good compliance. On the other hand, it is important not to impose unnecessary and unreasonable barriers to new businesses simply because they are new – although it must be recognized that 'newness' is definitely a risk factor from a fiscal perspective. A delicate line has to be walked in this respect. Of course, all such 'risk profiling' of taxpayers is simply a guide to the proper allocation of administrative resources (OECD 2001). It is an ingredient in good tax administration, not a substitute for it.

---

[10] For excellent discussions of how to carry out such studies, see, for example, National Audit Office (2004) and Gebauer, Nam, and Parsche (2003) on developed countries. Excellent examples of such work also exist in Latin America such as Engel, Galetovic, and Raddatz (1998) on Chile; Steiner and Soto (1999) on Colombia; Salim and D'Angela (2005) on Argentina; and Coba, Perelmuter, and Tedesco (n.d.) on Uruguay. As these studies show, every country has some degree of VAT evasion, ranging from relatively low estimates in EU countries such as the United Kingdom and the Netherlands to levels of evasion in countries such as Italy and Greece that are similar to those in Argentina, Colombia, and Uruguay – and greater than that in Chile.

Even in the relatively few such countries in which detailed VAT data are available in an accessible form, two characteristics are noticeable. First, considerable effort is generally required to put such data to any useful purpose, whether to analyze and improve the effects of VAT structure or to monitor and improve VAT administration.[11] Secondly, few developing or transitional countries have the resources or, it seems, the desire to make such an effort. This situation is curious. Tax administrations need to keep a close watch on trends and changes in taxpayer behavior to be able to allocate administrative resources effectively and to develop appropriate audit strategies. Data gathering and analytical capacity are clearly essential to do this. Yet not only do units devoted to such purposes seldom exist but even those most concerned with improving VAT administration seldom place much emphasis on the need to improve matters in this respect.[12]

One reason may be that those at the top of the tax administration give higher priority to other apparently more pressing needs such as dealing with issues concerning specific taxpayers or involvement in policy design. Good administrators may have useful, even essential, input into policy design (Bird 1989). But they should not be given major responsibility for policy design. That is not their job. Nor should good managers be involved in specific taxpayer issues. Their task is to set up the system correctly, including appropriate dispute settlement mechanisms, not to become involved in particular cases. Good tax administration is primarily a 'middle-range' problem of developing and implementing a process capable of achieving its policy goals (such as revenue and equity) efficiently and effectively. Both a good information base and the capacity to utilize that information effectively are essential tools for this task.

Good data are also needed to formulate good revenue policy. As an example, information on the revenue forgone as a result of different exemptions and exclusions is essential in determining the revenue and distributive effects of various policy options. A regular reporting system with respect to such 'tax expenditures' is needed to ensure that revenues forgone through tax policy measures such as VAT exemptions intended to achieve distributional or allocative goals are subject at least periodically to some form of

---

[11] For example, see the *Compendium of GST/HST Statistics (2004 Edition)* recently released by the Canada Revenue Agency (CRA) (2005). Not only does this appear to be the first such data that have been made available in the over 15 years the GST has existed in Canada, but the data included, while of interest, are not very useful for analytical purposes. One can only hope that much better information exists within the CRA.

[12] In many countries the only administrative data most tax officials, even at high levels, have at hand are records of the amount that has been collected. Information on *what* is taxed – the tax base – is particularly scarce.

monitoring.[13] In the absence of such estimates, once an interest group has received a tax concession, it may enjoy the results forever after without having to demonstrate to anyone that the benefits it receives warrant the costs incurred. Better data (e.g., on a sectoral and commodity basis) are also often necessary to address such critical issues as the substitutability and complementarity of tariffs and VAT.

Little attention is paid to such issues in most developing and transitional countries. Nonetheless, our experience in many such countries is that with relatively little effort some approximate information on many such matters can be obtained. The reason little is done is not so much that it cannot be done at reasonable cost with available resources but that no one tries to do it. At present it is seldom in anyone's interest to make much effort along these lines. One reason is that the existence of information always has a 'public good' aspect so that not all the benefits can be captured by any one individual or group.[14] Another is that better information may have an adverse effect on the interests of some powerful people. Such factors seem sufficiently strong in most countries to ensure that most decisions about both tax policy and tax administration continue to be made more on the basis of faith than of evidence.

The preceding comments may be applied to any tax. Several features make them especially applicable to VAT, however. For instance, one unfortunate consequence of the adoption of VAT in replacement of other indirect taxes has been the virtual disappearance in most countries of any information on the composition of the effective base of consumption taxation. Most studies that deal with this issue infer the tax base indirectly from national income accounts or survey data.[15] Some facts important to understanding the way VAT really works are surprisingly difficult to uncover in many countries. Consider the real nature of the VAT base. Bird (1999) estimated that in 1994 over 90% of all VAT collections in Poland (which adopted a VAT in 1993) were from imports and the traditional excise sector (alcohol, tobacco, and fuel). The implication is that the immediate result of introducing VAT in Poland was actually to *reduce* sales taxes collected on the nonimport nonexcise sector

---

[13] For a brief discussion, see Messere, de Kam, and Heady (2003) and for an extended treatment, Bruce (1990).

[14] One way to keep private information that indicates that all is not well is simply to hide it in the bottom drawer – a practice we have observed in a number of countries – or, these days, perhaps to direct it to an inactive URL.

[15] For an interesting recent example, though a simple one, of the information that can be drawn from VAT revenue data about the tax base for EU member states, see Mathis (2004).

from over 5% of GDP to less than 2% of GDP. Such estimates do not imply that introducing VAT was not a good idea. However, they do suggest that anyone who thought the economic impact of Poland's new VAT was similar to that in, for example, Germany just because it 'looked similar' was not looking at reality.

Similar data gaps in most developing and transitional countries make it difficult to estimate the likely revenue consequences of base and rate changes in VAT. Such problems should not exist since almost all the needed information is generated in the normal process of administering VAT. Seldom, however, are such data made available in a usable form even to local tax offices, let alone used either in allocating administrative resources or in improving tax policy.

VAT is the only tax that requires the government not only to collect substantial money from the private sector but also to pay much of it back to the same people in the form of input tax credits. Since any VAT invoice constitutes a potential claim on public funds, and falsifying such claims is perhaps the most common form of VAT fraud, it is critical from an administrative perspective to have a detailed knowledge of the 'normal' or 'expected' pattern of credits and liabilities for firms in all the different lines of business subject to VAT. Again, however, although the normal operation of an invoice-credit VAT generates such information (Table 9.1), it is striking how seldom such data are either collected in usable form or used for devising a risk management strategy. Perhaps even more surprising is that this whole question has not until very recently received much attention from the international community of VAT experts.[16]

A final general observation is simply that, as with all taxes in all countries, no VAT in any country, however well designed and well administered it may be initially, will forever remain the same. Times change and so must taxes. Keeping up in taxation requires an ability to read the winds – to detect important emerging tax issues, to work out in detail how best they may be dealt with, and to devote time and energy to changing tax design and administration to cope with changing circumstances. Life is more difficult in all aspects for those concerned with tax matters in developing and transitional countries simply because, almost by definition, such countries are not only more likely to change – especially if they succeed in growing and developing – but also likely to be more vulnerable than most developed

---

[16] See, however, the many useful suggestions in Silvani (1992), and the more recent simple estimates in Ebrill et al. (2001) and Harrison and Krelove (2005). Unfortunately, the data to do more along these lines do not exist in most countries.

countries to winds from abroad, and they generally have much less capacity to cope with all these problems.

DEALING WITH THE SMALL AND SHADOWY

We discussed the treatment of the informal sector briefly in Chapter 5. Here, we consider some further aspects of this question together with the vexing issue of the appropriate treatment of small business under VAT. As mentioned earlier, many have expressed concerns about the compliance costs VAT imposes on small business. These concerns are legitimate. A recent study of Croatia, for example, found VAT compliance costs to average 31% of VAT revenues for businesses with fewer than six employees (Blažić 2004). Similar results have been found in many other countries (Hanford and Hasseldine 2003). Such concerns have led many VAT countries to introduce various forms of special treatment for small traders. As we discussed in Chapter 7, one key decision point in VAT design related to this issue is the appropriate 'threshold' at which to require firms to register for VAT. Another such point is whether small firms, whether included in the VAT system or not, should be subjected to some 'simplified' tax. Thresholds range from none in some countries (e.g., Sweden) to an annual turnover of over U.S.$600,000 in Singapore (Table 7.1). Some countries differentiate by line of business. Some permit voluntary registration of those below the threshold.[17] Some impose a simple presumptive tax (usually based on gross receipts) on small sellers, although few make much effort to ensure that the rate or rates applied bear some relation to the VAT that should be collected.[18]

Simplified Regimes

In addition to simply collecting a little money from some people who otherwise might not be taxed, advocates of simplified special regimes usually have

---

[17] Interestingly, many U.S. states with retail sales taxes actually provide compensation for compliance costs to vendors, especially small vendors: see Due and Mikesell (1994).

[18] For example, in Korea self-employed taxpayers that have less than about U.S.$50,000 in annual sales are taxed presumptively, with tax liability estimated at sales in the taxable period times the average rate of value added to sales for the same type of business times the VAT rate of 10% (Korea National Tax Service 2005). Table 7.1 provides other examples. Data reported by Joosung Jun (personal communication) show that the 'prescribed ratios' used under this simplified system generally understate the actual ratios, in some sectors by as much as one-third, although in a few sectors (notably hotels) they overstate the actual ratios. Of all VAT registrants in Korea 44.4% utilize the simplified system (or are exempt), but in total these 1.8 million firms account for only 0.3% of VAT collections.

additional goals such as relieving small taxpayers from some of the compliance burden imposed by a relatively complex tax like VAT and hence encouraging the growth of small business. Another aim sometimes mentioned is to begin to 'educate' taxpayers by, as it were, sending them to fiscal kindergarten before admitting them as full members of the regular taxpaying population. Other plausible rationales for such systems may be to reduce opportunities for corruption and harassment of taxpayers, to reduce administrative costs of dealing with small taxpayers, and, by encouraging better record-keeping, to improve tax administration in general (Engelschalk 2004). A further aim is often both to discourage the growth of the informal economy and to increase revenues from this sector by equalizing tax burdens between the formal and informal sectors to some extent.

Such arguments appear to assume that there is no difficulty in determining which firms are small. They are like giraffes: one knows one when one sees one. This assumption is wrong in many developing and transitional countries. It is in the nature of the tax business that the 'clients' are not willing customers; indeed, most of them would be delighted to get out of the system and they often try to do so. Not only genuinely small businesses may look 'small.' Profitable large- or medium-sized businesses may also try to signal that they are small for tax purposes. Moreover, firms may be losing money but still functioning precisely because they do not pay over taxes such as VAT that they collect as agents but spend as though they were principals. Tax administrations in poorer countries are universally constrained in terms of resources and skills. Often, they have to choose whether to go after the larger firms that are already in the tax net (where potential tax revenue payback may be higher) or to pursue instead the less immediately lucrative and apparently smaller taxpayers that are largely outside that net.[19] Many have chosen to attempt to cope with the latter and indeed to some extent with the whole issue of the 'untaxed' shadow economy by adopting some form of specific presumptive tax regime in lieu of VAT (and often other taxes as well). Doing so, however, runs two risks. In the long run the very existence of presumptions of various sorts in many VAT systems in itself provides evidence of the inability or unwillingness to rely on taxpayer self-assessment as the first line of administration. Recourse to this approach thus both signals a general lack of trust between government and citizen and in all likelihood probably further delays the development of the kind

---

[19] As noted in Chapter 2 with respect to Barbados, such a country may be making a perfectly rational allocation of its scarce administrative resources by chasing those in the system rather than seeking those who are hiding.

of taxpayer culture (Nerré 2002) that must be developed over time if an inherently self-assessed tax such as VAT is ever to function adequately. The second risk is more immediate. How can countries with (by definition) weak administrations keep out of the simplified system large and medium enterprises that try to look like small enterprises and thus hide themselves from the tax collector's eye?

Two conditions must be satisfied to ensure that simplified systems satisfy either the fiscal or the nonfiscal rationalizations commonly offered in their defense. First, one has to ensure that as the truly small become bigger they will graduate into the normal tax system. Second, and of more immediate importance, one must also ensure that those who are in the normal system already – or who should be in that system – cannot easily migrate into the simplified system by taking on the disguise of smallness to shield themselves from taxation. The temptation to shelter from the fiscal blast within such systems is likely to be especially strong when, as experience suggests is usually the case, the effective tax rates applied to those who make it to the 'safe harbor' of the simplified system are considerably lower than those in the normal tax system. If the simplified rate is higher than the normal tax (including compliance costs), presumably no one would be in the simplified system. Since in most countries where simplified options are available, they appear to be extensively utilized, one must presume that the effective tax is lower.[20] Since such systems are often introduced in response to strong political protests from segments of the business community, it seems plausible and is indeed evident from experience in a number of countries that the effective rate may be markedly lower.

In practice, most developing and transitional countries have difficulty in distinguishing between truly small firms that may not keep good books and records but are potentially (and legally) taxable and other firms with activities that are clearly large enough to fall within the tax system but are tax evaders. Some in the latter group may be completely off the fiscal radar – so-called ghosts. Others are more like icebergs in that the portion of their activities visible to the authorities may be minuscule compared to the hidden reality (Bird and Wallace 2004). Special (simplified and presumptive) substitutes for 'real' taxes such as VAT may in some ways seem a feasible

---

[20] Often the number of taxpayers enrolled in simplified systems is trumpeted as evidence of their success in drawing into the tax net many who would otherwise escape. It may equally, however, demonstrate that many who should be in the normal tax system have managed to find a safe, and legal, haven in the simplified system. The evidence in Ukraine, for example, is that there has been substantial 'migration' into the simplified (and sheltered) system (World Bank 2003).

approach to reach at least some evaders. But this approach also fragments the tax system and is hence inconsistent with good tax administration.

Whenever a 'disconnect' is created between a special tax regime and the general tax system, problems are likely to emerge. A country can no more sustain two national tax regimes for long than two national currencies. The equivalent to Gresham's law (bad money drives out good) in the tax field is that the availability of a low-tax alternative inevitably weakens the 'normal' regime. In reality each regime constitutes an integral part of the other and changes in either will affect the entire tax system. Whether the aim of a special tax regime is to supplement a normal VAT by replacing its complexities with a simplified regime for small business or to move some 'shadowy' firms into the fiscal light, explicit transition arrangements are needed to link the special regime to the more general tax system within the context of the prevailing tax administration constraints. Unfortunately, in practice little attention seems to have been paid to this critical issue in most countries with such regimes.

An additional problem such systems impose for VAT is that since firms within special tax regimes are generally not included in the VAT chain, the number of transactions legally outside the VAT system is increased. Of course, since purchases from these taxpayers by regular VAT sellers cannot be used to claim input credits, they have an incentive voluntarily (or perhaps under pressure from their customers) to enter the VAT system. How effective such an incentive is likely to be, however, is far from clear given the general difficulties most developing and transitional countries face in policing the fringes of VAT. For example, other registered sellers – some of which may themselves be conducting significant 'shadow' business – may agree to issue VAT receipts for such 'outside' entities in their own name for a cut of the gains, a practice that seems not uncommon in countries with large shadow economies and weak tax auditing capacity. Attempts to supplement a VAT by some kind of simplified system may thus end up making matters worse by creating the risk of migration to the less expensive system, particularly when, as is too often the case, once firms are safely ensconced in the 'small' sector, they are able to remain there almost indefinitely with little or no risk of audit or exposure.

Chasing Shadows

Many devices intended to chase 'shadows,' small or otherwise, back into the fiscal light may be found around the world. At one level, tax officials may simply walk along the street, sweeping hawkers and peddlers into the tax net, entering premises and confiscating records, and so on. A much more sophisticated (and more productive) approach is to follow the audit trail, starting with those who are in the tax net and working outward. Even in the most undeveloped economies it is difficult for anyone engaged in business to any significant extent never to have potentially traceable contacts with someone who is already known to the tax authorities. Alternatively, operating on the premise that even tax evaders must eat and drink – and perhaps even drive a BMW – the authorities may attempt to tap some of the tax potential of the shadow world through methods related to consumption patterns. Such methods may range simply from imposing consumption taxes as such (as we discussed in Chapter 5) to introducing various 'fiscal gimmicks' intended to catch at least the more unwary among the unwilling.

Many countries have, for example, tried a 'tax lottery' approach, under which consumers can use VAT receipts (receipts containing the VAT registration number of the seller) to win a prize or even as partial payment for other taxes. Another device is to encourage credit card use. For example, even a country as developed as Korea allows 20% of credit card expenditure to be deducted from taxable income and has a lottery system based on VAT receipts (Korea National Tax Service 2005).[21] Few such schemes seem to have been systematically evaluated, however. In one study Berhan and Jenkins (2005) found that the costs (notably the additional compliance costs) created by a particular 'clever' scheme used in Northern Cyprus to reward VAT compliance appeared to be considerably larger than any additional revenue conceivably induced by the scheme. Equally unrewarding results are reported for Bolivia in the same study. If one reason for special treatment of small firms is recognition of their high compliance costs, as many argue, it is obviously important to be aware that compliance costs may be imposed on the economy as a whole by schemes intended to increase VAT revenues by discouraging operations in the cash and informal economy.

A quite different approach to the perceived and real problems of dealing with small taxpayers is the so-called VAT withholding found in some countries. Argentina, for example, requires specified larger registrants to withhold at rates of 10.5% on goods and 16.8% on services, in effect presuming (at a standard rate of 21%) that taxable inputs account for 50% of sales of goods

---

[21] A somewhat similar system, in effect lowering the effective VAT rate on credit (and debit) card purchases, is used in Argentina. Consumers get a 3% rebate for purchases subject to VAT from the bank that issued their card.

but only 20% of services (Kaplan 2005).[22] This practice assumes that VAT will not be reported properly by small firms and hence requires those selling to such firms to 'withhold' an additional VAT on such sales to make up for the VAT those firms are supposed to collect (but are expected not to remit even if they do collect) on their own sales. Such 'dual price' systems are usually imposed at arbitrary rates – there appear to be no data supporting the 'input' assumptions noted earlier, for example – and make little logical or administrative sense. Nonetheless, they are sufficiently common, and are suggested sufficiently often in countries in which they do not now exist, to call for closer examination than they seem so far to have received. For example, what is the best way to determine the appropriate 'withholding' rates (essentially presumptive taxes) in different circumstances? To what extent is such 'withheld' VAT ever credited against VAT actually reported by the firms from which they have been withheld?

Officials in many countries (Turkey, Argentina, Indonesia) insist that withholding schemes have improved VAT compliance substantially. Although we have seen no data on this, we suspect that in many cases little withheld VAT is credited so that the net effect on revenue is indeed positive (see later discussion). Moreover, as with VAT on imports, this approach may thus provide an effective way of taxing unregistered firms. But of course this tax, like most 'simplified' systems for small business, is not really a VAT in any meaningful way but rather a variety of turnover tax with the attendant economic problems of cascading, distortions, and so on.

Different varieties of VAT withholding exist. The simplest and perhaps most widespread is related to the refund problem discussed earlier. Exporters may be required to withhold VAT on purchases made from (purported) VAT registrants. They may only claim refunds if such withholding is less than the VAT paid. A related approach is to extend the requirement to withhold VAT on purchasers to other large taxpayers (notably public-sector agencies). Finally, in a few cases a sort of 'reverse withholding' is applied, for example, on commercial imports or sales by utilities to businesses. The seller imposes a surcharge (usually 1%–2%) on the VAT with respect to such sales on the assumption that the buyers are cheating on their own VAT.

Such systems actually existed long before VAT in countries such as Egypt (the 'additions and deductions' system) and Indonesia (the 'MPO-MPS'

---

[22] The withholding rate for services is 8.4% with respect to services subject to a reduced 10.5% rate (e.g., farming, some construction, and some health services). Other special withholding regimes also exist in Argentina (Kaplan 2005) and Venezuela (Evans 2003).

system). Both these systems essentially combined withholding (buyer 'taxes' seller) and 'reverse withholding' (seller surcharges buyer). The details of these now defunct systems are not considered here; briefly, an earlier (unpublished) study by one of the present authors in Egypt led to three conclusions. First, as we have suggested is still common with VAT withholding systems, the determination of withholding rates was not evidence based but largely arbitrary. Second, in the very few cases in which such 'withheld' tax was credited, the firms in question would almost certainly have filed and paid tax in any case. Third, in the end, for the most part the approach amounted to little more than an arbitrary supplementary turnover tax on small businesses (and their – often visibly relatively lower-income – customers). Field observations in Argentina several years ago suggested that the withholding scheme there had similar characteristics. Given the apparently growing popularity of VAT withholding, more serious empirical research – research that requires in-depth access to individual taxpayer accounts and thus can usually be done only by the tax administration itself – is needed.

One reason special regimes and devices of various sorts have sprung up in VATs in many developing and transitional countries around the world is that the normal tax regime is considered – somewhat paradoxically, often by the very people who established it in the first place – to be too complex, sometimes too harshly applied, and perhaps also unduly prone to corruption, extortion, and harassment.[23] Insulating selected (and often largely self-selected) taxpayers from such problems does not make the problems disappear. On the contrary, it likely makes them more difficult to solve, both by complicating tax administration and by reducing political pressures to fix more basic problems with tax administration. Information is the lifeblood of effective VAT administration. Every effort should be made to prevent breaking the information chain between potential registrants, rather than to encourage firms to do so, as most simplified systems in effect do. In the end there is no way to administer VAT well except by doing so. Papering over the cracks by layering on alternative regimes, approaches, and gimmicks only postpones and makes more difficult and costly the day of reckoning that will inevitably arrive.

---

[23] See, for example, Engelschalk (2004), Djankov et al. (2002), and the annual "Doing Business" reports, for example, World Bank and International Finance Corporation (2006). It should be noted that 'simplified' systems may sometimes actually increase problems, for example, by increasing compliance costs: when options are provided, rational taxpayers can choose between them rationally only by calculating tax burdens under both the standard and the optional approach.

ELEVEN

The Political Economy of VAT

This chapter differs from the rest of the book in that issues discussed relate more to the political economy of taxation in general than to the specific economic and administrative aspects of VAT as such. We discuss this broader issue for two reasons. One reason is simply that in many developing and transitional countries controversies about VAT have become one of the central ways in which tax issues arise in the political arena.[1] For better or worse, VAT has often become the 'poster child' of tax reform, so VAT reform is inevitably closely related to tax reform in general. The second reason, more directly related to this book, is that the performance of VAT in any country inevitably reflects politics – both short-run factors such as the calculations of particular interest groups and long-run factors such as the nature of political institutions.[2] This critical political dimension of the policy process is often simply taken as given by those directly concerned with VAT design and implementation. Ideally, however, those so engaged should be as aware as possible of the manner in which such factors may impact on (and in turn be affected by) such central elements of VAT design and implementation as exemptions.[3] For instance, being forewarned that a particular sector is

---

[1] See, for example, Brautigam, Fjeldstad, and Moore (in press). We are grateful to Odd-Helge Fjeldstad for helpful discussions of some of these issues.

[2] A common joke among development economists some years ago was along the following lines: "What difference would it make to development policy in country X if all the political scientists in the world disappeared?" The expected answer, of course, was "No difference at all." While no doubt serving its intended purpose of making economists feel perhaps a bit more useful (at least in relative terms), this joke is very inaccurate indeed. As we have begun to understand with the recent upsurge of the political economy literature, few elements matter more to improving policy design and implementation in any country than deeper understanding of the way politics works in that country.

[3] We do not discuss here the interesting question of the 'political' role played by the IMF with respect to tax reform in many developing and transitional countries, although one of

politically 'untouchable' may enable policy designers to work around the problem in a way that does less damage to the tax as a whole than might otherwise be the case.

Unfortunately, despite the proliferation of real world examples available for study, few careful 'political economy' studies of VAT implementation have yet been done in developing or transitional countries, and none seems to have been carried out in any rigorous analytical framework. Economists are just beginning to study the political economy of tax policy.[4] So far, most such work has taken the form of cross-country comparative studies employing rather aggregative and approximate variables to measure the various complex phenomena at play in the real world. There is still a long way to go before anyone can even approach rigorous analysis of the factors that really determine specific policies such as the adoption or design of a VAT in any country (Acemoglu 2005).[5] In the long run we may eventually be able to provide clear and directly useful guidance to those engaged in the precarious art of policy design and implementation in developing and transitional countries. Right now, however, the best we can do here is to tackle these big issues in much the same way that we earlier discussed many of the smaller but important questions that have to be resolved with respect to VAT in developing and transitional countries – by telling stories and drawing analogies.

To illustrate, in countries that already have a VAT an important question is whether VAT revenues will increase in relative importance over time. Giving a clear and simple answer to this question for any particular country is difficult not only because different conditions prevail in different countries but also because answering it requires a deep understanding of the political

us once took part in this activity. We can say, however, that contrary to what some outside observers seem to think, policy determination is a 'game' in which, in our experience, most players are well aware of their role. To illustrate with a small but important issue discussed in Chapter 7, one reason IMF experts often argue so strongly for one rate is not that they do not understand optimal tax theory but that they think that once administrative considerations are factored in, on balance it makes sense to do so. Another reason may be, however, that they see one of their roles in the policy process as acting as a balancing force against the many interests usually arguing for favorable treatment of this or that sector as well as providing an 'outsider' against whom conflicting local interests may perhaps form a common front. As the leader of one such mission once said to his colleagues – privately, late at night in his hotel room – "Well, today we were attacked by the Left as fascists and by the Right as communists. We must be doing something right!"

[4] For some interesting beginnings, see Urrutia, Ichimura, and Yukawa (1989); Thirsk (1997); and Perry, Whalley, and McMahon (2000).

[5] Two books by Persson and Tabellini (2000, 2003) summarize much of the early theoretical and empirical research.

and economic forces determining the level and structure of revenues. In the end the political factors shaping tax systems in general are likely to be more important in determining the answer than the economic and administrative aspects of VAT discussed in earlier chapters. This does not mean that such fundamental economic factors as the increasing openness to trade and the income elasticity of the expenditures subject to VAT do not matter. But the level and the structure of taxation in any country reflect deep-seated factors that, in the absence of severe shocks, do not change quickly.[6]

The last half-century has been tumultuous. Unsurprisingly, most countries have found it difficult to achieve a sustainable policy balance given the conflicting and changing forces, external and internal, economic and political, that they have faced. Both the facts that presumably should govern policy in principle and the intellectual fashions that sometimes seem to shape it in practice have changed markedly over the last few decades in most developing and transitional countries. It is not surprising that to some extent tax policies in these countries have also changed over time.

Often, however, such changes amount to less than might at first appear. Over the last few decades, for example, taxes have not increased in Latin America (Bird 2003b). Some rates have risen, especially for VAT, but many have declined, mainly for income taxes. Tax collections as a share of national income have, on average, actually declined a bit in the region. In the world as a whole, Latin American countries continue to be below average in terms of the size of their public sectors relative to their levels of per capita income (Inter-American Development Bank 1998). Fiscal stability in Latin America goes even further than this. Countries that had relatively high taxes at the end of the 1970s were still above the regional average in the 1990s. The tax mix also changed little in most countries over this period.

Two small examples make the point. In 1980–82 Guatemala's tax ratio (taxes as a percentage of GDP) was 9.8%, of which only 2.8% was from personal income taxes; in 1995–99, the comparable figures were 8.9% and 2.2%. At the other extreme, although Nicaragua's tax ratio rose from 23.6%

---

[6] An early version of the 'model' (to use the word loosely) sketched in this section was suggested for Canada with respect to the growth of government expenditures in Bird (1970a) and major tax reforms (Bird 1970b). For a detailed illustration of the changing configuration of political and economic factors that shape the evolution of tax systems over time, see the case of Britain, discussed at length in Daunton (2001, 2002). Similar studies could presumably be done in most countries: for a partial example, see the treatment of Brazil and South Africa in Lieberman (2003). A useful study that came to our attention too late to be considered here is Inter-American Development Bank (2006). This book is a stimulating attempt to evaluate systematically the 'politics of policies' in recent Latin American experience.

in 1981–83 to 26.2% in 1995–99, the share of taxes on domestic consumption remained dominant although declining a bit, from 49% to 46%.[7] Tax *rates* in these countries did not necessarily change in the same way as tax *ratios*. For example, the VAT rate in Nicaragua rose from 6% to 15% over this period. But that is precisely the point: despite the various crises, political and economic, affecting Latin America in the latter third of the 20th century, and the sometimes dramatic changes in tax laws as a result, the reality of taxation changed surprisingly little as evidenced by the relative constancy in both tax levels and tax structures across and within countries. A closer look is required.

THE CASE OF MEXICO

In a recent analysis of Mexico, Jorge Martinez-Vazquez (2001) notes that one of the most striking features of the various major tax changes that have taken place in that country over the years has been the limited effect they have had on Mexico's tax to GDP ratio, which has remained almost constant. He suggests several possible explanations for this constancy. The reforms in tax structure (1) may have been undermined by unrelated ad hoc measures or (2) may have been offset by administrative deterioration, or (3) one or both of the preceding may have occurred less by accident than by intention.

Mexico's tax system presents a paradox. An important problem facing Mexico, as well as many other developing countries, is its persistent inability to raise adequate revenues to finance basic public sector goods and services adequately. Significant tax policy and tax administration reforms have given Mexico a tax structure that in many ways is comparable to that in many developed countries. Nonetheless, Mexico's tax system has continued to perform poorly in its fundamental task of raising adequate revenues.[8] Indeed, Mexico's tax effort has not changed significantly for a quarter of a century. Tax yields have moved both up and down over the last two decades. Overall, however, they have remained surprisingly stable, averaging between 15% and 16% of GDP for total federal revenues (which exclude social

---

[7] The figures for the earlier period are from Tanzi (1987); the more recent figures are from Stotsky and WoldeMariam (2002).

[8] There is, of course, no absolute scale against which one can assess the adequacy of the size of the sustainable public sector in any country. The share of government in GDP reflects, among other things, collective preferences of a country for public goods and services vis-à-vis private consumption. From an economic standpoint such preferences cannot be judged right or wrong. However, there appears to be a fairly general consensus in Mexico that the current level of revenues is inadequate.

security funds and subnational governments) and between 10% and 11% for tax revenues (which exclude oil and other nontax revenues). From 1980 to 2003, tax revenues rose only from 10.9% to 11.3% of GDP, and total federal revenues only went up from 15.3% to 16.8%.[9]

This poor revenue performance is hard to explain, given the significant changes made in the tax system over this period. VAT, for example, has clearly been improved both as a revenue collector and in its allocative and distributive impact (Martinez-Vazquez 2001). The VAT rate (15%) is similar to or slightly below international averages. The same is true of most other taxes. Nonetheless, Mexico's apparently modern and 'average' tax system has been unable to generate much more than 11% of GDP in tax revenues. This outcome is even more surprising because the major objective of several major tax reforms in the last few decades has been explicitly to increase the revenue yield of the tax system in order to be able to improve the quality and quantity of public services.

Several factors seem to account for Mexico's enduring low tax effort. Some factors are common to many developing and transitional countries – including both supply factors such as tax 'handles' (such as the share of more easily taxed imports in final consumption) and demand factors such as corruption, the quality of governance, and tax morale (Bird, Martinez-Vazquez, and Torgler 2006). However, several country-specific factors appear to have played an important role in Mexico's lackluster performance. For instance, the good fundamental structure of Mexico's tax system has over the years been undermined by sundry ad hoc policy measures. In the case of VAT, for example, Mexico zero-rated (rather than exempted) a wide list of domestic goods and services such as agricultural goods, foodstuffs, medicines, and equipment used in agriculture. As a result of the government's taking this path, VAT's revenue yield was undermined and its administration complicated. In all likelihood, the outcome was also increased evasion and reduced confidence of taxpayers in the fairness of the system, hence probably reducing voluntary compliance.

Tax administration in Mexico has also faltered. Complex policies like extensive domestic zero-rating do not take adequately into account the ability of the tax administration to enforce the resulting equally complex

[9] The behavior of the government budget deficit also suggests revenue inadequacy. The sustained deficits during the 1980s (up to 10% of GDP) suggest taxes were too low to cover the level of expenditures desired by the government. Reduced deficits after 1993 may suggest either that Mexico has reached some sort of equilibrium vis-à-vis its desired level of tax effort (as we suggest in the text) or alternatively that external pressures have imposed fiscal discipline on the federal budget.

administrative procedures.[10] Moreover, not only has Mexico's tax administration largely failed to modernize, but it may plausibly be said to have
gone backwards during the 1990s as earlier efforts to improve its efficiency
were not sustained.[11] Persistently high levels of tax evasion demonstrate that
Mexico's tax administration is not capable of enforcing the current tax system at an acceptable level. In terms of VAT efficiency, for example, Mexico
is clearly one of the poorest performers in Latin America (see Table 4.2).

The frequent statements of Mexican authorities on the need for higher
revenue collections have not been matched by performance. The real
policy – at times implicit but sometimes quite explicit – appears more to
have been one of keeping the ratio of revenues to GDP at a relatively constant
level. This constancy of tax effort has been achieved in two ways. First, any
marked increase in revenues – whether resulting from an elastic response
of the tax structure to economic growth, enlargement of the tax base, or
increased revenues from petroleum – has generally been quickly followed
by such discretionary measures as lower tax rates, with the result of keeping
the tax ratio more or less constant. During the 1980s, for instance, when
petroleum revenues went up, nonpetroleum revenues were reduced, and
vice versa. The chronology of tax concessions in Mexico broadly parallels
periods in which the built-in elasticity of the system would otherwise have
increased relative revenue yields.[12] Secondly, if policy did not do the job,
then administration did. Changes in the actual ratio of revenues to GDP
were offset by discretionary changes in tax administration effort. Changes
in the level of enforcement or effort by the tax administration have been
asymmetric. It is not so much that tax enforcement efforts were relaxed
when government revenues were up but rather that enforcement was tight-
ened (in the form of so-called tax crusades) when government revenues
were dramatically down as a result of economic crises and business cycle
downturns.

---

[10] Matters were not helped by the fact that Mexico, as did some other countries (see
Chapter 7), in effect incorporated some relatively high-rate excise taxes into a 'VAT' collection system.

[11] Vázquez-Caro (2005) provides an illuminating (if largely implicit) comparison of Mexico's
administration against a 'benchmark' derived from a group of developed countries.

[12] To some extent this may be explained by rivalry between competing bureaucracies.
Martinez-Vazquez (2001) suggests that a common, although not explicitly stated, policy within the Ministry of Finance during much of the last two decades has been that any
increase in revenues should be spent by the ministry itself in the form of rate reductions
or tax expenditures rather than on the expenditure side of the budget by line ministries
and other budget units.

Why were such efforts made to keep the tax ratio (and also, it appears, the relative distribution of tax burdens) relatively constant over time? While further research is needed to investigate this question, one interesting possibility is that to a considerable extent taxation in Mexico may be a matter of 'negotiated' tax burdens that are in a sense agreed upon between government authorities and representatives of the private sector. Tax policy (and tax administration effort) in Mexico appears in practice to be determined to a substantial extent through periodic discussions and agreements between an (unofficial) compact of large taxpayers and government authorities willing to compromise on the overall level of taxes demanded in order to reach political agreement. If this conjecture is correct, in order for Mexico to raise its tax effort – or by inference to alter in any significant way the distribution of the tax burden – explicit agreement between government and the private sector on the desirability and level of the higher tax effort or the changed distribution is needed. A country's tax system, as do its other important political institutions, largely reflects the equilibrium reached by contending political forces.

BALANCING EQUITY, EFFICIENCY, AND SUSTAINABILITY

Mexico is hardly the only country in this position. Similar relative constancy can be seen in other countries in Latin America (e.g., Colombia, McLure and Zodrow 1997)[13] and elsewhere (e.g., India, Rao and Rao 2005) over the decades, with repeated tax reforms that have little lasting effect.[14] Major changes in taxation generally require major change either in the political reality of a country or in its economic circumstances. In normal times a 'good' tax reform – one intended to raise more revenue in a more efficient and equitable fashion, for instance – seems to be like a 'good' seat belt law. That is, if everything else stays the same, lives would be saved (the tax ratio would increase). However, things do not stay the same: some people drive faster when they are belted in, so death rates (tax ratios) show little change. Countries may tend to achieve an equilibrium position with respect to the size and nature of their fiscal systems reflecting largely the balance

---

[13] It should be noted, however, that an econometric analysis by Garcia Molina and Gómez (2005) found that the introduction of VAT in 1974 was one of only 2 (of 23) tax reforms in the 1973–2000 period that resulted in a real increase in tax revenues in Colombia.

[14] Nor is this phenomenon to be observed only in developing or transitional countries. Daunton (2001, 2002), for instance, provides an extremely detailed account of the way similar (generally implicit) 'negotiations' have shaped British tax policy for centuries.

of political forces and institutions, then remain there until 'shocked' into a new equilibrium.

Two alternative explanations may lie behind this process. Either – somewhat improbably – 'supply' ('capacity') factors may change over time in such a way as to offset all attempts to raise tax ratios. Or, more plausibly, ideas as to the 'proper' tax level – 'demand' factors – may change over time. Some evidence supports the latter position. For example, the two major explicit aims of tax policy in the period after the Second World War in most emerging countries around the world were, first, to raise revenue – and lots of it – in order to finance the state as the 'engine of development' and, second, to redistribute income and wealth. Then, as now, income and wealth were markedly unequally distributed in many developing countries, and especially in Latin America, so the need for redressing the balance through the budget seemed obvious to most analysts (if not to those who might be adversely affected). The ability of taxes to do the job was largely unquestioned. Indeed, both revenue and redistribution could, it was generally thought, be achieved best by imposing high effective tax rates on income, essentially because the depressing effects of taxes on investment and saving were considered to be small. Indeed, an extra bonus of high rates was sometimes argued to be that they made it easier to lead balky private investors by the very visible hand of well-designed fiscal incentives into those channels most needed for developmental purposes. In short, to exaggerate only a bit, the conventional wisdom at the time was essentially that all developing countries needed to do to solve their fiscal problems was to "learn to tax" (Kaldor 1963) – and to most that meant to tax in a properly progressive fashion.

Views on the appropriate role and structure of taxation began to change in the 1970s and 1980s, however. By 1990, most economists and policymakers believed that high tax rates (especially on income) not only discouraged and distorted economic activity but were largely ineffective in redistributing income and wealth. Reflecting this new view, income tax rates on both persons and corporations were cut sharply and are now almost universally in the 20%–30% range in Latin America, as elsewhere in the world (Shome 1999). On the other hand, reflecting – indeed, to some extent leading – worldwide trends, VAT is now the mainstay of the revenue system in the region, as in the world more generally. Other factors have been at play also. For example, taxes on international trade have declined with trade liberalization and the WTO. Together with increased competition for foreign investment, the result has been to move international concerns from the bottom to the top of the tax policy action list. At the same time, in many countries a new issue has risen to prominence on the fiscal menu as decentralization made the question of setting up adequate subnational tax systems an increasing concern, not least in Latin America (Inter-American Development Bank 1997).

The tax policy world is thus very different in many respects at the beginning of this century than it was in the middle of the last century. Ideas matter. As Blyth (2002, 274) says, "neither material resources nor the self-interest of agents can dictate . . . ends or tell agents what future to construct. Ideas do this." Or, in the more colorful words of Keynes (1936, 283–84): "practical men, who believe themselves to be quite free from any intellectual influences, are usually the slaves of some defunct economist. . . . Soon or late, it is ideas, not vested interests, which are dangerous for good or evil." Ideas about tax policy have clearly changed over time. Have institutions and interests also changed?

Some years ago Best (1976) analyzed Central American tax policy in a 'class' framework. He argued that in principle changes in tax level structure (e.g., the degree of emphasis on income taxation) essentially reflected the changing political balance of power among landlords, capitalists, workers, and peasants. Shortly after his article appeared, an explicitly 'Leftist' regime (the Sandinistas) took over in Nicaragua. What happened to taxes? Three things: Firstly, as Best (1976) would have predicted, the tax ratio rose very quickly, from 18% to 32% of GDP within the first five years of the Sandinista regime. Secondly, however, almost all the increase in tax revenue was derived from (probably) regressive indirect taxes and not from the (at least nominally) progressive income taxes. Thirdly, and in many ways most interestingly, once Nicaragua's tax ratio was increased, it stayed up there even a decade (and three subsequent governments) after the defeat of the Sandinistas.[15]

As this example suggests, political ideas definitely matter in taxation, but they do not necessarily dominate. Economic and administrative realities also matter. The fiscal reality found at any point of time in any country reflects a changing mixture of ideas, interests, and institutions. Few real-world tax structures have been designed with any particular objective in mind. On the contrary, they often seem like Topsy to 'have just growed' in ways shaped by both the changing local environment and the changing external context. In the case of the United States, for example, "economic crises and wars

---

[15] Peacock and Wiseman (1961) many years earlier had explained a similar discrete jump in tax effort and public expenditure in Great Britain as a "displacement effect": general perceptions about what is a tolerable level of taxation tend to be quite stable until these perceptions are shocked by social upheavals, and levels of taxation that would have been previously intolerable become acceptable and remain at that level after the social perturbations have disappeared.

helped create a consensus for an income tax that falls most heavily on the wealthiest taxpayers. The consensus [was] forged in the period of 1860 to 1920" (Weisman 2002, 366). The lengthy debate about taxes that took place over this period was not really about taxes at all but rather about what kind of society Americans wanted.

Since 1970 or so, the ideas on the relevant balance between taxes and society that were forged over the first half of the 20th century seem to many to have changed, as evidenced by the death of death taxes in developed countries such as Canada (Bird 1978) and, it now seems, the United States as well (Graetz and Shapiro 2005) and the very limited success of developing countries in achieving the high levels of income taxation to which many of them aspired in the postcolonial period (Bird and Zolt 2005). So far, however, reality in terms of both tax levels and the distribution of tax burdens seems to have changed rather less than ideas about what it should be.

LESSONS FROM HISTORY?

Consider some recent analyses of the way the Western democracies got into the business of big government and fiscal redistribution in the first place.[16] Alesina and Angeletos (2003) argue that two distinct 'models' of redistributive taxation exist in developed countries. One model is the United States with relatively low taxes and low redistribution. The other model is a country such as Sweden with high taxes and high redistribution. The difference, they suggest, is essentially due to self-fulfilling expectations. In the United States, they argue, the general belief is that effort is causally related to income. Those who make the effort, and consequently receive the income, are entitled to retain the fruits of their efforts. The resulting distributional inequality is considered to be fair since it reflects, or so it is believed, differential effort to a considerable degree.[17] Relatively low taxes are the result. On the other hand, since taxes are low, so are tax distortions.

---

[16] One might perhaps question the relevance of historical or even comparative experience in analyzing and understanding the problems of developing countries today. As Messere, de Kam, and Heady (2003, v) say, however, "Today's industrialized countries were yesterday's developing or transitional economies and for tax policy purposes the demarcation line between them is more likely to be the relative efficiency and integrity of the tax administration, rather than such economic criteria as GDP per capita." Of course, as we noted earlier with respect to Mexico, the way a tax administration functions is determined largely by more fundamental political factors.

[17] A striking confirmation of the power of this view in the United States may be seen in Graetz and Shapiro's (2005) tale of the way in which supporting death (estate) taxes has become political 'death' in recent decades.

The result is that high effort is indeed likely to yield high income, thus fulfilling initial expectations.

In some European countries such as Sweden, on the other hand, Alesina and Angeletos (2003) suggest that the pervasive belief appears to be that high income reflects not so much high effort as it does good connections (or even corruption). The result is strong popular support for high taxes. Since high taxes discourage effort, the connection between high effort and high income is indeed greatly weakened. This belief too is thus strongly grounded in the prevalent social reality. In both cases, as Alesina and Angeletos (2003) see it, ideas (perceptions) about the nature of social and economic reality shape fiscal outcomes that move reality to conform more closely to such perceptions, thus reinforcing the initial ideas.

Lindert (2002, 2003) takes a quite different approach to the two distinct fiscal equilibria observable in modern democratic societies. He starts at the same point: in some countries (such as the United States), the size of government is relatively small; in others (such as Sweden), it is relatively large. Lindert stresses, however, that low tax levels are not synonymous with low distortionary costs of taxation. In fact, he argues that the United States actually has more progressive tax policies in many respects than does Sweden, so its taxes, though lower in aggregate, are more distortionary.[18] Lindert's explanation is that with a larger government share of economic activity, bad tax policy choices can be more damaging. Democratic governments take care to avoid such choices, he says, because voters notice the effects of policy choices that affect their livelihoods adversely through discouraging investment and growth; hence they support more progrowth (and less progressive) tax structures. The result is that a country like Sweden when compared to the United States has lower effective tax rates on capital income and lower property taxes. On the other hand, it also has relatively higher taxes on labor income, on consumption, and especially on activities that are considered socially damaging (smoking, drinking, environmental damage, etc.).

Approaching the same tangle of political and economic factors influencing policy outcomes from a quite different angle, two recent studies of subnational debt policy in the United States (Inman 2003) and Canada (Bird and Tassonyi 2003) reach conclusions similar to Lindert's (2002). These studies suggest that democratic polities do learn from experience and that voters

---

[18] Steinmo (1993) had earlier made the same point. Cnossen (2002) argues that in fact effective tax rates on elastic factor supplies (especially capital) are roughly similar in the United States and the EU. Mintz et al. (2005), however, show that while marginal effective rates are close to U.S. levels in some EU countries (e.g., Germany), they are much lower in others, including Sweden.

do, over time, tend to reward parties that follow more prudent economic policies. Those who think that populists who promise the moon immediately to credulous voters invariably win should consider more carefully the meaning of Abraham Lincoln's famous dictum to the effect that one can fool all of the people some of the time and some of the people all of the time, but that one can never fool all of the people all of the time. Economic history appears to suggest that at least in societies with the 'error-correction mechanism' we call 'democracy,' Lincoln was broadly right. Or, as Blyth (2002, 274) puts essentially the same point: "Political economies . . . are . . . evolutionary systems populated by agents who learn and apply those lessons in daily practice."

The critical point seems to be that adequate feedback mechanisms are in place to warn when sustainable limits are being breached (Jakee and Turner 2002). Such mechanisms may take the form of the 'exit' mechanisms favored by economists, as when overtaxed resources flee a jurisdiction. Or they may be the 'voice' mechanisms stressed by political scientists, as when governments are changed to put into power those who will carry out more prudent policies.[19] But whatever form they take, such mechanisms must exist if any tax system is to be sustained in a country. Of course, no government is always competent; none is omniscient; and not all are always well intentioned. Mistakes will be made. A central problem facing all societies is finding ways to minimize the severity of such mistakes. In the story that Lindert (2002, 2003) tells, the way this is done is partly by muting the antigrowth aspects of pro-redistribution spending policy through a more progrowth tax policy. In addition, redistributive spending policy in such conditions tends to be itself largely 'progrowth' (e.g., by focusing on developing human capital). Redistributive policies that in themselves might be unsustainable in the long run as a result of the excessive distortionary costs on resource allocation they impose are thus made sustainable both by spending wisely (in ways that encourage growth) and by taxing wisely (reducing the distortionary costs of taxation).[20]

All this seems rather neat. Still, there are some obvious problems in reconciling the Alesina-Angeletos and Lindert views even in democracies assumed

---

[19] See Hirschman (1970) for the seminal discussion of these mechanisms.

[20] In the story told by Bird and Tassonyi (2003), much the same end is achieved by subjecting subnational governments to constant pressures from both exit (market forces) and voice (elections). Macroeconomic policies (subnational borrowing) that in themselves might lead to an unsustainable situation in the long run thus become sustainable over time by an evolution in both institutions (capital markets) and ideas (political rewards for conservative fiscal measures).

to function as well as in the stories told by these authors. For example, how can the United States simultaneously have both low taxes (and hence high reward to effort) and high tax rates on more elastic factor supplies (thus less progrowth policy)? Has the United States adopted low taxes to encourage efficiency and growth but done so in so inefficient a way that it may have decreased both? History matters in understanding not only why countries adopt different policies but what the effects of such policies are in the particular settings in which they have been adopted. To disentangle such issues, much more work is needed to resolve such conundrums – for example, by focusing in detail on such questions as the differential marginal tax rates applied in different countries to male workers between the ages of 25 and 45. Meaningful use of comparative international data requires close attention to such critical details.[21]

What does all this mean with respect to understanding tax policy and especially the role of VAT in developing and transitional countries? A recent study of American tax history concluded that "the search for the right balance is an endless process. . . . The consensus supporting the legitimacy of the income tax is likely to remain undisturbed. But its progressive nature will always be debated as long as we care about reconciling the competing demands of social equity, economic incentives and the need to pay for an expanding government" (Weisman 2002, 366).

Looking at Latin America with this perspective in mind, no real consensus on the 'right balance' for tax policy appears as yet to have been achieved. Some developed countries, notably the United States, may now be groping toward a new, less progressive consensus with respect to taxation (Graetz and Shapiro 2005). But this implies nothing with respect to what may be 'right' for other developed countries. Every country has to develop its own viable consensus on the right balance between equity and efficiency in taxation.

One point is clear: developed countries have clearly reached different equilibrium positions. Despite all the talk about globalization, there has been surprisingly little convergence in either tax levels or structures among OECD countries in recent decades. Nor is there much reason to expect such convergence in the near future (Messere, de Kam, and Heady 2003). Equally, there is no reason to expect strong tax policy convergence among emerging

---

[21] For a recent review of the use and limitations of the importance of a more historical approach to economics, see Guinnane, Sundstrom, and Whatley (2004). Reder (2004) notes that economists have found 'strong economics' (the neoclassical paradigm) so useful that they are unlikely to be willing to make the investment needed to do such 'strong history.' Perhaps not, but those interested in understanding the world must hope that someone will.

economies in Latin America or elsewhere. As always with public policy, no one size fits all. What is right – or at least feasible – for Chile or Brazil, for example, is likely to continue to differ from what may be sustainable in Colombia or Honduras.

What matter are not only how high taxes are (revenue adequacy), but also how the tax level has been (implicitly) chosen, how the taxes are actually imposed, and how the funds thus raised are used. History suggests, for instance, that one critical factor is the clarity of the linkage between expenditure and revenue decisions established in the budgetary and political process.[22] As Wicksell (1896 [1958]) argued long ago, allocative decisions in the public sector will be made efficiently only if they are financed efficiently. What this means is that 'benefit taxation' – broadly understood in this context as taxes deliberately chosen to finance specific expenditures in the full knowledge of the allocative consequences of both expenditures and taxes – is in principle the best way to run a country from either an economic or a political perspective. Of course, as Wicksell stressed, such a 'good' tax system would only be politically sustainable provided that the resulting distribution of income and wealth accorded broadly with what was politically acceptable. What is considered to be a 'just' distribution of income may be very different in different countries, but the distributive outcome is always and everywhere a high-profile matter.

The central question of tax policy thus in a sense concerns the way to make the so-called wicksellian connection (Breton 1996) operational so that good decisions – that is, decisions that reflect people's real preferences as closely as practically feasible – will be made on both sides of the budget. This question cannot be separated from the question of the perceived justice of the system or the institutional structure – how 'democratic' it is – within which political decisions are reached and expressed. The only way we know to help relevant decision makers make *right* decisions is to ensure that they – and ideally all those affected – are as aware as possible of all the relevant consequences. The key to good fiscal outcomes in any country is thus to have a public finance system that links specific expenditure and revenue decisions as transparently as possible. What all this really means is that if any country is to have a better tax system – better in the sense of giving the people what they want – it must have a better political system that translates citizen preferences into policy decisions as efficiently as possible. "Democracy," as Churchill once said, "is

---

[22] The discussion here focuses on taxation. To the extent public expenditures are financed from charges, nontax revenues, and borrowing, other considerations enter into play, but these issues cannot be discussed further adequately here.

the worst form of Government except all those other forms that have been tried from time to time."[23]

In any system, democratic or nondemocratic, taxation is of course always and everywhere a contested concept. Some pay and some do not. Some pay more than others. Some receive compensating services; some do not. Such matters are – and in democratic states, can be – resolved only through political channels. Indeed, history suggests that the need to secure an adequate degree of consensus from the taxed is one of the principal ways in which, over the centuries, democratic institutions have spread (Sokoloff and Zolt 2005). No nondictatorial government in this age of information and mobility can stay in power for long without securing a certain degree of consent from the populace, not least in the area of taxation. State legitimacy thus rests to a considerable extent on the 'quasi-voluntary compliance' of citizens with respect to taxation (Levi 1988). To secure such compliance, tax systems must, over time, in some sense represent the basic values of at least a minimum supporting coalition of the population.[24]

The central problem in many Latin American countries, for instance, is clearly inequality (de Ferranti et al. 2004). On the other hand, the key, and related, governance problem in most of the same countries is lack of accountability. A better tax system is critical to the solution of both problems. Reforms that link taxes and benefits more tightly, for example, such as decentralization and more reliance on user charges, may help accountability, if not inequality.[25] Reforms that replace highly regressive and inelastic excises by a less regressive and more elastic VAT may reduce inequality – especially of course if the increased revenues are invested in growth-facilitating activities such as education and infrastructure.[26] The most important function of the tax system in most developing countries is to provide (non-inflationary)

---

[23] This quotation actually had a somewhat different implication in its original context but nonetheless seems largely right even if one's main concern is growth: as Lindert (2004, 344), concludes, history tells us that "the average democracy has been better for economic growth than the average autocracy."

[24] Daunton (2001, 2002) shows that a great deal of attention was paid to precisely this task in Britain, with quite different tax levels and tax mixes found most suitable to the 'consensus-maintaining' objective over the years.

[25] Another such reform is earmarking (Bird and Jun 2005), but like the others mentioned, this, too, may instead of improving matters worsen them if it is captured by a particular interest, as may happen all too easily even in developed and democratic countries. There is no such thing as a free lunch when it comes to institutional design.

[26] Note that one implication is that to be relevant, analysis of the incidence of policy changes must consider both sides of the budget: as Break (1974) noted, the 'differential' tax analysis beloved of economists (and illustrated by all the studies cited in Table 5.1) is not necessarily the most relevant approach to incidence for policy purposes.

funding for pro-poor and progrowth spending programs, particularly in human capital. The best way to achieve this goal in most countries is likely through a broad-based nondistortionary consumption tax such as VAT, as has long been recognized (e.g., Heady 2004).

What countries actually do is always and inevitably determined in the first instance by political and not economic calculations. Countries vary enormously in the effectiveness and nature of their political systems. Some may be close to 'failed states' in which institutions are so ineffective that it does not matter much what they attempt to do: it will not work. Others may be 'developmentalist' and wish to use their fiscal systems as part of a relatively dirigiste interventionist policy. Still others may be of a more laissez-faire disposition. Some may be more populist, some more elitist, some more predatory.

The dominant policy *ideas* in any country (about equity and fairness, efficiency, and growth), as do the dominant economic and social *interests* (capital, labor, regional, ethnic, rich, poor), and the key *institutions*, both political (democracy, decentralization, budgetary) and economic (protectionism, macroeconomic policy, market structure), interact in the formulation and implementation of a VAT as they do with respect to tax and budgetary policy in general. Uniform results are unlikely to emerge from this constantly boiling cauldron with its different mixes of ingredients in each country. The changing interplay of ideas, interests, and institutions affects both the level of taxation and its structure, including the role of the VAT as well its design and administration. Taxation is one of the clearest arenas in which to witness the working out of these complex forces.

Viewed in this sweeping perspective, few developing or transitional countries have as yet completed even the earlier parts of the long cycle that produced the (more or less) redistributive and (more or less) growth-facilitating fiscal states now found in most developed countries – the long preparatory period during which the idea of the desirability and even necessity of a larger state and a more or less progressive fiscal system became established to different degrees in different countries. Some countries in Latin America, for example, might be argued to have moved more from the colonial inequality of land-based maldistribution to the modern inequality of capital-based maldistribution. Warriner (1969) once noted, despairingly, that many Latin Americans did not seem to know what a good land reform means – probably because they had never seen one. Equally, one might perhaps speculate that, in most countries of the region, as Engerman and Sokoloff (2002) almost – but not quite – say, most people do not really know what either moderate or justifiable inequality might mean since they have never seen it.

Many governments in developing and transitional countries, not just those in Latin America, are in dire straits. Even countries that have reached relatively safe harbors politically, achieving a certain degree of legitimacy and stability, almost always feel – often correctly – that they are in an economically precarious situation. The budget is politically and economically constrained. Life is difficult. Nothing can be done. All this may be true to some extent, but it is also both too much a counsel of despair and too easy a way out. Even in the most hopeless situations something usually can be done to improve matters. No doubt there will continue in most countries to be considerable dispute over what should be done to improve tax systems. Indeed, in most developing and transitional countries it would be better if there were even more such dispute because unless and until an adequate degree of political consensus on what should be done is achieved, no significant tax changes are likely to be made. Much of the problem in many developing and transitional countries is simply that there is no implicit "social contract between governments and the general population of the kind that is embedded in taxation and fiscal principles and practices in politically more stable parts of the world" (Lledo, Schneider, and Moore 2004, 39).

History tells us that such principles do not become embedded either painlessly or quickly. The specific substantive suggestions that Lledo, Schneider, and Moore (2004) make to improve matters such as better VAT administration on a broader base are already the stuff of countless existing reports. We agree. Most countries should do all (or most of) the good things that experts such as we recommend. However, the real question is: Why have so many done so little? Lledo, Schneider, and Moore (2004, 40) suggest, rather wistfully, that if Latin American countries are to improve their tax systems, they should "improve political institutions in ways that broaden and deepen social contracts. For example, create more responsive and less clientelistic political parties, more cohesive and less polarised party systems, and improved capacity of civil society to monitor government and participate in tax debates."

In other words, what they say is that there can be no good taxation without good representation. They are right. But is it useful to advise countries they should be something other than what they are? To return to the more low-level tax policy and administrative issues with which this book is primarily concerned, it can equally be said that in the end if a country needs or wants better VAT policy or administration, it can have it: the answer lies in their own hands. This too is correct. But even those who may want to do the right thing often need some help in finding out just what is right and how it can best be done. In most developing and transitional countries, one good thing is usually to establish and run as good a VAT as possible. Those who wish to do so will, we hope, find some useful guidance in the present book.

WHAT'S IN A NAME?

As both an example of the importance of getting the politics of VAT right and a suggestion about how that might be done, consider two apparently minor questions about VAT design. Should a VAT be quoted separately from prices? And should it be called a VAT? Each of these questions actually delves deep into the institutional cauldron. Neither has a simple or unique answer. Both need much more consideration than they seem to have received in most countries.

It may be a surprise to many outside North America to learn that retail sales taxes like those in most U.S. states are invariably stated as a separate explicit charge imposed on the posted price when the consumer arrives at the cash register. While this process is cumbersome and unwelcome – no one ever has the correct change ready! – the very fact that it is annoying can perhaps be considered good for democracy, at least if one believes that citizens should be fully aware of the cost of government. Equally obviously, however, such transparency makes it more difficult to increase tax rates (or reduce exemptions) because everyone is instantly aware of, and generally reacts adversely to, tax increases. In contrast, in most countries – Canada being a notable exception to this rule[27] – VAT is included in posted prices and hence not immediately obvious to the consumer at the point of sale (although it may often be stated explicitly on the cash register statement or invoice). Visible, or invisible: does it matter?

It is sometimes argued that it may not be worth imposing a VAT unless the rate is at least 10% because of the relatively high administrative cost of this form of sales tax. We suggested in Chapter 7 that this seems exaggerated and that some countries have VATs that function well at lower rates. We did not mention that another factor that seems to have led some countries to move to VAT was the belief that one could not impose retail sales taxes at rates much over 10% without producing both substantial consumer resistance and, probably, increased tax evasion. While this is again an exaggeration – in most Canadian provinces people have for years paid combined and highly visible federal-provincial taxes of about 15% on consumer purchases – it

---

[27] The visibility of VAT in Canada and the resulting public awareness of the tax was noted earlier as an important reason why its rate has not increased over time but decreased.

seems intuitively plausible that it is easier to introduce (or increase) a VAT if people are not reminded that the tax exists by adding it separately to the quoted price every time they buy something.[28]

If VAT is relatively invisible, having a better, broader base may be easier, for example, by taxing a wide range of services. Such a base is undoubtedly more desirable on both administrative and economic grounds than one eroded by popular resistance to taxes on food, medicines, school books, and so on. On the other hand, there is a strong democratic argument for separate quotation: people should know what they are paying for and what they are getting from government. If the price of more transparency in this sense is a 'defective' VAT in terms of more exemptions as well as lower spending because tax rates are lower, then the price might be considered worth paying.[29] Since deciding which way to go on this issue is entirely a political matter, it is striking that almost every country with a VAT – regardless of how democratic it is – has essentially decided to hide the tax from the public. While understandable in the interests of those in decision-making positions, this is clearly no way to build a democratic consensus in support of fiscal equilibrium.[30] It is thus surprising that there seems to be no serious discussion either in the policy process or in the academic literature of the 'importance of being visible' as a factor shaping not only the level and structure of taxation but also the evolution of political institutions.[31]

Finally, what's in a name? Does it matter what a sales tax is called? Many governments around the world think that it does, as indicated by the many

---

[28] One reason some U.S. conservatives have resisted VAT and argued for replacing the income tax by a national retail sales tax is that they think a 'hidden' VAT would lead to a larger government – as indeed the evidence for developed countries in Keen and Lockwood (2006) supports – while on the other hand replacing the (largely withheld) income tax by a highly visible RST would result in a smaller government sector.

[29] Note that even democrats might still like taxes to be hidden to some extent for the same reason as people sometimes support forced saving schemes of various types: namely, as a way of forcing themselves to behave more rationally in the long run (Elster 1979). Or they may do so for reasons similar to those of some supporters of social security systems: namely, to force others to behave more rationally (and thus ultimately in their own best interests) in the long run (Musgrave 1986).

[30] The incentive to avoid separate VAT quotation on final sales to consumers is especially strong in countries with weak administrations that fear, probably with reason, that one result would be even more false claims for input tax claims. One of the authors recalls being asked (in a country with a strong tax administration) for his gasoline receipts by an acquaintance who ran a farm and was entitled to refunds of the taxes on his own gasoline purchases, which were supposedly made for business purposes. Would-be tax cheats are everywhere, and all governments have to be concerned not to make their life too easy.

[31] For early reflections along this line with respect to developed countries, see Tanzi (1970) and Bird (1982).

taxes that have been named after expenditures considered politically attractive – the 'Education Tax,' the 'Employer Health Tax,' the 'Hospital Tax,' the 'Security Levy,' and so on. Sometimes the revenues from such taxes are in fact earmarked to the indicated objective. Often, however, this is not done: the name is the game.[32] Perception obviously matters in politics, and labels affect perception.

A good name can sometimes do as much to help a tax as a bad one can do to kill it.[33] Would a VAT by another name be more or less likely to be accepted? Many countries now call their VAT a GST – an acronym that has the useful dual meaning of Goods and Services Tax or General Sales Tax. Might some who teeter on the edge of moving to a VAT, or perhaps substantially raising the rate of an existing VAT, gain from going further and calling the new (or increased) levy something like, say, the Deficit Reduction Levy – though that may imply an undesired temporal limitation – or, for instance, the 'No Child Left Behind Tax' in support of increased education expenditures? Social security systems have done well by linking their 'contributions' – to a fiscal economist, a tax by another name – loosely to expenditures that people desire. Can or should VAT follow a similar path, at least to some extent?

The roles of judicious labeling and – though we are not advocating that this be done – perhaps even tying of VAT revenues to specific 'desired' activities are yet other issues that need to be considered more carefully than anyone seems to have done. Marketing matters. Those who want serious reform in VAT policy or VAT administration in any country need to spend as much (or more) time in studying the dark art of political salesmanship as in analyzing the details or data of VAT theory and practice to which most of this book has been devoted.

---

[32] For a recent detailed discussion of the theory and practice of earmarking, see Bird and Jun (2005).

[33] Graetz and Shapiro (2005), for instance, stress the role of the label 'death tax' as one key to the repeal of the U.S. estate tax.

TWELVE

Where Do We Go from Here?

The famous Russian author Leo Tolstoy once wrote that all happy families were alike. Most countries with value-added taxes seem relatively happy. But this does not mean that all 'good' VATs are alike. And of course not all VATs are equally 'good.' By definition, all VATs are value-added taxes in the sense that, as do happy families, they share many important common characteristics. Nonetheless, value-added taxes have a variety of sizes and styles, with different prices attached. No one would expect that a rich person in a cold country looking for the right boots in which to go skiing would buy the same footwear as a poor one in a hot country looking for a little protection for his or her feet. Equally, it seems unlikely that the best VAT for a country like, say, Switzerland – rich, with an excellent tax administration and a solid revenue system – would be the same as that for a country like, say, Liberia – poor, recently emerged from a violent conflict, with few administrative resources and in dreadful fiscal shape. Not only will one size not fit all, but VATs inevitably play different roles in different countries. The right VAT for the moment in any particular country may often be very context-specific.

All this is obvious. Somewhat strangely, however, for decades most developing and transitional countries have been told almost without exception that, so to speak, what is right for Switzerland (or France or Canada) is also right for them. Sometimes it may be. Often, however, it is not. Too often, countries in the market for a VAT have been in the position of someone searching for a good pair of shoes in the old Soviet Union just before the collapse: the only model on display in the store window is ugly, fits badly, and costs too much. But it is, or so it seems, the only choice available.

213

THE ASIAN EXAMPLE

In reality, however, many models of VAT are on the market, and still others may be developed. Consider the important case of Asia, where many different varieties of VAT exist and, for the most part, seem to flourish. Every country has its own story, as a few examples will illustrate.[1]

In 1977, Korea led the way with VAT in Asia. Korea also pioneered with a large-scale attempt to utilize the cross-checking feature of VAT for more effective enforcement, although this attempt did not prove particularly successful (Choi 1990) and was subsequently dropped. Korea has continued to experiment with innovative attempts to improve VAT enforcement in difficult sectors. For instance, since 1999 it has permitted those who make purchases with credit cards to deduct 20% of the amount spent from taxable income – presumably in order to obtain more information on the sales made by smaller firms. Credit card usage in Korea rose from 16% of private consumption expenditure in 1998 to a high of 42% in 2006. However, there appears to be no solid information whether this approach, which clearly reduces income tax revenues, has boosted VAT revenues by a greater amount. A recent study of related schemes in Bolivia and Northern Cyprus suggests that the answer may be negative (Berhan and Jenkins 2005). But of course Korea is a very different country, with a much better tax administration, so the answer may be different there.

Indonesia was next to join the VAT parade in Asia, in 1985. Indonesia moved to VAT as part of one of the best-prepared and best-analyzed tax reforms ever implemented in a developing country (Gillis 1985). Indeed, this reform is perhaps the only such reform in a developing country to be carried out not in response to a crisis but in anticipation of one expected when oil revenues declined in the future. Indonesia's original 'clean' VAT, however, soon became cluttered with a number of additional rates and more exemptions, in a pattern often seen, although more recently Indonesia has again returned to a uniform standard rate system.[2]

In 1986, Taiwan, setting a pattern subsequently followed by both Japan and Singapore, imposed a VAT rate of only 5%, well below the 10% that an IMF study around the same time (Tait 1988) said was the minimal sensible rate. Taiwan's VAT is unusual in several additional ways. For reasons peculiar to

---

[1] The adoption and subsequent evolution of VAT followed a somewhat different path in the transitional Central Asian countries emerging from the former Soviet Union, but these countries are not discussed here: see Baer, Summers, and Sunley (1996).

[2] For an interesting analysis of the distortionary and revenue effects of the VAT in Indonesia, see Marks (2005).

the island's recent history, for example, the VAT was actually imposed by local governments. Unsurprisingly, this system turned out to be unsatisfactory for two reasons. First, taxes accrued to the locations in which companies filed taxes rather than those where consumption (or production) took place. Second, rebates to exports often had to be paid by jurisdictions other than those that had collected the taxes on inputs. Both problems have also been experienced to some extent elsewhere (e.g., Brazil) when VAT is operated below the national level.

Despite such problems, VAT worked surprisingly well in Taiwan from the beginning, apparently in large part because of the heavily computerized administrative system that was put in place from the beginning. This system has enabled the tax administration to successfully 'match' VAT invoices, thus providing a powerful (if costly) check on evasion (Jenkins, Kuo, and Sun 2003). It has also enabled Taiwan to be one of the few VAT jurisdictions in the world that do not collect any VAT at import from registered tax-payers. Instead, as with cross-border sales within the European Union and in Québec, Canada, VAT is deferred until the goods are sold. While other countries, such as Singapore, treat imports by certain major exporters in this way, Taiwan appears to be the only instance in which such deferral of VAT on imports by registrants is a generalized practice.[3]

Japan's VAT, adopted in 1989, differed even more from the by-then well-established 'world norm,' which was modeled to a considerable extent on European experience. Not only did Japan impose a standard national VAT rate of only 3%, it also imposed a 1% 'local' tax collected by the national government but with all the proceeds being distributed to local govern-ments.[4] Even more interesting, in contrast to all other VAT countries, Japan does not use the invoice-credit method but instead applies a 'subtraction' approach, under which taxpayers deduct total purchases (including pur-chases from exempt businesses) rather than adding up VAT actually paid on purchase invoices (Schenk 1995). This treatment is especially interesting since the threshold of VAT was quite high – about U.S.$250,000 – when VAT was introduced, compared to, say, the zero threshold in Korea. The subtrac-tion approach means that even purchases from the many small businesses excluded from the VAT system, on which no VAT is charged, give rise to

---

[3] As World Bank (2003) notes, Ukraine in effect did much the same by allowing imports to be cleared provided imports promised to pay within 90 days of release – a practice that appears to have facilitated fraud in some cases.

[4] Of course, other countries (e.g., Germany, Morocco) similarly distribute a share (or, in Australia, all) of VAT proceeds to subnational governments, but Japan's characterization of a certain number of percentage points of its VAT as 'local' appears to be unique.

'input credits' – not in the sense of actual credits, of course, but in the sense that the value of all inputs, including those from unregistered firms, are deductible in determining the base on which 'output VAT' is levied.

China also followed its own unique path when it introduced a VAT in 1994. As we discussed earlier, China's VAT is not the destination-based consumption-type tax found in most countries but rather an origin-based production-type tax that also excludes from the tax base many services subject to a separate business tax collected by local governments. China also did not extend zero-rating automatically to all exports but instead allowed different presumptive credits on different types of exports, a practice that gave rise to some external criticism (as being equivalent to subsidization of such favored exports as semiconductors) and has subsequently been moved closer to world norms. Only in 2004 did a move toward a consumption-type VAT begin in three northeast provinces as part of an effort to stimulate investment in this region. To keep costs under control, even in these provinces tax credits were applied only to selected investments and were limited to firms that were in business prior to the introduction of the reform (Wong and Bird 2005). The provinces were required to cover 25% of the cost of crediting VAT on investment – the same share as they receive of VAT revenues. Another interesting feature in China is that all taxpayers are required to use official VAT invoices in order to claim input credits.[5]

Finally, the ongoing VAT saga in India also deserves mention. As we discussed in Chapter 8, India has been attempting for decades to rationalize its incredibly complex consumption tax structure. At the central level, where for constitutional reasons only goods are taxed, its long-standing extended excise system first was changed to a sort of VAT at the manufacturing level (MANVAT) and then moved on through what was called MODVAT to its present CenVAT. In effect, India's central sales tax has gradually been moving closer to a full VAT on goods, although it is still some distance away from this goal. More recently, after many years of discussion and a few abortive attempts in some individual states (e.g., Maharashtra), India in 2005 began a major attempt to reform the important sales taxes imposed at the state level by introducing more uniform state VATs in 21 of the 29 states, though these levies are also still clearly some distance away from that goal, and in particular it is not clear how this system will deal with the critical problem of interstate trade (Rao and Rao 2005).

---

[5] China has an exceptionally ferocious tax administration. Li (2004) reports that, since 1994 when the current VAT came into effect, nearly 200 persons have been sentenced to death for VAT fraud, and most of them have been executed.

Much more could be said about each of the cases mentioned as well as about the local peculiarities of VATs in other Asian countries. But even this summary discussion suffices to underline one of our main points in this book: there is much to be learned from close study of the very diverse experience with VAT found not just in Asia but throughout the world. Numerous experiments with different VAT structures and administrative techniques have been going on for years all over the world. Much has been learned, but as we have often noted, there is much more that as yet we do not fully understand.

VAT, YES, BUT WHAT VAT?

Much of this book may be read, by those so inclined, as a state-of-the-art survey pointing out a variety of researchable questions. Many readers, however, are probably less interested in finding out what we do not know about VAT than they are in learning what we do know. In Chapter 3, we argued that a VAT was usually the right way for developing and transitional countries to impose general consumption taxes. Throughout the book, however, we have in effect shown that there really is no such thing as 'a VAT.' Rather, there are many possible VATs, both in principle and, as we have just discussed, in practice. So the real question is, What type of VAT should any particular country adopt?

One way to approach this question is to take the standard IMF treatise on the 'modern VAT' (Ebrill et al. 2001) seriously. That book argues persuasively that the core feature of a modern VAT is that it is a 'self-assessed' tax. This argument is inarguably correct: like all mass taxes in developed countries, a good tax is one that essentially 'runs itself,' that is, one that, once established, basically becomes part of standard business operations so that the role of the tax administration is not to assess tax but to guard the 'borders' of the system and to verify that those who should be 'self-assessing' are behaving as they should be.

Ebrill et al. (2001) set out seven 'preconditions' that must be established for such a self-assessed tax to function properly, as set out in the left-hand column of Table 12.1. The right-hand column of this table is our capsule summary of what conditions might obtain in a country that failed the precondition test completely. To add some verisimilitude to what might otherwise be a bald and unconvincing narrative, we have, no doubt provocatively, filled in the space between these two columns with a totally subjective appraisal (on an arbitrary scale ranging from 1 – poor – to 5 – excellent) assessing the extent to these preconditions seem to be

Table 12.1. *Good and Bad Prospects for VAT Success: A Subjective Appraisal*

Preconditions	Canada	South Africa	Jamaica	Colombia	Egypt	Ukraine	Liberia	The Opposite
Simple, clear, stable law	5	5	3	2	1	1	1	Bad, changing, law
Good taxpayer service	5	4	2	2	1	1	1	No service
Simple procedures	5	4	3	2	1	1	1	Obscure and complex
Effective enforcement	5	3	2	2	1	1	1	No real enforcement
Reasonable audit	5	3	2	2	1	1	1	No audit
Strict penalties	5	3	2	2	1	1	1	No effective penalties
Good review	5	3	1	1	1	1	1	No review

Note: 5 = excellent; 4 = very good; 3 = good; 2 = fair; 1 = poor.

218

satisfied in the countries listed, in all of which we have some recent personal experience.

In summary, Table 12.1 suggests (1) that a modern VAT should work well in Canada; (2) that a 'standard' VAT model should also work, although in some ways not all that well in Jamaica and Colombia; and (3) that (for very different reasons not spelled out in the table) this model is much less likely to prove successful in Egypt, Ukraine, and Liberia. As we discuss later, Liberia does not have a VAT at present. South Africa, about which we know less than we do about the other countries, is of course a sort of 'dual economy' in the sense that it combines a well-developed modern sector – to which VAT mainly applies – and a large 'small business' sector, where, as in most countries, the reality and impact of the country's well-structured VAT are quite different. These summary remarks are of course based not only on our (inevitably only partially informed) assessment about the extent to which the various preconditions are met or not in the different countries shown but also on our assessment (based on varying degrees of involvement and knowledge) of how well we think VAT actually does work in these countries. Still, we doubt that most informed observers would disagree with the picture shown in this table suggesting that many countries that already have VATs fall far short of the 'ideal' conditions for a 'modern' 'self-assessed' tax.

Much the same conclusion emerges from any systematic comparison of what might be called the 'fiscal architecture' (Wallace 2003) that underlies any tax system. The conditions set out in Table 12.1 relate only to the structure and functioning of the tax administration and not to the underlying economic and political structure of the country within which that administration has to operate. But one cannot take a tax administration out of its environment. If one takes into consideration not only the 'quality' of the tax administration (as in Table 12.1) but also the size and location of the country, the level and distribution of income and wealth, the importance and pattern of international trade, the relative size and nature of the 'informal' sector, the relative importance of 'final' and 'intermediate' sales, as well as more nebulous but nonetheless important factors such as the prevailing level of 'trust' in government and 'taxpayer morale' two additional points become clear.

First, the level, structure, and effectiveness of taxation – including VAT – vary enormously from country to country and over time within countries as these underlying factors change (Bird, Martinez-Vazquez, and Torgler 2006). Second, the nature and effectiveness of any tax administration will also vary with these factors as well as with policy choices, as will not only the extent to which conditions such as those set out in Table 12.1 are satisfied but also what satisfying such conditions means in terms of providing a foundation for a modern self-assessed tax such as VAT (Vázquez-Caro 2005). To design and implement a modern tax such as VAT, one must, as Ebrill et al. (2001) say, satisfy conditions such as those set out in Table 12.1 – that is, have the right kind of tax structure and tax administration. However, as we discussed in Chapter 11, to get to this position a country may sometimes require fundamental changes in underlying economic and political conditions. In effect, one must have the right kind of clientele (taxpayers) to make a self-assessed VAT work as it should.

If one adds these general administrative and political economy considerations to the many criticisms recently made of VATs in developing countries as inequitable, inefficient, and growth-retarding (see Chapters 4 and 5), the conclusion may seem to be that only a developed country should ever have a VAT. Nonetheless, as argued earlier, we think VAT is the right way to impose general consumption taxes in almost all circumstances. Our basic argument is simple: (1) almost every developing and transitional country needs a general consumption tax; (2) VAT is the best form of such a tax – the one with the fewest bad effects. The case for VAT remains strong.

For this reason, for example, even in the least developed of the countries mentioned in Table 12.1 (Liberia), it can be argued that the existing limited general sales tax imposed on manufacturing and imports should be moved closer to a normal VAT by replacing the present 'ring' system of exempting imports by registered manufacturers by a VAT credit system under which VAT would be applied to all taxable imports and this import VAT could then be credited (by registered firms) against output VAT due. Such a change makes both administrative and economic sense. Administratively, it would no longer be the (very weak) tax office that had to prove that a duty-free import had been improperly claimed. Instead, a taxpayer would have to demonstrate, by filing a return, that it was entitled to offset VAT on imports against VAT on sales. Economically, evidence in many countries in Africa strongly suggests that a high proportion of potentially creditable sales tax levied on imports is not in fact utilized as a deduction against tax due on sales in large part because the supplies are being diverted to the 'informal sector' (Glenday 2006).[6] To the extent that the informal sector is being 'fed' by the diversion of tax-free imports, stopping this leakage would constitute a major step towards restoring the competitive balance between formal and informal sectors. Even a very poor country such as Liberia can, with a limited VAT, thus to some extent both have more cake (revenue) and at the same time stimulate a healthier pattern of development. What more can one ask?

[6] Keen (2006a) sets out the analytical underpinnings of this argument in detail.

CONCLUSION

To return to another theme that has run throughout this book, whether one is concerned with the question of whether a country such as Liberia should adopt a VAT or the more pervasive question of how countries such as Ukraine and Egypt might improve existing VATs to make them more administrable, more efficient, and often more equitable, it is critical to pay close attention to the many particular features of both tax design and tax administration we have discussed earlier. Thresholds, for example, should not be set too low (Chapter 7). On the other hand, self-selected 'small' taxpayers should not be hived off into a separate 'simple' system and forgotten, as too often happens (Chapter 10). One rate may not be enough in light of distributional considerations, but including numerous 'excise' rates in a VAT system is a mistake, as is striving for too much equity through excessive domestic zero-rating. Such details matter, and striking the right balance on them for any particular country is not a simple task.

There is a huge gap between what we need to know to do the VAT 'right' in developing and transitional countries and what we now know. This book makes only a partial attempt to fill this gap. We cannot do much of the job that needs to be done. But we can and do attempt to define its importance in some detail and to suggest both some partial answers and some promising lines of inquiry. One question that needs more exploration, for example, is whether there is a taxonomy within which countries can be placed in designing VAT. One size might not fit all. But might 8 (or 6, or 12) VAT structures encompass all possible designs that would be both feasible and desirable? Some interesting pioneer work along these lines, albeit only in general conceptual terms, was done some years ago (Shoup 1990). Subsequently, however, the question of whether (say) eight sizes (VAT designs) might fit all has been left aside in the 'rush to VAT.' It is time to go back and take another look at this question, and we do so to some extent in this book.[7]

A second approach that might prove rewarding might be to recast the familiar (if usually implicit) decision-tree approach to tax design.[8] For example, one might first set out more clearly and in more detail than is usual the implications of different decisions that may be made with respect to critical 'nodal' points (e.g., with respect to zero-rating) for other aspects

---

[7] For an attempt to sketch such a taxonomy with respect to the almost contemporaneous 'rush to decentralization' in many countries, see Devarajan and Reinikka (2003).

[8] For an example of the application of this approach to the design of user charges, see Bird and Tsiopoulos (1996).

of VAT design. Next, the optimal sequence of such decisions for particular countries (or groups of countries) might be assessed – for instance in terms of 'best practice.'[9] Ideally, such an analysis would include sensitivity analysis assessing how dependent the 'rightness' of particular decisions is with respect to different characteristics of the environment within which the VAT is expected to function. Alternatively, this approach might perhaps be viewed as a 'risk analysis' since the degree of reliability of our knowledge with respect to various salient characteristics affecting outcomes is likely to differ widely.

Many elements of such an approach are to be found in the existing literature, notably in the useful IMF book *The Modern VAT* (Ebrill et al. 2001). To a considerable extent we follow similar lines in this book, which may thus be read in part as a complement to and commentary on the Ebrill book. As yet, however, surprisingly little has been done either to set out the relevant decision points and their interdependence in a systematic fashion or to quantify them in any meaningful way – although some interesting recent work on VAT thresholds provides a useful first step in this direction.[10] Much more such work is needed before the many countries around the world currently facing critical VAT issues have anything to turn to other than 'expert opinion' – biased as it inevitably often is by the particular experience of the experts in question – in formulating policy decisions. In this book we have both discussed some 'nodal' decisions in which the 'right' way (in given circumstances) seems clear and highlighted some of the critical questions that remain to be resolved by future investigation.

To improve the VATs now in place in developing and transitional countries around the world requires getting the details right for the case at hand. Only thus can countries begin to move closer to the conceptual ideal of a smoothly functioning self-assessed general consumption tax that not only does not impede economic growth but provides the basis for a good tax administration lie. This task can be done, and indeed to a considerable extent has been well done in many respects in a few countries (notably, Chile and Singapore). But many more developing and transitional countries need better VATs if they are to establish a sound revenue system for present and future prosperity. There is much to be done.

---

[9] For a recent interesting example of this approach in the field of tax administration, see Vázquez-Caro (2005).

[10] See Keen and Mintz (2004). Another useful example of such work, although – like this book – less formally rigorous in structure, is Harrison and Krelove (2005).

Annex

Table A.1. *VAT – When, Where, and at What Rates*

	Date VAT Introduced	Standard Rate at Introduction	Standard Rate (%)	Other Rates (%)[a] (reduced or increased)
Albania	1996	12.5	20	—
Algeria	1992	13	17	7
Argentina	1975	16	21	10.5, 27
Armenia	1992	28	20	—
Australia	2000	10	10	—
Austria	1973	8	20, 16[b]	10, 12
Azerbaijan	1992	28	18	—
Bangladesh	1991	15	15	10–350[c]
Barbados	1997	15	15	7.5[d]
Belarus	1992	28	18	10
Belgium	1971	18	21	6, 12
Benin	1991	18	18	—
Bolivia	1973	10	13[e]	—
Bosnia and Herzegovina	2006	17	17	—
Botswana	2002	10	10	—
Brazil	1967	17.6	20.5[f]	Multiple
Bulgaria	1994	18	20	—
Burkina Faso	1993	15	18	—
Cambodia	1999	10	10	—
Cameroon	1999	18.7	19.3	—
Canada[g]	1991	7	6	—
Cape Verde	2004	15	15	—
Central African Republic	2001	18	18	—
Chad	2000	18	18	—
Chile	1975	20	19	—

(continued)

Table A.1 *(continued)*

	Date VAT Introduced	Standard Rate at Introduction	Standard Rate (%)	Other Rates (%)[a] (reduced or increased)
China	1994	17	17[h]	4, 6, 13[i]
Colombia	1975	10	16	2–45
Congo, Republic of	1997	18	18.9	5
Cook Islands	1997	n/a	10	1
Costa Rica	1975	10	13	5, 10
Côte d'Ivoire	1960	8	18	—
Croatia	1998	22	22	—
Cyprus	1992	5	15	5, 8
Czech Republic	1993	23	19	5
Denmark	1967	10	25	5[j]
Dominican Republic	1983	6	16	—
Ecuador	1970	4	12	—
Egypt	1991	10	10	5, 20, 30
El Salvador	1992	10	13	—
Equatorial Guinea	2005	15	15	—
Estonia	1992	10	18	5
Ethiopia	2003	15	15	—
Faroe Islands	1992	n/a	25	—
Fiji	1992	10	12.5	—
Finland	1994	22	22	8, 17
France	1948	13.6	19.6[k]	2.1, 5.5[l]
French Polynesia*	1998	n/a	10, 16[m]	6
Gabon	1995	18	18	10
Georgia	1992	28	18	—
Germany	1968	10	16	7
Ghana	1998	10	12.5	—
Greece	1987	18	19	4.5, 9[n]
Guadeloupe and Martinique	n/a	n/a	8.5	2.1
Guatemala	1983	7	12	5
Guinea	1996	18	18	—
Guinea-Bissau	n/a	n/a	10	—
Haiti	1982	7	10	—
Honduras	1976	3	12	15
Hungary	1988	25	20	5, 15
Iceland	1990	24.5	24.5	14
India[o]	2005	12.5	12.5	Multiple
Indonesia	1985	10	10	—
Ireland	1972	16.4	21	4.8, 13.5
Israel	1976	8	16.5	—
Italy	1973	12	20	4, 10

	Date VAT Introduced	Standard Rate at Introduction	Standard Rate (%)	Other Rates (%)[a] (reduced or increased)
Jamaica	1991	10	16.5	8.5[p]
Japan[q]	1989	3	5	—
Jordan	2001	13	16	4
Kazakhstan	1992	28	15	—
Kenya	1990	17	16	14
Korea (Republic)	1977	13	10	—
Kyrgyz Republic	1992	28	20	—
Latvia	1992	12	18	5
Lebanon	2002	10	10	—
Lesotho	2003	14	14	5, 15[r]
Lithuania	1994	18	18	5, 9
Luxembourg	1970	8	15	3, 6, 12
Macedonia	2000	19	19	5
Madagascar	1994	20	20	—
Malawi	1989	35	17.5	—
Mali	1991	17	15	10
Malta	1995	15	18	5
Mauritania	1995	14	14	—
Mauritius	1998	10	15	—
Mexico	1980	10	15	10[s]
Moldova	1992	28	20	5, 8
Mongolia	1998	10	15	—
Morocco	1986	19	20	7, 10, 14
Mozambique	1999	17	17	—
Namibia	2000	15	15	—
Nepal	1997	10	13	—
Netherlands	1969	12	19	6
Netherlands Antilles*	1999	2	5	3
New Zealand	1986	10	12.5	—
Nicaragua	1975	6	15	—
Niger	1986	12	19	—
Nigeria*	1994	5	5	—
Norway	1970	20	25	8, 13
Pakistan	1990	12.5	15	—
Palestine Autonomous Areas*	1976	8	17	—
Panama	1977	5	5	15
Papua New Guinea	1999	10	10	—
Paraguay	1993	12	5, 10[t]	—
Peru	1973	20	19	—
Philippines	1988	10	12	—

(continued)

Table A.1 *(continued)*

	Date VAT Introduced	Standard Rate at Introduction	Standard Rate (%)	Other Rates (%)[a] (reduced or increased)
Poland	1993	22	22	3, 7
Portugal	1986	17	21	5, 12[u]
Romania	1993	18	19	9
Russia	1992	28	18	10
Rwanda	2001	15	18	—
Samoa	1994	10	12.5	—
Senegal	1980	20	18	—
Serbia/Montenegro[v]	2003	17, 20	17, 18	8
Singapore	1994	3	5	—
Slovak Republic	1993	23	19	—
Slovenia	1999	19	20	8.5
South Africa	1991	10	14	—
Spain	1986	12	16	4, 7[w]
Sri Lanka	1998	12.5	15	5, 18
Sudan	2000	10	10	—
Suriname*	1999	7	10[x]	8, 25
Sweden	1969	11.1	25	6, 12
Switzerland	1995	6.5	7.6	2.4, 3.6[y]
Taiwan	1986	5	5	—
Tajikistan	1992	28	20	—
Tanzania	1998	20	20	—
Thailand	1992	7	7	—
Togo	1995	18	18	—
Trinidad and Tobago	1990	15	15	—
Tunisia	1988	17	18	6, 10, 29
Turkey	1985	10	18	1, 8, 26, 40
Turkmenistan*[z]	1992	28	15	—
Uganda	1996	17	18	—
Ukraine	1992	28	20	—
United Kingdom	1973	10	17.5	5
Uruguay	1968	14	23	14
Uzbekistan	1992	30	20	15
Vanuatu	1998	12.5	12.5	—
Venezuela	1993	10	14	8–16.5
Vietnam	1999	10	10	5
Zambia	1995	20	17.5	—
Zimbabwe	2004	15	15	—

Notes: A dash indicates that there are no rates other than the standard rate. An asterisk denotes jurisdictions that are an exception to the rule that countries levying VAT-type taxes generally zero-rate exports. "n/a" indicates information not available.

[a] Rates are in tax-exclusive form (i.e., specified as a proportion of the net of tax price).

[b] The standard rate of 16% applies in Jungholz and Mittelberg.

^{c} Rates ranging from 10% to 350% represent supplementary taxes on luxury goods and services.

^{d} The reduced rate of 7.5% applies to hotel accommodation.

^{e} The official listed tax rate of 14.943% applies to the taxable amount inclusive of VAT.

^{f} The formal rates are tax-inclusive. The figures shown in the table are the most common rate of state VAT (ICMS), which is levied at 25 rates from 1% to 250%. There are also a limited national VAT (IPI) levied on the industrial sector at rates ranging up to 350% as well as a local tax (ISS) on some services.

^{g} The federal GST was lowered to 6% in 2006. Three provinces applied a VAT (HST) jointly with the federal VAT at a combined rate of 14%. Québéc levies its own VAT (QST). Five provinces apply their own retail sales taxes. In one province (Alberta) and three northern territories, the federal GST is the only sales tax.

^{h} VAT is imposed on the supply of tangible goods and specified services. Credit is allowed for investment goods only in a few provinces. A local business tax is applied to some services at rates of 5%–10%.

^{i} Small producers and traders taxed at these rates cannot claim VAT credits.

^{j} Since only 20% of the taxable base is taken into account for 'artists' products,' the effective rate is 5%.

^{k} Rate is 8.5% in DOM (Départements d'Outre-Mer), excluding French Guyana.

^{l} Reduced rates in Corsica and DOM range from 0.9% to 13%.

^{m} VAT rates are 10% on services and 16% on goods. Exports of goods and services are exempt rather than zero-rated.

^{n} Rates up to 30% lower may be applied in some regions.

^{o} VAT was introduced in most (21) states in 2005. Reduced rates of 1% and 4% apply to certain goods. Other goods, mainly petroleum products, are subject to an increased rate that, depending on the state, may range from 15% to 40%. A central service tax applies to some services, and a low-rate central sales tax applies to interstate sales.

^{p} Motor vehicles are subject to higher rates of up to 113.95%.

^{q} Rate includes 1% local tax.

^{r} Reduced rate of 5% applies to electricity and telephone services.

^{s} Rate applies in frontier zones.

^{t} The standard rate of 10% applies to all supplies of goods and services unless a specific provision of the new tax law allows a reduced tax base that reduces the effective tax rate to 5%. Examples of supplies that qualify for a reduced base include international freight services and certain imports of goods.

^{u} In the Azores and Madeira the standard rate is 15% and the reduced rates are 4% and 8%.

^{v} VATs in Serbia and Montenegro were established in 2005 and 2003, respectively. The standard rate is 17% in Montenegro and 18% in Serbia. The reduced rate applies only in Serbia.

^{w} The Canary Islands have a standard rate of 4%, a reduced rate of 2%, and an increased rate of 12%.

^{x} A rate of 8% applies to services, and a rate of 25% applies on certain luxury goods not produced in Suriname.

^{y} The reduced rate of 3.6% applies to the supply of accommodation.

^{z} Certain exports to CIS countries are not zero-rated.

Sources: Table A.1 is based largely on various publications of the International Bureau of Fiscal Documentation, supplemented by IBFD (2006); Annacondia and van der Corput (2005); Ernst and Young (2006), PricewaterhouseCoopers (2006), and information obtained directly from a few countries. In most cases, the 'current' rates shown relate to late 2005 or early 2006.

Table A.2. *VAT – Some Indicators*

Country	GDP per capita (U.S.$ 1995)	Private Consumption (% GDP)	Sales, Turnover, or VAT (% GDP)	Total Revenue (% GDP)	Total Tax Revenue (% GDP)	VAT / Total Tax (%)	VAT Efficiency	VAT Productivity
Albania	915.3	90.5	6.2	19.4	14.8	42.2	0.35	0.31
Algeria	1,588.0	49.4	1.4	32.4	30.3	4.7	0.17	0.08
Argentina	8,150.0	70.3	3.9	14.0	12.7	30.9	0.27	0.19
Australia	23,187.4	60.0	2.4	24.1	22.0	10.8	0.40	0.24
Azerbaijan	388.7	73.4	3.6	17.7	16.8	21.4	0.27	0.20
Belarus	1,358.2	58.6	5.9	29.1	26.8	21.9	0.50	0.29
Belgium	29,993.7	54.1	8.7	43.9	43.0	20.1	0.76	0.41
Bolivia	959.5	76.1	5.4	17.9	14.4	37.1	0.47	0.36
Brazil	4,539.7	61.7	2.0	25.9	20.6	9.9	0.16	0.10
Bulgaria	1,467.7	69.3	8.4	33.6	26.2	32.0	0.60	0.42
Cameroon	661.9	71.1	3.2	16.1	12.4	26.0	0.24	0.17
Canada	22,118.6	56.5	2.7	21.8	19.7	13.4	0.67	0.38
Chile	5,241.9	65.9	8.0	22.0	18.0	44.4	0.64	0.42
China	772.8	46.8	4.1	6.8	6.4	63.8	0.52	0.24
Colombia	2,319.8	63.9	4.5	12.2	10.6	42.3	0.44	0.28
Congo, Rep.	780.5	40.1	4.1	25.3	8.2	49.9	0.57	0.23
Costa Rica	3,851.9	66.9	4.6	20.4	18.2	25.2	0.53	0.35
Cote d'Ivoire	767.5	71.3	2.1	17.2	16.6	12.8	0.15	0.11
Croatia	5,025.3	58.4	14.8	43.1	40.9	36.1	1.15	0.67
Cyprus	13,509.0	67.2	4.8	31.4	25.0	19.2	0.48	0.32
Czech Republic	5,254.8	53.4	7.0	32.6	31.6	22.3	0.60	0.32
Denmark	37,586.6	49.2	9.9	37.8	33.0	29.9	0.80	0.39

228

El Salvador	1,748.6	86.6	11.4	10.6	52.8	0.50	0.43
Estonia	4,251.3	56.9	31.2	28.4	31.0	0.86	0.49
Ethiopia	111.5	77.8	20.6	13.3	16.1	0.18	0.14
Finland	30,511.0	49.7	32.1	27.8	30.4	0.77	0.38
Georgia	455.4	89.1	11.4	9.7	40.0	0.22	0.19
Germany	31,887.2	58.2	21.9	18.9	18.0	0.36	0.21
Greece	12,693.5	70.6	23.7	21.9	35.9	0.62	0.44
Guatemala	1,547.3	84.5	10.0	9.9	45.8	0.45	0.38
Guinea	602.6	77.6	11.6	10.9	5.5	0.04	0.03
Hungary	5,138.4	63.2	37.7	33.8	24.6	0.53	0.33
Iceland	30,206.7	58.6	30.6	26.4	35.6	0.66	0.38
Indonesia	993.2	69.7	17.3	16.1	18.4	0.42	0.30
Israel	16,657.3	56.5	42.2	36.2	30.2	1.07	0.61
Italy	20,391.4	60.1	40.5	38.2	15.6	0.50	0.30
Jamaica	2,157.3	65.8	33.1	25.2	36.5	0.93	0.61
Jordan	1,609.7	75.5	25.6	18.4	25.8	0.48	0.36
Kazakhstan	1,375.0	69.2	12.6	9.6	41.6	0.36	0.25
Kenya	335.1	74.7	25.8	21.2	23.5	0.42	0.31
Kyrgyz Republic	385.0	77.2	16.1	12.7	42.2	0.35	0.27
Latvia	2,464.8	63.1	31.6	27.4	30.0	0.73	0.46
Lesotho	540.5	84.8	44.1	34.4	13.8	0.40	0.34
Lithuania	2,125.5	63.2	25.8	24.2	35.9	0.76	0.48
Madagascar	242.0	85.4	11.1	10.7	14.7	0.09	0.08
Malta	9,874.4	62.9	33.0	27.7	19.2	0.56	0.36
Mauritius	4,011.4	62.7	22.2	18.8	21.9	0.44	0.27
Mexico	3,657.2	67.2	13.9	12.4	26.5	0.33	0.22
Moldova	634.8	87.0	26.9	23.0	37.6	0.50	0.43
Mongolia	424.4	66.3	24.2	17.2	32.0	0.55	0.37
Morocco	1,384.5	63.0	29.1	24.4	23.1	0.45	0.28

(continued)

Table A.2 (continued)

Country	GDP per capita (U.S.$ 1995)	Private Consumption (% GDP)	Sales, Turnover, or VAT (% GDP)	Total Revenue (% GDP)	Total Tax Revenue (% GDP)	VAT / Total Tax (%)	VAT Efficiency	VAT Productivity
Nepal	234.9	76.8	2.4	10.4	8.6	28.2	0.32	0.24
New Zealand	17,481.3	60.9	6.3	31.9	29.6	21.4	0.83	0.51
Nicaragua	437.4	88.2	9.3	31.9	28.7	32.5	0.70	0.62
Norway	37,509.9	46.3	9.0	41.5	33.9	26.7	0.81	0.38
Pakistan	507.8	74.1	2.7	16.3	12.8	21.4	0.25	0.18
Papua New Guinea	960.1	61.9	0.0	22.7	21.2	0.2	0.01	0.00
Paraguay	1,745.5	81.5	4.4	16.0	10.2	43.2	0.54	0.44
Peru	2,322.4	70.9	6.4	16.8	14.0	45.9	0.50	0.36
Philippines	1,135.2	68.4	1.7	16.3	14.7	11.9	0.26	0.17
Poland	3,536.8	63.3	7.8	33.2	29.8	26.2	0.56	0.35
Portugal	12,507.0	62.0	7.5	34.8	31.1	24.0	0.63	0.39
Romania	1,309.2	81.7	6.1	29.9	26.2	23.2	0.39	0.32
Russian Federation	2,285.6	53.1	4.7	21.8	18.7	25.0	0.44	0.23
Singapore	26,478.0	39.1	1.4	31.0	15.1	9.4	0.90	0.35
Slovak Republic	4,191.8	54.5	7.3	36.3	32.0	22.9	0.67	0.37
South Africa	3,970.6	63.0	6.0	27.2	25.6	23.6	0.68	0.43
Sri Lanka	868.4	71.6	3.6	17.2	14.7	24.7	0.25	0.18
Sudan	300.4	83.7	1.1	7.7	6.3	16.7	0.13	0.11
Sweden	30,207.4	49.0	6.6	39.1	34.3	19.3	0.54	0.26
Switzerland	45,864.8	61.0	3.8	24.7	23.0	16.6	0.82	0.50

Tajikistan	362.5	76.2	5.5	10.0	9.6	57.5	0.36	0.27
Thailand	2,722.9	55.1	3.6	16.1	14.1	25.3	0.93	0.51
Tunisia	2,378.2	60.6	6.9	29.6	26.0	26.6	0.63	0.38
Turkey	3,096.7	66.9	6.1	26.1	21.2	28.7	0.51	0.34
Uganda	341.1	79.9	2.1	11.6	10.8	19.2	0.15	0.12
Ukraine	857.0	56.1	7.1	25.2	22.3	31.9	0.63	0.36
United Kingdom	21,684.5	65.4	6.7	36.5	34.6	19.3	0.58	0.38
Uruguay	6,270.1	73.1	7.8	28.8	25.9	30.2	0.46	0.34
Vanuatu	1,259.1	60.9	6.4	22.8	20.1	31.8	0.84	0.51
Venezuela	3,367.4	68.1	4.7	18.6	13.3	35.3	0.43	0.29
Vietnam	353.0	68.5	3.8	19.6	16.4	23.3	0.56	0.38
Zambia	389.8	83.6	5.4	18.7	18.1	29.9	0.37	0.31
All countries (83 countries)	7,178.2	66.6	5.4	24.5	21.0	27.3	0.51	0.32
Western Hemisphere (15 countries)	3,221.1	72.7	5.6	19.5	16.3	35.9	0.49	0.36
Countries w/GDP between U.S.$1,500 and U.S.$5,000 (23 countries)	2,847.4	65.4	5.6	23.4	20.0	30.0	0.55	0.36

Notes: Data are averaged for the period 1998–2000; data are for the central government only.

Sources: Government Finance Statistics, IMF 2003; World Development Indicators, World Bank.

References

Acemoglu, D. (2005) "Constitutions, Politics, and Economics: A Review Essay on Persson and Tabellini's *The Economic Effects of Constitutions*," *Journal of Economic Literature*, 43 (4): 1025–48.

Afonso, J., and L. de Mello (2000) "Brazil: An Evolving Federation," Paper presented to IMF Seminar on Decentralization, Washington, DC <http://www.imf.org/external/pubs/ft/seminar/2000/fiscal/afonso.pdf>

Agha, A., and J. Haughton (1996) "Designing VAT Systems: Some Efficiency Considerations," *Review of Economics and Statistics*, 78 (2): 303–8.

Aguirre, C. A., and P. Shome (1988) "The Mexican Value-Added Tax (VAT): Methodology for Calculating the Tax Base," *National Tax Journal*, 41 (4): 543–54.

Ahmad, E., and N. Stern (1987) "Alternative Sources of Government Revenue: Illustrations from India, 1979–80," in D. Newbery and N. Stern, eds., *The Theory of Taxation for Developing Countries* (New York: Published for the World Bank by Oxford University Press), 281–332.

Ainsworth, R. T. (2005) "The One-Stop Shop for VAT and RST: Common Approaches to EU-U.S. Consumption Tax Issues," *Tax Notes International*, 37 (8): 693–714.

Aizenman, J., and Y. Jinjarak (2005) "The Collection Efficiency of the Value Added Tax: Theory and International Evidence," Working Paper 11539, National Bureau of Economic Research, Cambridge, MA, July.

Aizenman, J., and Y. Jinjarak (2006) "Globalization and Developing Countries – a Shrinking Tax Base?" Working Paper 11933, National Bureau of Economic Research, Cambridge, MA, January.

Alesina, A., and G. Angeletos (2003) "Fairness and Redistribution: U.S. versus Europe," Working Paper 9502, National Bureau of Economic Research, Cambridge, MA, February.

Alesina, A., and R. Wacziarg (1998) "Openness, Country Size and Government," *Journal of Public Economics*, 69 (3): 305–21.

Alm, J., and H. López-Castaño (2005) "Payroll Taxes in Colombia," in R. M. Bird, J. M. Poterba, and J. Slemrod, eds., *Fiscal Reform in Colombia: Problems and Prospects* (Cambridge, MA: MIT Press), 225–45.

Alm, J., J. Martinez-Vazquez, and F. Schneider (2004) "'Sizing' the Problem of the Hard-to-Tax," in J. Alm, J. Martinez-Vazquez, and S. Wallace, eds., *Taxing the Hard-to-Tax* (Amsterdam: Elsevier), 12–55.

Angermann, F. (2000) "Tax Aspects of Investing in Real Estate in Germany," *Bulletin for International Fiscal Documentation*, 54 (4): 186–96.

Annacondia, F., and W. van der Corput (2003) "VAT Registration Thresholds in Europe," *International VAT Monitor*, 14 (1): 71–72.

Annacondia, F., and W. van der Corput (2005) "Overview of General Turnover Taxes and Tax Rates," *International VAT Monitor*, 16 (2): 2–11.

Appleyard, D. R., A. J. Field, Jr., and S. L. Cobb (2006) *International Economics*, 5th ed. (New York: McGraw-Hill/Irwin).

Artana, D., and Naranjo, F. (2003) *Fiscal Policy Issues in Jamaica: Budgetary Institutions, the Tax System, and Public Debt Management*, Economic and Sector Study Series, Region 3 (Washington, DC: Inter-American Development Bank).

Auditor General (1999) *Report of the Auditor General of Canada* (Ottawa: Government of Canada).

Auerbach, A. J., and R. H. Gordon (2002) "Taxation of Financial Services under a VAT," *American Economic Review (Papers and Proceedings)*, 92 (2): 411–16.

Aujean, M., P. Jenkins, and S. Poddar (1999) "A New Approach to Public Sector Bodies," *International VAT Monitor*, 10 (4): 144–49.

Auriol, E., and M. Warlters (2005) "Taxation Base in Developing Countries," *Journal of Public Economics*, 89 (4): 625–46.

Australia (2001) *International Benchmarking of GST Administration* (Canberra: Australian Taxation Office). <http://www.ato.gov.au/fsmke/gstadmin.pdf>

Australia (2003) *Tax Basics for Non-Profit Organizations* (Canberra: Australian Taxation Office). <http://www.ato.gov.au/content/downloads/N7966.pdf>

Baer, K., O. P. Benon, and J. A. Toro Rivera (2002) *Improving Large Taxpayers' Compliance: A Review of Country Experience*. Occasional Paper 215 (Washington, DC: International Monetary Fund).

Baer, K., V. P. Summers, and E. M. Sunley (1996) "A Destination VAT for CIS Trade," *MOCT-MOST, Economic Policy in Transitional Countries*, 6 (3): 87–106.

Bagchi, A. (2005) "State VATs in Operation: Promises and Problems," *ICRA Bulletin: Money and Finance*, January–June, 29–44.

Bagchi, A., R. M. Bird, and A. Das-Gupta (1995) "An Economic Approach to Tax Administration Reform," Discussion Paper 3, International Centre for Tax Studies, Faculty of Management, University of Toronto, November. <http://www.rotman.utoronto.ca/iib/icts/ICTS03.pdf>

Bagchi, A., and S. Poddav (2006) "GST for India: Some Basic Questions," Times News Network, September 14. <http://economictimes.indiatimes.com/articleshow/1988867.cms>

Bahl, R., R. M. Bird, and M. B. Walker (2003) "The Uneasy Case for Discriminatory Taxation of Carbonated Beverages: The Case of Ireland," *Public Finance Review*, 31 (5): 510–33.

Bakker, C., and P. Chronican (1985) *Financial Services and the GST: A Discussion Paper* (Wellington: Victoria University Press for the Institute for Policy Studies).

Barlow, R., and W. Snyder (1994) "The Tax That Failed: The VAT in Niger," *Public Budgeting & Finance*, 14 (3): 77–89.

Bartlett, B. (2004) "Agenda for Tax Reform," *Tax Notes* 105 (12): 1531–39.

Baunsgaard, T., and M. Keen (2005) "Tax Revenue and (or?) Trade Liberalization," Working Paper WP/05/112, International Monetary Fund, Washington, DC, June.

Bennett, R. J. (1991) "The New VAT on Construction of Commercial Property: The Fall-Out on Urban Regeneration," *Fiscal Studies*, 12 (1): 78–87.

Berhan, B. A., and G. P. Jenkins (2005) "The High Cost of Controlling GST and VAT Evasion," *Canadian Tax Journal*, 53 (3): 720–36.

Best, M. H. (1976) "Political Power and Tax Revenues in Central America," *Journal of Development Economics*, 3 (1): 49–82.

Beyer, V. L. (2001) "Japan's Consumption Tax: Settled in to Stay," *Tax Notes International*, 22 (8): 921–25.

Bibi, S., and J.-Y. Duclos (2004) "Poverty-Decreasing Indirect Tax Reforms: Evidence from Tunisia," CIRPEE Working Paper 04-03, Tunis, January.

Bird, R. M. (1970) *Taxation and Development: Lessons from Colombian Experience* (Cambridge, MA: Harvard University Press).

Bird, R. M. (1970a) *The Growth of Government Spending in Canada* (Toronto: Canadian Tax Foundation).

Bird, R. M. (1970b) "The Tax Kaleidoscope: Perspectives on Tax Reform in Canada," *Canadian Tax Journal*, 18 (5): 444–78.

Bird, R. M. (1976) *Charging for Public Services: A New Look at an Old Idea* (Toronto: Canadian Tax Foundation).

Bird, R. M. (1978) "Canada's Vanishing Death Taxes," *Osgoode Hall Law Journal*, 16 (1): 133–45.

Bird, R. M. (1982) "Closing the Scissors, or the Real Public Sector Has Two Sides," *National Tax Journal*, 35 (4): 477–81.

Bird, R. M. (1989) "The Administrative Dimension of Tax Reform in Developing Countries," in M. Gillis, ed., *Lessons from Tax Reform in Developing Countries* (Durham, NC: Duke University Press), 315–46.

Bird, R. M. (1991) "Sources of Indirect Tax Revenue in Jamaica," in R. Bahl, ed., *The Jamaican Tax Reform* (Cambridge, MA: Lincoln Institute of Land Policy), 461–77.

Bird, R. M. (1992) *Tax Policy and Economic Development* (Baltimore: Johns Hopkins University Press).

Bird, R. M. (1992a) "Taxing Tourism in Developing Countries," *World Development*, 20 (8): 1145–58.

Bird, R. M. (1993) "Federal-Provincial Taxation in Turbulent Times," *Canadian Public Administration*, 36 (4): 479–96.

Bird, R. M. (1994) "The Cost and Complexity of Canada's VAT: The GST in an International Perspective," *Tax Notes International*, 8 (1): 37–47.

Bird, R. M. (1994a) *Where Do We Go from Here? Alternatives to the GST* (Toronto: KPMG Centre for Government).

Bird, R. M. (1995) "Indirect Tax in Belarus: VAT by Subtraction," *Tax Notes International*, 11 (9): 589–95.

Bird, R. M. (1999) "Tax Policy and Tax Administration in Transitional Countries," in G. Lindencrona, S.-O. Lodin, and B. Wiman, eds., *International Studies in Taxation Law and Economics* (London: Kluwer Law International), 59–75.

Bird, R. M. (2000) "Tax Incentives for Investment in Developing Countries," in G. Perry, J. Whalley, and G. McMahon, eds., *Fiscal Reform and Structural Change in Developing Countries*, Vol. 1 (London: Macmillan for International Development Research Centre), 201–21.

Bird, R. M. (2001) *Intergovernmental Fiscal Relations in Latin America: Policy Designs and Policy Outcomes* (Washington, DC: Inter-American Development Bank).

Bird, R. M. (2002) "Why Tax Corporations?" *Bulletin for International Fiscal Documentation*, 56 (5): 194–203.

Bird, R. M. (2003) "A New Look at Local Business Taxes," *Tax Notes International*, 30 (7): 695–711.

Bird, R. M. (2003a) *Taxing Electronic Commerce: A Revolution in the Making*, C. D. Howe Institute Commentary 187 (Toronto: C. D. Howe Institute).

Bird, R. M. (2003b) "Taxation in Latin America: Reflections on Sustainability and the Balance between Efficiency and Equity," ITP Paper 0306, International Tax Program, Rotman School of Management, University of Toronto, June. <http://www.rotman.utoronto.ca/iib/ITP0306.pdf>

Bird, R. M. (2004) "Managing Tax Reform," *Bulletin for International Fiscal Documentation*, 58 (2): 42–55.

Bird, R. M. (2004a) "Administrative Dimensions of Tax Reform," *Asia-Pacific Tax Bulletin*, 10 (3): 134–50.

Bird, R. M. (2005) "Value-Added Taxes in Developing and Transitional Countries: Lessons and Questions," in R. Sthanumoorthy, ed., *State-Level VAT in India: Issues, Challenges and Experiences* (Hyderabad: ICFAI University Press), 220–48.

Bird, R. M. (2005a) "Taxing E-Commerce: The End of the Beginning?" *Bulletin for International Fiscal Documentation*, 59 (4): 130–40.

Bird, R. M. (2005b) "Taxing Sales Twice: International Experience with Multilevel Sales Taxes," *State Tax Notes*, 37 (11): 803–9.

Bird, R. M. (2005c) "VAT in Ukraine: An Interim Report," ITP Paper 0503 Revised; International Tax Program, Rotman School of Management, University of Toronto, December. <http://www.rotman.utoronto.ca/iib/ITP0503.pdf>

Bird, R. M. (2007) "VAT in Ukraine: An Interim Report," in R. W. McGee, ed., *Taxation and Public Finance in Transition and Developing Countries* (New York: Springer).

Bird, R. M., and S. Banta (2000) "Fiscal Sustainability and Fiscal Indicators in Transitional Countries," in A. Shapleigh, F. Andic, and S. Banta, eds., *Transition Economies and Fiscal Reforms. Proceedings of the Conference on Central and Eastern Europe and the New Independent States*, Istanbul, July 1999 (Washington, DC: USAID), 13–42.

Bird, R. M., and M. Casanegra de Jantscher, eds. (1992) *Improving Tax Administration in Developing Countries* (Washington, DC: International Monetary Fund).

Bird, R. M., and L. De Wulf (1973) "Taxation and Income Distribution in Latin America: A Critical Review of Empirical Studies," *IMF Staff Papers*, 20 (4): 639–82.

Bird, R. M., and R. D. Ebel, eds. (2007) *Fiscal Fragmentation in Decentralized Countries: Subsidiarity, Solidarity, and Asymmetry* (Cheltenham, UK: Edward Elgar).

Bird, R. M., and P.-P. Gendron (1998) "Dual VATs and Cross-Border Trade: Two Problems, One Solution?" *International Tax and Public Finance*, 5 (3): 429–42.

Bird, R. M., and P.-P. Gendron (2000) "CVAT, VIVAT and Dual VAT; Vertical 'Sharing' and Interstate Trade," *International Tax and Public Finance*, 7 (6): 753–61.

Bird, R. M., and P.-P. Gendron (2001) "VATs in Federal Countries: International Experience and Emerging Possibilities," *Bulletin for International Fiscal Documentation*, 55 (7): 293–309.

Bird, R. M., and P.-P. Gendron (2005) "VAT Revisited: A New Look at Value Added Taxation in Developing and Transitional Countries" (Washington, DC: USAID).

Bird, R. M., and J. Jun (2005) *Earmarking in Theory and Korean Practice*. ITIC Special Report (Washington, DC: International Tax and Investment Center).

Bird, R. M., J. Martinez-Vazquez, and B. Torgler (2006) "Societal Institutions and Tax Effort in Developing Countries," in J. Alm, J. Martinez-Vazquez, and M. Rider, eds., *The Challenges of Tax Reform in a Global Economy* (New York: Springer), 283–338.

Bird, R. M., and K. J. McKenzie (2001) *Taxing Business: A Provincial Affair?* C. D. Howe Institute Commentary 154 (Toronto: C. D. Howe Institute).

Bird, R. M., and B. D. Miller (1989) "The Incidence of Indirect Taxation on Low-Income Households in Jamaica," *Economic Development and Cultural Change*, 37 (2): 393–409.

Bird, R. M., and J. M. Mintz (2003) "Sharing the International Tax Base in a Changing World," in S. Cnossen and H.-W. Sinn, eds., *Public Finance and Public Policy in the New Century* (Cambridge, MA: MIT Press), 405–46.

Bird, R. M., J. M. Mintz, and T. A. Wilson (2006) "Coordinating Federal and Provincial Sales Taxes: Lessons from the Canadian Experience," *National Tax Journal*, 59 (4): 889–903.

Bird, R. M., and O. Oldman, eds. (1990) *Taxation in Developing Countries* (Baltimore: Johns Hopkins University Press).

Bird, R. M., and O. Oldman (2000) *Improving Taxpayer Service and Facilitating Compliance in Singapore*, PREM Note 48, World Bank, Washington, DC, December.

Bird, R. M., and E. Slack (2004) *International Handbook of Land and Property Taxation* (Cheltenham, UK, and Northampton, MA: Edward Elgar).

Bird, R. M., and M. Smart (2002) "Intergovernmental Fiscal Transfers: Lessons from International Experience," *World Development*, 30 (6): 899–912.

Bird, R. M., and A. Tassonyi (2003) "Constraining Subnational Fiscal Behavior in Canada: Different Approaches, Same Results?" in J. A. Rodden, G. S. Eskeland, and J. I. Litvack, eds., *Fiscal Decentralization and the Challenge of Hard Budget Constraints* (Cambridge, MA: MIT Press), 85–132.

Bird, R. M., and T. Tsiopoulos (1996) "User Charges in the Federal Public Sector," Treasury Board Secretariat, Ottawa. <http://www.tbs-sct.gc.ca/pubs_pol/opepubs/tb_h/ucfg_e.asp>

Bird, R. M., and S. Wallace (2004) "Is It Really So Hard to Tax the Hard-to-Tax?: The Context and Role of Presumptive Taxes," in J. Alm, J. Martinez-Vazquez, and S. Wallace, eds., *Taxing the Hard-to-Tax: Lessons from Theory and Practice* (Amsterdam: Elsevier), 121–58.

Bird, R. M., and S. Wallace (2005) "Revenue Maximizing Tax Rates," in J. Cordes, R. D. Ebel, and J. Gravelle, eds., *The Encyclopedia of Taxation and Tax Policy* (Washington, DC: Urban Institute), 347–49.

Bird, R. M., and S. Wallace (2006) "Taxing Alcohol in Africa: Reflections from International Experience," in S. Cnossen, ed., *Excise Tax Policy and Administration* (Pretoria: UNISA Press), 21–60.

Bird, R. M., and T. A. Wilson (2004) "A Tax Strategy for Ontario," ITP Paper 0407, International Tax Program, Rotman School of Management, University of Toronto, March. <http://www.rotman.utoronto.ca/iib/ITP0407.pdf>

Bird, R. M., and E. Zolt (2005) "Redistribution through Taxation: The Limited Role of the Personal Income Tax in Developing Countries," *UCLA Law Review*, 62 (6): 1627–96.

Bird, R. M., and E. Zolt (2005a) "Redistribution through Taxation: The Limited Role of the Personal Income Tax in Developing Countries," ITP Paper 0508, International Tax Program, Rotman School of Management, University of Toronto. <http://www.rotman.utoronto.ca/iib/ITP0508.pdf>

Bishop, M. (2000) "A Survey of Globalisation and Tax: The Mystery of the Vanishing Taxpayer," *The Economist*, January 29 Supplement.

Blažić, H. (2004) "Tax Compliance Costs of Small Business in Croatia," Occasional Paper 22, Institute of Public Finance, Zagreb, November.

Blyth, M. (2002) *Great Transformations: Economic Ideas and Institutional Change in the Twentieth Century* (Cambridge: Cambridge University Press).

Boadway, R., and M. Keen (2003) "Theoretical Perspectives on the Taxation of Capital Income and Financial Services," in P. Honohan, ed., *Taxation of Financial Intermediation: Theory and Practice for Emerging Economies* (New York: Published for the World Bank by Oxford University Press), 31–80.

Botes, M. (2001) "Regressivity of VAT – the First Decade's Experience in South Africa," *International VAT Monitor*, 12 (5): 237–44.

Bovenberg, A. L. (1994) "Destination- and Origin-Based Taxation under International Capital Mobility," *International Tax and Public Finance*, 1 (3): 247–73.

Brautigam, D., O.-H. Fjeldstad, and M. Moore, eds. (in press) "Capacity and Consent: Taxation and State-Building in Developing Countries" (Cambridge: Cambridge University Press).

Break, G. F. (1974) "The Incidence and Economic Effects of Taxation," in Alan S. Blinder et al., *The Economics of Public Finance* (Washington, DC: Brookings Institution), 119–237.

Breton, A. (1996) *Competitive Governments* (Cambridge: Cambridge University Press).

Breusch, T. (2005) "The Canadian Underground Economy: An Examination of Giles-Tedds," *Canadian Tax Journal*, 53 (2): 367–91.

Brin, D. (1998) *The Transparent Society* (Reading, MA: Perseus Books).

Bruce, N., ed. (1990) *Tax Expenditures and Government Policy* (Kingston, ON: John Deutsch Institute for the Study of Economic Policy, Queen's University).

Bryne, E. (2002) "Value Added Taxation in Norway," *Bulletin for International Fiscal Documentation*, 56 (8/9): 384–91.

Burman, L. (1999) *The Labyrinth of Capital Gains Tax Policy: A Guide for the Perplexed.* (Washington, DC: Brookings Institution).

Caiden, N., and A. Wildavsky (1980) *Planning and Budgeting in Poor Countries* (New Brunswick, NJ: Transaction Books).

Canada (1987) *Tax Reform 1987: Sales Tax Reform* (Ottawa: Department of Finance).

Canada Revenue Agency (CRA) (2005) *Compendium of GST/HST Statistics 2004 Edition (2002 Tax Year)* (Ottawa: Canada Revenue Agency). <http://www.cra-arc.gc.ca/agency/stats/gb02/pst/gst_hst/menu-e.html>

Capehart, R. (2000) "Proposing a State VAT: The Political Experience in West Virginia," in D. Kenyon, ed., *Proceedings of the 92nd Annual Conference on Taxation* (Washington, DC: National Tax Association).

Casanegra de Jantscher, M. (1990) "Administering the VAT," in M. Gillis, C. Shoup, and G. P. Sicat, eds., *Value Added Taxation in Developing Countries* (Washington, DC: World Bank), 171–90.

Casanegra de Jantscher, M., I. Coelho, and A. Fernandez (1992) "Tax Administration and Inflation," in R. M. Bird and M. Casanegra de Jantscher, eds., *Improving Tax Administration in Developing Countries* (Washington, DC: International Monetary Fund), 251–66.

Casanegra de Jantscher, M., and C. Silvani (1991) "Guidelines for Administering a VAT," in A. Tait, ed., *Value-Added Tax: Administrative and Policy Issues*, Occasional Paper 88, International Monetary Fund, 30–39.

Chambas, G. (2005) "Foreign Financed Projects in Developing Countries and VAT Exemptions," Paper presented at the VAT Conference, International Tax Dialogue, Rome, March 15–16. <http://www.itdweb.org/VATConference/documents/Presentations/Parallel5_Application%20of%20VAT%20to%20International%20Aid_GChambas%20.ppt>

Chapman, E. (2001) *Introducing a Value Added Tax: Lessons from Ghana.* PREM Note 61, World Bank, Washington, DC, December.

Chelliah, R. J., et al. (2001) *Primer on Value Added Tax* (New Delhi: Har-Anand).

Chen, D., and J. Mintz (2001) "Property and Casualty Insurance Taxation in G-7 Countries," *Tax Notes International*, 31 (1): 47–67.

Chen, D., and J. Mintz (2003) "Assessing Ontario's Fiscal Competitiveness," Report prepared for the Institute of Competitiveness and Prosperity, Toronto, November. <http://www.competeprosper.ca/research/ChenMintzReport_251103.pdf>

Chen, M. (2005) "Rethinking the Informal Economy: Linkages with the Formal Economy and the Formal Regulatory Environment," WIDER Research Paper 2005/10, Helsinki, April.

Chi, Z. (2003) "China's Export Tax Rebate Policy," *China: An International Journal*, 1 (2): 339–49.

Chia, N.-C., and J. Whalley (1999) "The Tax Treatment of Financial Intermediation," *Journal of Money, Credit and Banking*, 31 (4): 704–19.

Choi, K. (1990) "Value-Added Taxation: Experiences and Lessons of Korea," in R. M. Bird and O. Oldman, eds., *Taxation in Developing Countries* (Baltimore: Johns Hopkins University Press), 269–87.

Chown, V. (2001) "When Is a Building Not a Building?" *Tax Notes International*, 23 (6): 725–37.

Chu, K., H. Davoodi, and S. Gupta (2000) "Income Distribution and Tax and Government Social Spending Policies in Developing Countries," Working Paper 214, UNU/WIDER, December.

Cnossen, S. (1994) "Administrative and Compliance Costs of the VAT: A Review of the Evidence," *Tax Notes International*, 8 (25): 1649–68.

Cnossen, S. (1996) "VAT Treatment of Immovable Property," in V. Thuronyi, ed., *Tax Law Design and Drafting* (Washington, DC: International Monetary Fund), 231–45.

Cnossen, S. (1998) *Value-Added Taxes in Central and Eastern Europe: A Survey and Evaluation* (Paris: European Commission and OECD).

Cnossen, S. (1999) "What Rate Structure for Australia's GST?: The OECD Experience," *Tax Notes International*, 18 (21): 2137–50.

Cnossen, S. (2002) "Tax Policy in the European Union: A Review of Issues and Options," *Finanzarchiv*, 58 (4): 466–558.

Cnossen, S. (2003) "Is the VAT's Sixth Directive Becoming an Anachronism?" *European Taxation*, 43 (12), 434–42.

Cnossen, S. (2004) "VAT in South Africa: What Kind of Rate Structure?" *International VAT Monitor*, 15 (1): 19–24.

Cnossen, S. (2005) *Theory and Practice of Excise Taxation: Smoking, Drinking, Gambling, Polluting and Driving* (Oxford: Oxford University Press).

Cnossen, S. (2005a) "The Role and Rationale of Excise Taxes in the ASEAN Countries," *Bulletin for International Fiscal Documentation*, 59 (12): 503–13.

Cnossen, S., ed. (2006) *Excise Tax Policy and Administration* (Pretoria: UNISA Press).

Cnossen, S., and C. S. Shoup (1987) "Coordination of Value-Added Taxes," in S. Cnossen, ed., *Tax Coordination in the European Community* (Deventer: Kluwer), 59–84.

Coba, P., N. Perelmuter, and M. P. Tedesco (n.d.) "Evasión fiscal en Uruguay: Un análisis sobre el impuesto al valor agregado," Montevideo: Banco Central de Uruguay.

Cockfield, A. (2002) "Designing Tax Policy for the Digital Biosphere: How the Internet Is Changing Tax Laws," *Connecticut Law Review*, 34 (2): 333–403.

Conrad, R. F. (1990) "The VAT and Real Estate," in M. Gillis, C. Shoup, and G. P. Sicat, eds., *Value Added Taxation in Developing Countries* (Washington, DC: World Bank), 95–103.

Cooper, G. S. (2001) "Tax Year in Review – Australia," *Tax Notes International*, 22 (1): 8–11.

Cornford, F. (1908) *Microcosmographia Academica* (Cambridge: Bowes & Bowes).

Crandall, W., and J.-P. Bodin (2005) "Revenue Administration Reform in Middle Eastern Countries, 1994–2004," Working Paper WP05/203, International Monetary Fund, Washington, DC.

Cukierman, A., S. Edwards, and G. Tabellini (1992) "Seignorage and Political Instability," *American Economic Review*, 82 (3): 537–55.

Dahlby, B. (2005) "Dealing with the Fiscal Imbalances: Vertical, Horizontal and Structural," Working Paper, C. D. Howe Institute, Toronto, September.

Daly, M. (2006) "WTO Rules on Direct Taxation," *The World Economy*, 29 (5): 527–57.

Das-Gupta, A., and I. Gang (1996) "A Comparison of Sales Taxes," *Public Finance*, 51 (2): 217–25.

Das-Gupta, A., and I. Gang (2003) "Value Added Tax Evasion, Auditing and Transactions Matching," in J. McLaren, ed., *Institutional Elements of Tax Design and Reform*. World Bank Technical Paper 539 (Washington, DC: World Bank), 25–48.

Das-Gupta, A., and D. Mookherjee (1998) *Incentives and Institutional Reform in Tax Enforcement* (New Delhi: Oxford University Press).

Daunton, M. (2001) *Trusting Leviathan: The Politics of Taxation in Britain 1799–1914* (Cambridge: Cambridge University Press).

Daunton, M. (2002) *Just Taxes: The Politics of Taxation in Britain 1914–1979* (Cambridge: Cambridge University Press).

David, I., and S. Poddar (2004) "Now Fix the Rest of the GST," *National Post* (Toronto), February 6, FP15.

Decoster, A., and I. Verbina (2003) "Who Pays Indirect Taxes in Russia?" WIDER Discussion Paper 2003/58, Helsinki, August.

De Ferranti, D., et al. (2004) *Inequality in Latin America: Breaking with History?* World Bank Latin American and Caribbean Studies (Washington, DC: World Bank).

De Wulf, L., and J. B. Sokol, eds. (2005) *Customs Modernization Handbook* (Washington, DC: World Bank).

Desai, M. A., and J. R. Hines, Jr. (2002) "Value-Added Taxes and International Trade: The Evidence," University of Michigan, November. <http://www.people.hbs.edu/mdesai/vats.pdf>

Devarajan, S., and R. Reinikka (2003) "Making Services Work for Poor People," *Finance and Development*, September, 48–51.

Diamant, A., and M. McKinney (2005) "GST/HST: Procurement Cards," *Canadian Tax Highlights*, 13 (9): 2.

Diamond, P. A., and J. A. Mirrlees (1971) "Optimal Taxation and Public Production I: Production Efficiency," *American Economic Review*, 61 (1): 8–27.

Díaz-Cayeros, A., and C. E. McLure (2000) "Tax Assignment," in M. M. Giugale and S. B. Webb, eds., *Achievements and Challenges of Fiscal Decentralization: Lessons from Mexico* (Washington, DC: World Bank), 177–99.

Dijkgraaf, E., and R. H. J. M. Gradus (2003) "Cost Savings of Contracting Out Refuse Collection," *Empirica*, 30 (2): 149–61.

Djankov, S., et al. (2002) "The Regulation of Entry," *Quarterly Journal of Economics*, 118 (1): 1–37.

Doernberg, R. L., et al. (2001) *Electronic Commerce and Multijurisdictional Taxation* (London: Kluwer Law International).

Dresch, S. P., A. Lin, and D. K. Stout (1977) *Substituting a Value-Added Tax for the Corporate Income Tax* (Cambridge, MA: Published for the National Bureau of Economic Research by Ballinger Publishing Company).

Due, J. F. (1957) *Sales Taxation* (Urbana: University of Illinois Press).

Due, J. F., and J. Mikesell (1994) *State Sales Tax Administration* (Washington, DC: Urban Institute).

Dungan, D. P., and T. A. Wilson (1993) *Fiscal Policy in Canada: An Appraisal* (Toronto: Canadian Tax Foundation).

Ebel, R. D., and L. Kalambokidis (2005) "Value-Added Tax, State," in J. Cordes, R. D. Ebel, and J. Gravelle, eds., *The Encyclopedia of Taxation and Tax Policy* (Washington, DC: Urban Institute), 464–67.

Ebrill, L., J. Stotsky, and R. Gropp (1999) *Revenue Aspects of Trade Liberalization* (Washington, DC: International Monetary Fund).

Ebrill, L., M. Keen, J.-P. Bodin, and V. Summers (2001) *The Modern VAT* (Washington, DC: International Monetary Fund).

Edgar, T. (2001) "Exempt Treatment of Financial Intermediation Services under a Value-Added Tax: An Assessment of Alternatives," *Canadian Tax Journal*, 49 (5): 1133–1219.

Edmiston, K., and R. M. Bird (2004) "Taxing Consumption in Jamaica: The GCT and the SCT," ITP Paper 0414, International Tax Program, Rotman School of Management, University of Toronto, December. <http://www.rotman.utoronto.ca/iib/ITP0414.pdf>

Edmiston, K., and R. M. Bird (2006) "Taxing Consumption in Jamaica," *Public Finance Review*, 20 (10): 1–31.

Edmiston, K., and W. F. Fox (2006) "A Fresh Look at the VAT," in J. Alm, J. Martinez-Vazquez, and M. Rider, eds., *The Challenges of Tax Reform in a Global Economy* (New York: Springer), 249–66.

Elster, J. (1979) *Ulysses and the Sirens* (Cambridge: Cambridge University Press).

Emini, C. A. (2000) "Long Run vs. Short Run Effects of a Value-Added Tax: A Computable General Equilibrium Assessment for Cameroon," CREFA Cahier de Recherche 00-12, Université Laval, Québec, June.

Empowered Committee of State Finance Ministers (2005) *A White Paper on State-Level Value Added Tax* (New Delhi: Empowered Committee of State Finance Ministers).

Emran, M. S., and J. E. Stiglitz (2005) "On Selective Indirect Tax Reform in Developing Countries," *Journal of Public Economics*, 89 (4): 599–623.

Engel, E., A. Galetovic, and C. Raddatz (1998) "Estimación de la evasión del IVA mediante el método de punto fijo," Santiago de Chile: Servicio de Impuestos Internos. <www.sii.cl/aprenda_sobre_impuestos/estudios/tributarios5.htm>

Engel, E., A. Galetovic, and C. Raddatz (2001) "A Note on Enforcement Spending and VAT Revenue," *Review of Economics and Statistics*, 83 (2): 384–87.

Engelschalk, M. (2004) "Creating a Favorable Tax Environment for Small Business," in J. Alm, J. Martinez-Vazquez, and S. Wallace, eds., *Taxing the Hard-to-Tax: Lessons from Theory and Practice* (Amsterdam: Elsevier), 276–311.

Engerman, S. L., and K. L. Sokoloff (2002) "Factor Endowments, Inequality, and Paths of Development among New World Economies," Working Paper 9259, National Bureau of Economic Research, Cambridge, MA, October.

Ernst & Young (2006) *Worldwide VAT and GST Guide* (London: Ernst & Young Global Limited).

European Commission (1996) *A Common System of VAT: A Programme for the Single Market* (Brussels: European Commission).

European Commission (1997) *Value Added Tax: A Study of Methods of Taxing Financial and Insurance Services* (Brussels: European Commission).

European Commission (2006) *VAT Rates Applied in the Member States of the European Union: Situation at 1 September 2006* (Brussels: European Commission). <http://ec.europa.eu/taxation_customs/resources/documents/taxation/vat/how_vat_works/rates/vat_rates_2006_en.pdf>

Evans, R. (2003) "Focus on Venezuela's VAT Withholding Regime," *International VAT Monitor*, 14 (2): 110–14.

Fedeli, S. (1998) "The Effects of Interaction between Direct and Indirect Tax Evasion: The Cases of VAT and RST," *Public Finance*, 53 (3–4), 385–418.

Federation of Tax Administrators (1997) *Sales Taxation of Services: 1996 Update* (Washington, DC: Federation of Tax Administrators).

Feldstein, M., and P. Krugman (1990) "International Trade Effects of Value-Added Taxation," in A. Razin and J. Slemrod, eds., *Taxation in the Global Economy* (Chicago: University of Chicago Press), 263–82.

Fjeldstad, O.-H. (2005) *Revenue Administration and Corruption*. Ulstein Anti-Corruption Resource Centre, U4 Issue 2: 2005, Chr. Michelsen Institute, Bergen.

Floyd, R. H. (1973) "GATT Provisions on Border Tax Adjustments," *Journal of World Trade Law*, 7 (5): 489–99.

Fox, W. F. (2000) "Subnational VAT or Retail Sales Tax: What Is Tax Policy's Panacea?" in D. Kenyon, ed., *Proceedings of the 92nd Annual Conference on Taxation* (Washington, DC: National Tax Association).

Fox, W., and C. Wallich (2001) "Fiscal Federalism in Bosnia-Herzegovina: The Dayton Challenge," in R. M. Bird and T. Stauffer, eds., *Intergovernmental Fiscal Relations in Fragmented Societies* (Basel: Helbig and Lichtenhahn), 397–434.

Frenkel, J. A., A. Razin, and E. Sadka (1991) *International Taxation in an Integrated World* (Cambridge, MA: MIT Press).

Fullerton, D. (1982), "On the Possibility of an Inverse Relationship between Tax Rates and Government Revenues," *Journal of Public Economics*, 19 (1): 3–22.

Fullerton, D., and G. Metcalf (2002) "Tax Incidence," in A. Auerbach and M. Feldstein, eds., *Handbook of Public Economics*, Vol. 4 (Amsterdam: North-Holland), 1787–1872.

Gale, W. G., and J. Holtzblatt (2002) "The Role of Administrative Issues in Tax Reform: Simplicity, Compliance, and Administration," in G. R. Zodrow and P. Mieszkowski, eds, *United States Tax Reform in the 21st Century* (Cambridge: Cambridge University Press), 179–214.

Gallagher, M. (2004) "Assessing Tax Systems Using a Benchmarking Methodology," Research Paper, Fiscal Reform in Support of Trade Liberalization Project, USAID, Washington, DC, April.

Gallagher, M. (2005) "Benchmarking Tax Systems," *Public Administration and Development*, 25 (2): 125–44.

Garcia Molina, M., and A. P. Gómez (2005) "Han aumentado el recaudo las reformas tributarias en Colombia?" *Revista de Economía Institucional*, 7 (12): 43–61.

Gauthier, B., and M. Gersovitz (1997) "Revenue Erosion through Exemption and Erosion in Cameroon, 1993," *Journal of Public Economics*, 64 (3): 407–24.

Gebauer, A., C. W. Nam, and R. Parsche (2003) "Is the Completion of EU Single Market Hindered by VAT Evasion?" CESifo Working Paper 974, June.

Gemmell, N., and O. Morrissey (2003) "Tax Structure and the Incidence on the Poor in Developing Countries," Centre for Research on Economic Development and International Trade Research Paper 03/18, University of Nottingham, October.

Gendron, P.-P. (2005) "Value-Added Tax Treatment of Public Bodies and Non-Profit Organizations," *Bulletin for International Fiscal Documentation*, 59 (11): 514–26.

Gendron, P.-P. (2006) "Value-Added Tax Treatment of Financial Services: A Developing Country Perspective," ITP Paper 0606, International Tax Program, Rotman School of Management, University of Toronto, August. <http://www.rotman.utoronto.ca/iib/ITP0606.pdf>

Gendron, P.-P., J. M. Mintz, and T. Wilson (1996) "VAT Harmonization in Canada: Recent Developments and the Need for Flexibility," *International VAT Monitor*, 7 (6): 332–42.

Genser, B. (1996) "A Generalized Equivalence Property of Mixed International VAT Regimes," *Scandinavian Journal of Economics*, 98 (2): 253–62.

Genser, B. (2000) "VAT Reform in Federal States," in H.-G. Petersen and P. Gallagher, eds., *Tax and Transfer Reform in Australia and Germany* (Berlin: Berliner Debatte Wissenschaftsverlag), 305–18.

Gerhanxi, K. (2004) "The Informal Sector in Developed and Less Developed Countries: A Survey," *Public Choice*, 120 (3–4): 267–300.

Giles, D., and L. Tedds (2005) "Response to Breusch's Critique," *Canadian Tax Journal*, 53 (2): 392–95.

Gillis, M. (1985) "Micro- and Macroeconomics of Tax Reform: Indonesia," *Journal of Development Economics*, 19 (3): 221–54.

Gillis, M., C. Shoup, and G. P. Sicat, eds. (1990) *Value Added Taxation in Developing Countries*. (Washington, DC: World Bank).

Gjems-Onstad, O. (2004) "Refund of Input VAT to Norwegian NPOs," *International VAT Monitor*, 15 (4): 244–46.

Glenday, G. (2006) "Towards Fiscally Feasible and Efficient Trade Liberalization," Report prepared for USAID, Washington, DC, May.

Go, D. S., M. Kearney, S. Robinson, and K. Thierfelder (2005) "An Analysis of South Africa's Value Added Tax," World Bank Policy Research Working Paper 3671, August.

Gonzalez, D. (1998) "Estudio comparado del impuesto de valor agregado" (Buenos Aires: Prepared for CIAT, Centro Interamericano de Administraciones Tributarias).

Goorman, A. (2005) "Duty Relief and Exemption Control," in L. De Wulf and J. B. Sokol, eds., *Customs Modernization Handbook* (Washington, DC: World Bank), 215–41.

Gooroochurn, N. (2004) "The Economy-Wide Effects of Tourism Taxation in a Distorted Economy: A General Equilibrium Analysis," Discussion Paper 2004/1, Tourism and Travel Research Institute, University of Nottingham.

Gooroochurn, N., and M. T. Sinclair (2003) "The Welfare Effects of Tourism Taxation," Discussion Paper 2003/2, Tourism and Travel Research Institute, University of Nottingham.

Gordon, R., and W. Li (2005) "Tax Structure in Developing Countries: Many Puzzles and a Possible Explanation," Working Paper 11267, National Bureau of Economic Research, Cambridge, MA, April.

Graetz, M. J., and I. Shapiro (2005) *Death by a Thousand Cuts: The Fight over Taxing Inherited Wealth* (Princeton, NJ: Princeton University Press).

Grandcolas, C. (2005) "The Occasional Failure in VAT Implementation: Lessons for the Pacific," *Asia-Pacific Tax Bulletin*, 10 (1): 6–13.

Greenaway, D., and C. Milner (1993) "The Fiscal Implications of Trade Policy Reform: Theory and Evidence," UNDP–World Bank Trade Expansion Program, Occasional Paper 9, November.

Greenbaum, A. (1999) "The Australian GST – a 'Brave New World' for Both Consumers and Business," *Tax Notes International*, 19 (18): 1743–52.

Grubert, H., and J. Mackie (2000) "Must Financial Services Be Taxed under a Consumption Tax?" *National Tax Journal*, 53 (1): 23–40.

Guérard, M. (1973) "The Brazilian State Value-Added Tax," *International Monetary Fund Staff Papers*, 20: 118–69.

Guinnane, T. W., W. A. Sundstrom, and W. C. Whatley, eds. (2004) *History Matters: Essays on Economic Growth, Technology, and Demographic Change* (Stanford, CA: Stanford University Press).

Hamilton, B., and J. Whalley (1989) "Reforming Indirect Taxes in Canada: Some General Equilibrium Estimates," *Canadian Journal of Economics*, 22 (3): 561–75.

Hanford, A., and J. Hasseldine (2003) "Factors Affecting the Costs of UK VAT Compliance for Small and Medium-Sized Enterprises," *Environment and Planning C: Government and Policy*, 21 (4): 479–92.

Harberger, A. C. (2006) "Taxation and Income Distribution: Myths and Realities," in J. Alm, J. Martinez-Vazquez, and M. Rider, eds., *The Challenges of Tax Reform in a Global Economy* (New York: Springer), 13–37.

Harrison, G., and R. Krelove (2005) "VAT Refunds: A Review of Country Experience," Working Paper WP 05/218, International Monetary Fund, November.

Hartman, D. A. (2004) "The Case for Border-Adjusted Taxation in the United States," *Tax Notes International*, 35 (13): 1183–98.

Hartman, D. A. (2004a) "More on Why Border-Adjusted U.S. Tax Reform Is Needed," *Tax Notes International*, 36 (6): 549.

Hasseldine, J. (2005) "Measuring and Reducing Administrative Costs and Tax Compliance Costs," Paper presented to Global VAT Conference, Rome, March. <http://www.itdweb.org/VATConference/documents/Presentations/Parallel1_Measuring%20&%20Reducing%20Administrative%20Costs%20&%20Tax%20Compliance%20Costs_JHasseldine.PPT>

Haughton, J. (2005) "An Assessment of Tax and Expenditure Incidence in Peru," DFID-SG CAN-IDB, Lima, April.

Heady, C. (2004) "Taxation Policy in Low-Income Countries," in T. Addison and A. Roe, eds., *Fiscal Policy for Development: Poverty, Reconstruction and Growth* (London: Palgrave), 130–48.

Hellerstein, W. (2005) "U.S. Subnational State Sales Tax: The Streamlined Sales Tax Project," Paper presented to Global VAT Conference, Rome, March. <http://www.itdweb.org/VATConference/documents/Prof%20W%20Hellerstein%20-%20U.S.%20Subnational%20%20State%20Sales%20Tax%20Reform%20-%20Streamlined%20Sales%20Tax.doc>

Hendrix, M., and G. Zodrow (2003) "Sales Taxation of Services: An Economic Perspective," *Florida State University Law Review*, 30 (3): 411–33.

Heredia, J., and J. A. Fernandes (2003) "B2C in Europe through Madeira: Planning for the Near Future," *Tax Notes International*, 30 (5): 475–77.

Higgins, B. (1959) *Economic Development: Principles, Problems and Policies* (New York: W. W. Norton).

Hill, J. R. (1977) "Sales Taxation in Francophone Africa," *Journal of Developing Areas*, 11: 165–84.

Hines, J. R., Jr. (2004) "Might Fundamental Tax Reform Increase Criminal Activity?" *Economica*, 71 (283): 483–92.

Hirschman, A. O. (1970) *Exit, Voice and Loyalty* (Cambridge, MA: Harvard University Press).

Hong Kong (2006) *Broadening the Tax Base*, Consultation Document, July. <http://www.taxreform.gov.hk/eng/document.htm>

Huesca, L., and A. Serrano (2005) "El impacto fiscal redistributivo desagregado del impuesto al valor agregado en México: Vias de reforma," *Investigación Económica*, 64 (253): 89–122.

Hughes, G. (1987) "The Incidence of Fuel Taxes: A Comparative Study of Three Countries," in D. Newbery and N. Stern, eds., *The Theory of Taxation for Developing Countries* (New York: Published for the World Bank by Oxford University Press), 533–59.

Huizinga, H. (2002) "Financial Services VAT: VAT in Europe," *Economic Policy*, 17 (35): 499–534.

Hussey, W. M., and D. C. Lubick (1992) *Basic World Tax Code and Commentary* (Arlington, VA: Tax Analysts).

Inland Revenue Authority of Singapore (IRAS) (2006) *Goods and Services Tax: Major Exporter Scheme* (rev. ed.) (Singapore: IRAS). <http://www.iras.gov.sg/ESVPortal/resources/mesfinal.pdf>

Inman, R. P. (2003) "Transfers and Bailouts: Enforcing Local Fiscal Discipline with Lessons from U.S. Federalism," in J. A. Rodden, G. S. Eskeland, and J. I. Litvack, eds., *Fiscal Decentralization and the Challenge of Hard Budget Constraints* (Cambridge, MA: MIT Press), 35–83.

Inter-American Development Bank (IDB) (1997) *Latin America after a Decade of Reforms*. Economic and Social Progress in Latin America 1997 (Washington, DC: IDB).

Inter-American Development Bank (IDB) (1998) *Facing Up to Inequality in Latin America*. Economic and Social Progress in Latin America 1998–99 (Washington, DC: IDB).

Inter-American Development Bank (IDB) (2004) "Integration and Trade in the Americas: Fiscal Impact of Trade Liberalization in the Americas," Periodic Note, Washington, DC, January.

Inter-American Development Bank (IDB) (2006) *The Politics of Policies*. Economic and Social Progress in Latin America 2006 (Washington, DC: IDB).

International Bureau of Fiscal Documentation (IBFD) (2004) *Annual Report 2003–04* (Amsterdam: IBFD).

International Bureau of Fiscal Documentation (IBFD) (2006) "Practical Information on VAT," *International VAT Monitor*, 17 (1): 1–11.

International Monetary Fund (IMF) (2003) *Tax Law Drafting Samples: VAT*. <http://www.imf.org/external/np/leg/tlaw/2003/eng/tlvat.htm>

International Tax Dialogue (ITD) (2005) "The Value Added Tax: Experiences and Issues," Prepared for the ITD Conference on the VAT, Rome, March 15–16. <http://www.itdweb.org/VATConference/Documents/VAT%20-%20EXPERIENCE%20AND%20ISSUES.pdf>

Ishi, H. (2001) *The Japanese Tax System*, 3rd ed. (Oxford: Oxford University Press).

Jack, W. (2000) "The Treatment of Financial Services under a Broad-Based Consumption Tax," *National Tax Journal*, 53 (4): 841–51.

Jakee, K., and S. Turner (2002) "The Welfare State as a Fiscal Commons: Problems of Incentives versus Problems of Cognition," *Public Finance Review*, 30 (6): 481–508.

Jenkins, G. P., H. Jenkins, and C.-Y. Kuo (2006) "Is the Value Added Tax Naturally Progressive?" Working Paper 1059, Economics Department, Queen's University, Kingston, April.

Jenkins, G. P., and R. Khadka (1998) "Value Added Tax Policy and Implementation in Singapore," *International VAT Monitor*, 9 (2): 35–47.

Jenkins, G. P., and C.-Y. Kuo (2000) "A VAT Revenue Simulation Model for Tax Reform in Developing Countries," *World Development*, 28 (4): 763–74.

Jenkins, G. P., C.-Y. Kuo, and K.-N. Sun (2003) *Taxation and Economic Development in Taiwan* (Cambridge, MA: John F. Kennedy School of Government).

Kaldor, N. (1956) *Indian Tax Reform* (New Delhi: Government of India Ministry of Finance).

Kaldor, N. (1963) "Will Underdeveloped Countries Learn to Tax?" *Foreign Affairs*, 41 (2): 410–19.

Kaplan, H. E. (2005) "Aspects of VAT and Other Consumption Taxes Affecting Investments into Argentina," *Bulletin for International Fiscal Documentation*, 59 (8–9): 341–48.

Kay, J. A., and E. H. Davis (1990) "The VAT and Services," in M. Gillis, C. Shoup, and G. P. Sicat, eds., *Value Added Taxation in Developing Countries* (Washington, DC: World Bank), 70–82.

Keen, M. (2000) "VIVAT, CVAT and All That: New Forms of Value-Added Tax for Federal Systems," *Canadian Tax Journal*, 48 (2): 409–24.

Keen, M., ed. (2003) *Changing Customs: Challenges and Strategies for the Reform of Customs Administration* (Washington, DC: International Monetary Fund).

Keen, M. (2006) "VAT Attacks! Second Best Perspectives on the Value Added Tax," Paper presented to International Institute of Public Finance, Cyprus, August.

Keen, M. (2006a) "VAT, Tariffs and Withholding: Tax Design and the Informal Sector," Washington, DC: International Monetary Fund, September.

Keen, M., and J. E. Ligthart (2001) "Coordinating Tariff Reductions and Domestic Tax Reform," *Journal of International Economics*, 56 (2): 407–25.

Keen, M., and J. E. Ligthart (2004) "Information Sharing and International Taxation," Center Discussion Paper 2004–17, Tilburg University, November.

Keen, M., and J. E. Ligthart (2005) "Coordinating Tariff Reduction and Domestic Tax Reform under Imperfect Competition," *Review of International Economics*, 13 (2): 385–90.

Keen, M., and B. Lockwood (2006) "Is the VAT a Money Machine?," National Tax Journal, 59 (4): 905–28.

Keen, M., and J. Mintz (2004) "The Optimal Threshold for a Value-Added Tax," *Journal of Public Economics*, 88 (3/4): 559–76.

Keen, M., and S. Smith (1996) "The Future of Value-Added Tax in the European Union," *Economic Policy*, 11 (23): 375–411.

Keen, M., and S. Smith (2000) "Viva VIVAT!" *International Tax and Public Finance*, 7 (6): 741–51.

Keynes, J. M. (1936) *The General Theory of Employment, Interest and Money* (New York: Harcourt, Brace).

Kleiman, E. (1997) "National Price Levels: Do Taxes Matter?" *International Tax and Public Finance*, 4 (3): 361–77.

Kopczuk, W., and J. Slemrod (2006) "Putting Firms into Optimal Tax Theory," *American Economic Review (Papers and Proceedings)*, 96 (2): 130–34.

Korea National Tax Service (2005) "VAT Administration in Korea," Presented to Global Conference on VAT, Rome, March. <http://www.itdweb.org/VATConference/documents/Korea%20-%20Experiences%20in%20VAT%20Administration.ppt>

Kramer, J.-D. (1994) "The Introduction of Western Tax Law into Eastern European Countries Is Sometimes a Dubious Gift," *Tax Notes International*, 8 (1): 14–16.

Kreklewetz, R. G. (2004) "In Defence of Foods," *Canadian Tax Highlights*, 12 (5): 9.

Kreklewetz, R. G., and J. S. Seres (2005) "GST Health-Care Services Rebate," *Canadian Tax Highlights*, 13 (9): 7.

Kuo, C.-Y, T. McGirr, and S. Poddar (1988) "Measuring the Non-Neutralities of Sales and Excise Tax in Canada," *Canadian Tax Journal*, 36 (3): 655–70.

Laffer, A., and J. Seymour, eds. (1979) *The Economics of the Tax Revolt: A Reader* (New York: Harcourt Brace & Jovanovich).

Laffont, J.-J. (2004) "Management of Public Utilities in China," *Annals of Economics and Finance*, 5: 185–210.

Lanovy, V. (2005) "Concept of Reforming the Tax System of Ukraine." Prepared by the Task Force of the Secretariat of the President of Ukraine, Kyiv, September.

Leggett, A. (2005) "VAT Fraud and Control of Refunds and Credits: A Strategic Approach to Tackling VAT Losses," Presentation to Global Conference on VAT, March. <http://www.itdweb.org/VATConference/documents/Presentations/Parallel4_VAT%20Fraud%20&%20Control%20of%20Refunds%20&%20Credits_ALeggett.ppt>

Levi, M. (1988) *Of Rule and Revenue* (Berkeley: University of California Press).

Levin, J. V. (1968) "The Effect of Economic Development upon the Base of a Sales Tax: A Case Study of Colombia," *IMF Staff Papers*, 15: 30–99.

Li, J. (1997) "Counteracting Corruption in the Tax Administration in Transitional Economies: A Case Study of China," *Bulletin for International Fiscal Documentation*, 51 (11): 474–92.

Li, J. (2003) *International Taxation in the Age of Electronic Commerce: A Comparative Study* (Toronto: Canadian Tax Foundation).

Li, J. (2004) "Death and Taxes – Two Certainties Combined in the P. R. C. VAT System," *Tax Notes International*, 36 (10): 859–60.

Li, J. (2005) "Relationship between International Trade Law and National Tax Policy: A Case Study of China," *Bulletin for International Fiscal Documentation*, 52 (2): 77–86.

Lieberman, E. S. (2003) *Race and Regionalism in the Politics of Taxation in Brazil and South Africa* (Cambridge: Cambridge University Press).

Light, M. K. (2004) "Taxation and Economic Efficiency in Jamaica," Working Paper 04-33, International Studies Program, Andrew Young School of Policy Studies, Georgia State University, December.

Ligthart, J. E. (2004) "Consumption Taxation in a Digital World: A Primer," *Canadian Tax Journal*, 52 (4): 1076–1101.

Lindert, P. H. (2002) "Why the Welfare State Looks Like a Free Lunch," UC Davis Department of Economics Working Paper 02-7, November.

Lindert, P. H. (2003) *Growing Public: Social Spending and Economic Growth since the Eighteenth Century* (Cambridge: Cambridge University Press).

Lindert, P. H. (2004) "Voice and Growth: Was Churchill Right?" *Journal of Economic History*, 63 (2): 315–50.

Lledo, V., A. Schneider, and M. Moore (2004) "Governance, Taxes and Tax Reform in Latin America, IDS Working Paper 222, Institute of Development Studies, March.

Lockwood, B. (1993) "Commodity Tax Competition under Destination and Origin Principles," *Journal of Public Economics*, 52 (2): 141–67.

Lockwood, B., D. de Meza, and G. Myles (1994) "The Equivalence between the Destination and Non-Reciprocal Restricted Origin Tax Regimes," *Scandinavian Journal of Economics*, 96 (3): 311–28.

Lockwood, B., D. de Meza, and G. Myles (1994a) "When Are Origin and Destination Regimes Equivalent?" *International Tax and Public Finance*, 1 (1): 5–24.

Lockwood, B., D. de Meza, and G. Myles (1995) "On the European Union VAT Proposals: The Superiority of Origin over Destination Taxation," *Fiscal Studies*, 16 (1): 1–17.

López-Garcia, M. (1996) "The Origin Principle and the Welfare Gains from Indirect Tax Harmonization," *International Tax and Public Finance*, 3 (1): 83–93.

Mackenzie, G. A. (1992) "Estimating the Base of the Value-Added Tax (VAT) in Developing Countries: The Problem of Exemptions," *Public Finance*, 47 (2): 375–410.

Maktouf, L., and S. Surrey (1983) "Tax Expenditure Analysis and Tax and Budgetary Reform in Less Developed Countries," *Law and Policy in International Business*, 15 (3): 739–61.

Mann, A., and R. Burke (2002) "El gasto tributario en Guatemala," DevTech Systems, Inc., March.

Marks, S. V. (2005) "Proposed Changes to the Value Added Tax: Implications for Tax Revenue and Price Distortions," *Bulletin of Indonesian Economic Studies*, 41 (1): 81–95.

Martinez-Vazquez, J. (2001) "Mexico: An Evaluation of the Main Features of the Tax System," Working Paper 01–12, International Studies Program, Andrew Young School of Policy Studies, Georgia State University, November.

Martinez-Vazquez, J., and R. M. McNab (2000) "The Tax Reform Experiment in Transitional Countries," *National Tax Journal*, 53 (2): 273–98.

Mathis, A. (2004) "VAT Indicators," Working Paper 2/2004, Directorate-General Taxation and Customs Union, European Commission, Brussels, April.

Matthews, K., and J. Lloyd-Williams (2000) "Have VAT Rates Reached Their Limit? An Empirical Note," *Applied Economics Letters*, 7 (2): 111–15.

McCarten, W. (2006) "The Role of Organizational Design in the Revenue Strategies of Developing Countries: Benchmarking with VAT Performance," in J. Alm, J. Martinez-Vazquez, and M. Rider, eds., *The Challenges of Tax Reform in a Global Economy* (New York: Springer), 13–39.

McLure, C. E. (1980) "State and Federal Relations in the Taxation of Value Added," *Journal of Corporation Law*, 6 (1): 127–39.

McLure, C. E. (1997) "Taxation of Electronic Commerce: Economic Objectives, Technological Constraints, and Tax Laws," *Tax Law Review*, 52 (3): 269–423.

McLure, C. E. (1997a) "Electronic Commerce, State Sales Taxation, and Intergovernmental Fiscal Relations," *National Tax Journal*, 50 (4): 731–49.

McLure, C. E. (1999) "Tax Holidays and Investment Incentives: A Comparative Analysis," *Bulletin for International Fiscal Documentation*, 53 (8): 326–39.

McLure, C. E. (2000) "Implementing Subnational VATs on Internal Trade: The Compensating VAT (CVAT)," *International Tax and Public Finance*, 7 (6): 723–40.

McLure, C. E. (2003) "Taxation of Electronic Commerce in Developing Countries," in J. Alm and J. Martinez-Vazquez, eds., *Public Finance in Developing and Transitional Countries* (Cheltenham, UK: Edward Elgar), 283–323.

McLure, C. E., and G. Zodrow (1997) "Thirty Years of Tax Reform in Colombia," in W. R. Thirsk, ed., *Tax Reform in Developing Countries* (Washington, DC: World Bank), 57–125.

Messere, K. (1994) "Consumption Tax Rules," *Bulletin for International Fiscal Documentation*, 48 (12): 665–81.

Messere, K. (1999) "Half a Century of Changes in Taxation," *Bulletin for International Fiscal Documentation*, 53 (8/9): 340–66.

Messere, K., F. de Kam, and C. Heady (2003) *Tax Policy: Theory and Practice in OECD Countries* (Oxford: Oxford University Press).

Mikesell, J. L. (1999) "Structure of the Russian Federation's New Regional Sales Taxes," *Tax Notes International*, 18 (11): 1059–68.

Mikesell, J. L. (2007) "Developing Options for the Administration of Local Taxes: An International Review," *Public Budgeting and Finance*, 27 (1): 41–68.

Mintz, J. M., and S. Richardson (2002) "Taxation of Financial Intermediation Activities in Hong Kong," *Tax Notes International*, 23 (7): 771–93.

Mintz, J. M., D. Chen, Y. Guillemette, and F. Poschmann (2005) *The 2005 Tax Competitiveness Report: Unleashing the Canadian Tiger*, Commentary 216 (Toronto: C. D. Howe Institute).

Mintz, J. M., T. A. Wilson, and P.-P. Gendron (1994) "Sales Tax Harmonization Is the Key to Simplification," *Tax Notes International*, 8 (10): 661–78.

Mitra, P., and N. Stern (2003) "Tax Systems in Transition," Policy Research Working Paper 2947, World Bank, Washington, DC, January.

Moore, M. (2004) "Taxation and the Political Agenda, North and South," *Forum for Development Studies*, 1: 7–32.

Munk, K. J. (2006) "Tax-Tariff Reform with Costs of Tax Administration," Economics Working Paper 2006-14, School of Economics and Management, University of Aarhus, December.

Muñoz, S., and S. S. Cho (2003) "Social Impact of a Tax Reform: The Case of Ethiopia," IMF Working Paper 03/232, November.

Musgrave, R. A. (1986) "A Reappraisal of Social Security Financing," in R. A. Musgrave, *Public Finance in a Democratic Society*. Volume II. *Fiscal Doctrine, Growth and Institutions* (Brighton, UK: Wheatsheaf Books distributed by Harvester Press), 103–22.

National Audit Office (2004) HM Customs and Excise: *Tackling VAT Fraud*, Report by the Comptroller and Auditor General (London: The Stationery Office).

National Economic Development Office (1969) *Value Added Tax* (London: HMSO).

Nerré, B. (2002) "The Concept of Tax Culture," *Proceedings of the 94th Annual Conference* (Washington, DC: National Tax Association), 288–95.

Neumark Report (1963) *The EEC Reports on Tax Harmonization* (Amsterdam: International Bureau of Fiscal Documentation).

New Zealand (2001) "Tax and Charities: A Government Discussion Document on Taxation Issues Relating to Charities and Non-Profit Bodies," Policy Advice Division (Wellington: Inland Revenue Department). <http://www.taxpolicy.ird.govt.nz/publications/files/tax&charitiesdd.pdf>

New Zealand (2004) "GST Guidelines for Working with the New Zero-Rating Rules for Financial Services," Policy Advice Division (Wellington: Inland Revenue Department). <www.taxpolicy.ird.govt.nz/publications/files/gstguidelinezerorating.pdf>

Newbery, D., and N. Stern, eds. (1987) *The Theory of Taxation for Developing Countries* (New York: Published for the World Bank by Oxford University Press).

Oldman, Oliver (1968) "Controlling Income Tax Evasion," in Joint Tax Program of Organization of American States and Inter-American Development Bank, *Problems of Tax Administration in Latin America* (Baltimore: Johns Hopkins University Press), 296–344.

Olivei, G. P. (2002) "Exchange Rates and the Price of Manufacturing Products Imported into the United States," *New England Economic Review* (First Quarter): 3–18.

Organización de los Estados Americanos (OEA) (1993) *El impuesto al valor agregado y su generalización en América Latina* (Buenos Aires: Ediciones Interoceanicas S. A.).

Organisation for Economic Co-Operation and Development (OECD) (1988) *Taxing Consumption* (Paris: OECD).

Organisation for Economic Co-Operation and Development (OECD) (2001) Centre for Tax Policy and Administration "Risk Management – Practice Note," GAP003, May.

Organisation for Economic Co-Operation and Development (OECD) (2003) Committee on Fiscal Affairs "Report on the Use of Simplified Registration Systems," DAFFE/CF (2003) 43/ANN4, July.

Organisation for Economic Co-Operation and Development (OECD) (2004) *Consumption Tax Trends* (Paris: OECD).

Organisation for Economic Co-Operation and Development (OECD) (2004a) Centre for Tax Policy and Administration *Tax Administration in OECD Countries; Comparative Information Series (2004)* (Paris: OECD).

Organisation for Economic Co-Operation and Development (OECD) (2005) Centre for Tax Policy and Administration "Verification of Customer Status and Jurisdiction," Consumption Tax Guidance Series 3 (Paris: OECD).

Organisation for Economic Co-Operation and Development (OECD) (2006) Centre for Tax Policy and Administration *Tax Administration in OECD and Selected Non-OECD Countries: Comparative Information Series (2006)* (Paris: OECD).

Pagan, J. A., G. Soydemir, and J. A. Tijerina-Guajardo (2001) "The Evolution of VAT Rates and Government Tax Revenue in Mexico," *Contemporary Economic Policy*, 19 (4): 424–33.

Pallot, M. (2005) "GST and Financial Services," Presentation to Global Conference on VAT, March. <http://www.itdweb.org/VATConference/documents/Presentations/Parallel1_Treatment%20of%20Financial%20Services_MPalot.ppt>

Pallot, M., and D. White (2002) "Improvements to the GST Treatment of Financial Services – the Proposed New Zealand Approach," *International VAT Monitor*, 13 (6): 481–86.

Peacock, A., and J. Wiseman (1961) *The Growth of Government Expenditures in the United Kingdom* (Princeton, NJ: Princeton University Press).

Pellechio, A. J., and C. B. Hill (1996) "Equivalence of the Production and Consumption Methods of Calculating the Value-Added Tax Base: Application in Zambia," IMF Working Paper WP/96/67, June.

Perry, G., J. Whalley, and G. McMahon, eds. (2000) *Fiscal Reform and Structural Change in Developing Countries*, 2 vols. (London: Macmillan for International Development Research Centre).

Persson, T., and G. Tabellini (2000) *Political Economics: Explaining Economic Policy* (Cambridge, MA: MIT Press).

Persson, T., and G. Tabellini (2003) *The Economic Effects of Constitutions: What Do the Data Say?* (Cambridge, MA: MIT Press).

Petri, M., G. Taube, and A. Tsyvinski (2002) "Energy Sector Quasi-Fiscal Activities in the Countries of the Former Soviet Union," IMF Working Paper QP/02/60, March.

Piffano, H. (2005) *Notas sobre federalismo fiscal – Enfoques positivos y normativos* (e-Book, available at Se.Di.Ci – Servicio de Difusión de la Creación Intelectual, Universidad Nacional de La Plata, Argentina).

Piggott, J., and J. Whalley (2001) "VAT Base Broadening, Self Supply, and the Informal Sector," *American Economic Review*, 91 (4): 1084–94.

Poddar, S. (1990) "Options for a VAT at the State Level," in M. Gillis, C. Shoup, and G. P. Sicat, eds., *Value Added Taxation in Developing Countries* (Washington, DC: World Bank), 104–12.

Poddar, S. (2003) "Consumption Taxes: The Role of the Value-Added Tax," in P. Honohan, ed., *Taxation of Financial Intermediation: Theory and Practice for Emerging Economies* (New York: Published for the World Bank by Oxford University Press), 345–80.

Poddar, S. (2005) "Application of VAT to Public Bodies," Presented at the VAT Conference, International Tax Dialogue, Rome, March. <http://www.itdweb.org/VATConference/documents/Presentations/Parallel3_Application%20of%20VAT%20to%20the%20Public%20Sector_SPoddar.ppt>

Poddar, S., and M. English (1997) "Taxation of Financial Services under a Value-Added Tax: Applying the Cash Flow Approach," *National Tax Journal*, 50 (1): 89–111.

Poore, D. R. (2004) "Nonresident Vendors Required to Collect Provincial Sales Tax in Canada," *Tax Notes International*, 36 (4): 321–24.

PricewaterhouseCoopers (2006) Corporate Taxes 2005-2006: Worldwide Summaries. <http://www.pwc.com/extweb/pwcpublications.nsf/docid/9B2B76032544964C8525717E00606CBD>

Pugel, T. A. (2004) *International Economics*, 12th ed. (New York: McGraw-Hill/Irwin).

Purohit, M. C. (2006) *Value Added Tax: Experiences of India and Other Countries*, 4th ed. (New Delhi: Foundation for Public Economics and Policy Research).

Québec (2005) *General Information Concerning the QST and the GST/HST* (Québec: Ministère du Revenu du Québec). <http://www.revenu.gouv.qc.ca/documents/eng/publications/in/in-203-v(2005-04).pdf>

Québec (2006) *GST and QST – How They Apply to Residential Complexes* (Québec: Ministère du Revenu du Québec). <http://www.revenu.gouv.qc.ca/documents/eng/publications/in/in-261-v(2006–03).pdf>

Radian, Alex (1980) *Resource Mobilization in Poor Countries: Implementing Tax Policies* (New Brunswick, NJ: Transaction Books).

Rajaraman, I. (2004) "Fiscal Restructuring in the Context of Trade Reform," Working Paper 7, National Institute of Public Finance and Policy, New Delhi.

Rao, M. G., and R. K. Rao (2005) "Trends and Issues in Tax Policy and Reform in India," National Institute of Public Finance and Policy (New Delhi) Tax Research Unit Working Paper 1, October.

Reder, M. W. (2004) "The Tension between Strong History and Strong Economics," in T. W. Guinnane, W. A. Sundstrom, and W. C. Whatley, eds., *History Matters: Essays on Economic Growth, Technology, and Demographic Change* (Stanford, CA: Stanford University Press), 96–112.

Refaqat, S. (2003) "Social Incidence of the General Sales Tax in Pakistan," IMF Working Paper WP/03/216, November.

Reilly, R. F., and R. P. Schweis (1999) *Valuing Intangible Assets* (New York: McGraw-Hill).

Ring, R. J., Jr. (1999) "Consumers' Share and Producers' Share of the General Sales Tax," *National Tax Journal*, 52 (1): 79–90.

Riswold, S. (2004) "IMF VAT Policy in Sub-Saharan Africa," *Tax Notes International*, 33 (4): 385–405.

Rodrik, D. (1998) "Why Do More Open Economies Have Bigger Governments?" *Journal of Political Economy*, 106 (5): 997–1032.

Roller, L.-H., and L. Waverman (2001) "Telecommunications Infrastructure and Economic Development: A Simultaneous Approach," *American Economic Review*, 91 (4): 909–23.

Rousslang, D. J. (2002) "Should Financial Services Be Taxed under a Consumption Tax? Probably," *National Tax Journal*, 55 (2): 281–91.

Ruiz Almendral, V. (2003) "Autonomous Communities Taking Advantage of the Mechanism to Ensure the Neutrality of VAT," *International VAT Monitor*, 14 (5): 373–80.

Rutherford, T. F., M. K. Light, and F. Barrera (2005) "Equity and Efficiency Costs of Raising Tax Revenue in Colombia," in R. M. Bird, J. Poterba, and J. Slemrod, eds., *Fiscal Reform in Colombia* (Cambridge, MA: MIT Press), 93–138.

Salim, J. A., and W. D. D'Angela (2005) "Estimación del incumplimento en el IVA, Años 2000 a 2004," AFIP, Buenos Aires, July.

Sanchez-Ugarte, F., and J. Modi (1987) "Are Export Duties Optimal in Developing Countries? Some Supply-Side Considerations," in V. P. Gandhi, ed., *Supply-Side Tax Policy: Its Relevance to Developing Countries* (Washington, DC: International Monetary Fund), 279–320.

Sandford, C., M. Godwin, P. Hardwick, and I. Butterworth (1981) *Costs and Benefits of VAT* (London: Heinemann Educational Books).

Schatan, R. (2003) "VAT on Banking Services: Mexico's Experience," *International VAT Monitor*, 14 (4): 287–94.

Schenk, A. (1989) *Value Added Tax: A Model Statute and Commentary*. A Report of the Committee on Value Added Tax of ABA Section on Taxation (Washington, DC: American Bar Association).

Schenk, A. (1995) "Japanese Consumption Tax after Six Years: A Unique VAT Matures," *Tax Notes International*, 11 (21): 1379–93.

Schenk, A., and O. Oldman (2007) *Value Added Tax: A Comparative Approach* (Cambridge: Cambridge University Press).

Schenk, A., and H. H. Zee (2004) "Financial Services and the Value-Added Tax," in H. H. Zee, ed., *Taxing the Financial Sector: Concepts, Issues, and Practices* (Washington, DC: International Monetary Fund), 60–74.

Schneider, F., and R. Klinglmair (2004) "Shadow Economies around the World: What Do We Know?" Working Paper 0408, Department of Economics, Johannes Kepler University of Linz, April.

Scully, Gerald (1991) "Tax Rates, Tax Revenues, and Economic Growth," National Center for Policy Analysis, Policy Report 98. <http://www.ncpa.org/studies/s159/s159.html>

Shiells, C. R. (2005) "VAT Design and Energy Trade: The Case of Russia and Ukraine," *IMF Staff Papers*, 52 (1): 103–19.

Shome, P., ed. (1995) *Tax Policy Handbook* (Washington, DC: International Monetary Fund).

Shome, P. (1997) *Value Added Tax in India: A Progress Report* (New Delhi: Centax).

Shome, P. (1999) "Taxation in Latin America: Structural Trends and Impact of Administration," IMF Working Paper WP/99/19, February.

Shoup, C. S., ed. (1967) *Fiscal Harmonization in Common Markets*, Vols. 1–2 (New York: Columbia University Press).

Shoup, C. S. (1969) *Public Finance* (Chicago: Aldine).

Shoup, C. S. (1990) "Choosing among Types of VATs," in M. Gillis, C. Shoup, and G. P. Sicat, eds., *Value Added Taxation in Developing Countries* (Washington, DC: World Bank), 3–16.

Silvani, C. (1992) "Improving Tax Compliance," in R. M. Bird and M. Casanegra de Jantscher, eds., *Improving Tax Administration in Developing Countries* (Washington, DC: International Monetary Fund), 274–305.

Silvani, C., and P. dos Santos (1996) "Administrative Aspects of Brazil's Consumption Tax Reform," *International VAT Monitor*, 7 (3): 123–32.

Silvani, C., and S. Wakefield (2002) "The Relationship between Tax Rates and Tax Yield," Paper presented at 36th General Assembly of the Inter-American Centre of Tax Administrators (CIAT), Québec, May.

Sinn, H.-W., A. Gebauer, and R. Parsche (2004) "The IFO Institute's Model for Reducing VAT Fraud: Payment First, Refund Later," *CESifo Forum*, 5 (2): 30–34.

Slemrod, J. (1990) "Optimal Taxation and Optimal Tax Systems," *Journal of Economic Perspectives*, 4 (1): 157–70.

Smith, S. (1997) *The Definitive Regime for VAT* (London: Institute for Fiscal Studies).

Sokoloff, K. L., and E. M. Zolt (2005) "Inequality and Taxation: Evidence from the Americas on How Inequality May Influence Tax Institutions," *Tax Law Review*, 59 (2): 167–241.

State of Hawaii (2002) *An Introduction to the General Excise Tax* (Honolulu: Department of Taxation), June.

Steiner, R., and C. Soto (1999) "IVA: productividad, evasión y progresividad," Fedesarrollo, Bogotá.

Steinmo, S. (1993) *Taxation and Democracy: Swedish, British, and American Approaches to Financing the Modern State* (New Haven, CT: Yale University Press).

Sthanumoorthy, R., ed. (2005) *State-Level VAT in India: Issues, Challenges and Experiences* (Hyderabad: ICFAI University Press).

Stotsky, J. G., and A. WoldeMariam (2002) "Central American Tax Reform: Trends and Possibilities," IMF Working Paper WP/02/227, December.

Strasma, J. (1965) "Market-Enforced Self-Assessment for Real Estate Taxes," *Bulletin for International Fiscal Documentation*, 19 (9): 353–65, 397–414.

Surrey, S. S., and P. R. McDaniel (1985) *Tax Expenditures* (Cambridge, MA: Harvard University Press).

Swift, Z. L. (2003) *Why Worry about Tax Expenditures?* PREM Notes 77, World Bank, January.

Swinkels, J. (2005) "State Aid and VAT," *International VAT Monitor*, 16 (5): 311–16.

Swinkels, J. (2005a) "VAT Exemption for Medical Care," *International VAT Monitor*, 16 (1): 14–18.

Tait, A. A. (1988) *Value-Added Tax: International Practice and Problems* (Washington, DC: International Monetary Fund).

Tait, A. A., ed. (1991) *Value-Added Tax: Administrative and Policy Issues*, Occasional Paper 88 (Washington, DC: International Monetary Fund).

Tamaoka, M. (1994) "The Regressivity of a Value Added Tax: Tax Credit Method and Subtraction Method – a Japanese Case," *Fiscal Studies*, 15 (2): 57–73.

Tanzi, V. (1970) "International Tax Burdens: A Study of Tax Ratios in the OECD Countries," in *Taxation: A Radical Approach* (London: Institute for Economic Affairs).

Tanzi, V. (1987) "Quantitative Characteristics of the Tax Systems of Developing Countries," in D. Newbery and N. Stern, eds., *The Theory of Taxation in Developing Countries* (New York: Published for the World Bank by Oxford University Press), 205–41.

Tanzi, V., ed. (1992) *Fiscal Policies in Economies in Transition* (Washington, DC: International Monetary Fund).

Tanzi, V., ed. (1993) *Transition to Market: Studies in Fiscal Reform* (Washington, DC: International Monetary Fund).

Taylor, A. M., and M. P. Taylor (2004) "The Purchasing Power Parity Debate," *Journal of Economic Perspectives*, 18 (4): 135–58.

Technical Committee on Business Taxation (1997) *Report* (Ottawa: Finance Canada).

Terkper, S. E. (1996) "VAT in Ghana: Why It Failed," *Tax Notes International*, 11 (23): 1801–16.

Terkper, S. E. (2000) "Ghana Reintroduces VAT – Lessons Learned and Progress after a Year," *Tax Notes International*, 20 (11): 1253–68.

Thirsk, W. R., ed. (1997) *Tax Reform in Developing Countries* (Washington, DC: World Bank).

Thuronyi, V. (2003) *Comparative Tax Law* (The Hague/London/New York: Kluwer Law International).

Toro, J. (2005) "Implementing VAT: Problems and Experiences," Paper presented to Global VAT Conference, Rome, March. <http://www.itdweb.org/VATConference/documents/Presentations/Parallel3_Implementing%20VAT_Problems%20&%20Experiences%20_JToro.ppt>

Toye, J. (2000) "Fiscal Crisis and Fiscal Reform in Developing Countries," *Cambridge Journal of Economics*, 24 (1): 21–44.

Urrutia, M., S. Ichimura, and S. Yukawa (1989) *The Political Economy of Fiscal Policy* (Tokyo: United Nations University).

U. S. Chamber of Commerce (2004) "Sales and Use Tax in Louisiana." <http://uschamber.com/sb/business/P07/P07_4947.asp>

Valadkhani, A., and A. P. Layton (2004) "Quantifying the Effect of the GST on Inflation in Australia's Capital Cities: An Intervention Analysis," *Australian Economic Review*, 37 (2): 125–38.

Van den Berg, H. (2004) *International Economics* (New York: McGraw-Hill/Irwin).

Van Steenwinckel, J., and A. Theissen (2001) "VAT Treatment of Conveyances of Buildings and the Land on Which They Stand," *International VAT Monitor*, 12 (1): 25–28.

Varsano, R. (1995) "A tributação do comércio interestadual: ICMS versus ICMS partilhado," Texto par Discussão No. 382, Instituto de Pesquisa Economica Aplicade, Brasilia.

Varsano, R. (2000) "Subnational Taxation and Treatment of Interstate Trade in Brazil: Problems and a Proposed Solution," in S. J. Burki and G. Perry, eds., *Decentralization and Accountability of the Public Sector*, Annual World Bank Conference on Development in Latin America and the Caribbean 1999 (Washington, DC: World Bank).

Vázquez-Caro, J. (2005) "Benchmarking Complex Systems: The Search for a North Star," Bogotá, June (on file with the authors).

Vázquez-Caro, J., G. Reid, and R. M. Bird (1992) *Tax Administration Assessment in Latin America*. Latin America and Caribbean Technical Department, Regional Studies Program, Report 13 (Washington, DC: World Bank).

Verwaal, E., and Cnossen, S. (2002) "Europe's New Border Taxes," *Journal of Common Market Studies*, 40 (2): 309–30.

Waidyasekera, D. D. M. (1998) "Sri Lanka: Implementation of the Goods and Services Tax – an Evaluation," *Asia-Pacific Tax Bulletin*, 4 (10): 384–88.

Wallace, S. (2003) "Fiscal Architecture," Module prepared for course on Practical Issues of Tax Policy and Administration, World Bank, April.

Wanless, P. T. (1985) *Taxation in Centrally Planned Economies* (London: Croom Helm).

Warlters, M., and E. Auriol (2005) "The Marginal Cost of Public Funds in Africa," World Bank Policy Research Working Paper 3679, August.

Warriner, D. (1969) *Land Reform in Theory and Practice* (Oxford: Clarendon Press).

Wassenaar, M. C., and R. H. J. M. Gradus (2004) "Contracting Out: The Importance of a Solution for the VAT Distortion," *CESifo Economic Studies*, 50 (2): 377–96.

Webb, S. B. (2001) "Challenges and Prospects for Tax Reform," in M. M. Giugale, O. Lafourcade, and V. H. Nguyen, eds., *Mexico: A Comprehensive Development Agenda for the New Era* (Washington, DC: World Bank), 179–98.

Weekes, A. (2005) "Small Island Economies: The Barbados Perspective," Paper prepared for Global Conference on the Value Added Tax, Rome, March. <http://www.itdweb. org/VATConference/documents/Presentations/Parallel2_Special%20Topics_Island% 20Economies_Equity%20&%20Trade_AWeekes.ppt>

Weisman, S. R. (2002) *The Great Tax Wars* (New York: Simon & Schuster).

Westin, R. A. (2004) "Modifying the U.S. Tax Framework to Stimulate Employment without Violating GATT Principles," *Tax Notes International*, 34 (5): 523–34.

Whalley, J. (1992) "Taxation and the Service Sector," in R. M. Bird and J. M. Mintz, eds., *Taxation to 2000 and Beyond*, Canadian Tax Paper 93 (Toronto: Canadian Tax Foundation), 269–93.

Whalley, J., and D. Fretz (1990) *The Economics of the Goods and Services Tax* (Toronto: Canadian Tax Foundation).

Wickremasinghe, G., and P. Silvapulle (2005) "Exchange Rate Pass-Through to Manufactured Import Prices: The Case of Japan," Working Paper, Department of Econometrics and Business Statistics, Monash University, Caulfield, Australia.

Wicksell, K. (1896 [1958]) "A New Principle of Just Taxation," in R. A. Musgrave and A. Peacock, eds., *Classics in the Theory of Public Finance* (London: Macmillan), 72–118.

Wong, C. P. W., and R. M. Bird (2005) "China's Fiscal System: A Work in Progress," ITP Paper 0515, International Tax Program, Rotman School of Management, University of Toronto, October. <http://www.rotman.utoronto.ca/iib/ITP0515.pdf>

World Bank (2003) *Ukraine: Tax Policy and Tax Administration*, Report 26221-UA, World Bank, Kyiv, March.

World Bank and International Finance Corporation (2006) *Doing Business in 2006: Creating Jobs* (Washington, DC: World Bank and IFC).

Wu, S.-Y., and M.-J. Teng (2005) "Determinants of Tax Compliance – a Cross-Country Analysis," *Finanzarchiv*, 61 (3): 393–417.

Yang, P., and W. Jin (2000) "Ideas on the Perfection of China's Value Added Tax System," *International VAT Monitor*, 11 (3): 106–10.

Yang, X. (2005) "VAT Treatment of Government Procurement: A Comparative Analysis," *International VAT Monitor*, 16 (5): 342–48.

Yoingco, A. Q., and M. M. Guevara, eds. (1988) *The VAT Experience in Asia* (Singapore: Asian-Pacific Tax and Investment Research Center).

Youngman, J. M. (1996) "Tax on Land and Buildings," in V. Thuronyi, ed., *Tax Law Design and Drafting* (Washington, DC: International Monetary Fund), 264–91.

Yu, M. (2004) "Tax Authority Designates Trial Points for New VAT Regime," *Tax Notes International*, 33 (2): 145.

Zapata, J. G., and N. Ariza (2005) "Eficiencia y equidad de la política tributaria y su relación con el gasto público en la Comunidad Andina – el caso de Colombia," Bogotá, July.

Zee, H. H. (2005) "A New Approach to Taxing Financial Intermediation Services under a Value-Added Tax," *National Tax Journal*, 58 (1): 77–92.

Zee, H. H. (2006) "VAT Treatment of Financial Services: A Primer on Conceptual Issues and Country Practices," *Intertax*, 34 (10): 458–74.

Zuleta, J. C., and A. Leyton (2006) "Corruption in the Revenue Service: The Case of VAT Refunds in Bolivia," Washington, DC: World Bank. <http://info.worldbank.org/etools/docs/library/232168/PP%20PRESENTATION-CORRUPTION%20IN%20THE%20REVENUE%20SERVICE%20%20THE%20CASE%20OF%20VAT%20REFUNDS%20IN%20BOLIVIA%281%29_files/frame.htm>

Index